Repairing Rainbows

Dear Roni,
    Wishing you a
life filled with
beautiful rainbows.
        Lynda

LYNDA FISHMAN

Edited by Nancy Davis
Front cover design by Jonathan Fishman
Book design by Joanne Ward, Beeline Design & Communications

Second printing, October 2010

ISBN 978-0-9866074-0-0
Printed in Canada

For My Mother and Sisters

Rita Gordon Weinberg
September 23, 1930 – July 5, 1970

Carla Beth Weinberg
September 16, 1958 – July 5, 1970

Wendy Bonnie Weinberg
August 1, 1961 – July 5, 1970

And My Dad

Shloime Weinberg
November 2, 1925 – July 5, 1970 – October 15, 1999

Like kites without strings,
and butterflies with wings,

My mother taught me to soar with my dreams.

We paint our own rainbows

PREFACE

WHEN MOST PEOPLE meet a happily married, successful couple, they assume that their privileged and seemingly lucky life has always been that way. *Repairing Rainbows* is the true story of two people who, although they consider themselves fortunate and blessed, have an astonishing tale to tell.

I have my story and my husband Barry has his. Individually, they are tragic and shocking but our story together is one of love, strength and appreciation. Barry and I met when we were seventeen, just a few months after finishing high school. We were two young people essentially on our own but armed with courage and determination to create a meaningful life together. Today, we have been married for over thirty years and have three talented, wonderful children, two dogs and two cats.

Many people have encouraged me to write a book about my life; one that might inspire others faced with tragedy. How did we get through it and end up so normal? Barry and I know first hand that when a child loses a parent or a sibling, they also lose their childhood. But my intention was not to write a depressing book about tragedy and loss. Ours was an unusual and challenging journey from lost childhood to rewarding adulthood. All of our experiences and the people we met along the way were part of the lessons that shaped our lives. They gave us strength and wisdom, continuously motivating us to live courageously. Searching for the good parts reminded us to be thankful.

My hope is that, by sharing our heartbreaking yet triumphant story, others will be uplifted; that our journey and untiring search to find a glimmer of positivity in the darkest, most difficult times and knowing that we always have choices, will help others overcome their own struggles and obstacles.

I have been faithful to what I remember and have recounted everything as honestly as possible. All incidents are described to the best of my recollection. None of the names have been changed.

Lynda Fishman

PART ONE:

Silence

PROLOGUE

WHEN I WAS thirteen years old, my mother and two sisters were killed in a plane crash. Their Air Canada flight from Montreal to California had a stopover in Toronto and it went down just outside Toronto killing all 109 passengers and crew members.

It also killed my father's spirit. My father simply continued to exist, overcome by despair, in a state devoid of hope. His spirit was gone but his clock continued to tick. Burying a wife and two young children at the age of forty-four devastated him and left him with an intense sorrow from which he never recovered. In addition, the overwhelming responsibility of raising a daughter alone completely immobilized him.

In that plane crash, I lost my mother and two younger sisters. At thirteen years of age, I was faced with the responsibility of a father in a complete state of shock, a house to take care of and what felt like hundreds of well-meaning relatives and friends telling us exactly what to do and how to proceed with our shattered lives.

But I chose life. We always have choices.

CHAPTER 1

I WOKE ABRUPTLY to an ear-piercing scream and staggered out of the bedroom I shared with my cousins. The apartment was still dim, but in my dazed state I made out shadows, bumping into furniture like lost ghosts. I stood in the living room doorway, rubbing my eyes, dopey and puzzled in the faint morning light. Like a camera lens shifting from blurry to focused, the scene before me slowly sharpened. My grandmother wringing her hands together, her eyes bulging, her nostrils flaring in fear. My aunt, uncle and grandfather wailing like ragged banshees in their pyjamas: gasping screams, high-pitched shrieking, guttural noises. But in between I kept hearing the same three words, over and over.

"Oh my God, oh my God."

Everyone was going crazy. Why were they up so early? My aunt glanced at me and I felt my stomach drop. Her wide eyes were glazed over, her mouth frozen open and covered with her hand, tears streaming down her cheeks. Her face looked contorted. The blue silk of her nightdress shimmered eerily with each heaving breath. Then her hand dropped to her side and, for a moment, her face muscles seemed to go lax, her eyes blank. Her flat tone of voice muffled my grandparents' crying and filled the space between us.

"Your father just called to tell us that the plane crashed. They don't know yet if anyone has survived."

I looked around trying to digest why everyone was acting strangely. It was disturbing and confusing and slow. But in my disjointed state of mind, it hit me that something awful had just happened.

I stood frozen in one spot as my Mickey Mouse nightgown clung to my back in sweat. I felt cold. My mouth felt dry. I was terrified.

CHAPTER 2

A s my California cousin Steve and I approached the age of thirteen, his family was busy planning his Bar Mitzvah in Los Angeles, and we were all going to be there for the celebration. My parents decided that we would fly, instead of taking the train, and stay a whole month. Another cousin was getting married in Montreal at the end of June, and my mother wanted to wait until after her wedding. But I begged my mother to let me go with her parents, my Bubby and Zaida, as soon as school let out. I would have the whole apartment cleaned and set up for her arrival a week later, I promised. She reluctantly agreed. It was settled: Bubby, Zaida and I would leave on Sunday, June 28th; my mother and sisters would come the following Sunday; and my father the one after that, since he could only be away from his store for two weeks.

My sisters and I had never been on a plane but had been to the airport to pick up visitors. Waiting in the arrival area at Montreal's Dorval Airport was like waiting for a much-anticipated birthday present. You knew it was coming but could not wait to get it. When our visitors burst through those double doors, everyone hugged and helped carry bags, chatting all the way to the parking lot.

We could hardly believe that this time we would be the ones on the other side of those doors, tickets in hand, greeted by eager relatives. I wasn't sure what was more exciting: going somewhere on an airplane for the first time, or a whole week with my grandparents, organizing an apartment. I had just turned thirteen and already I felt like such a grown up.

Carla, my second youngest sister, learned how to play Peter, Paul and Mary's "Leaving on a Jet Plane" on the piano, and the three of us sang it over and over. "All my bags are packed. I'm ready to go..." We just could not wait to get on that jet plane.

We bought dresses and party shoes for the Bar Mitzvah, brand new toothbrushes with travelling cases and cosmetic bags to keep our bathroom items. None of us wore makeup yet, but we had plenty to fill those brightly coloured little bags. We each had our own suitcase which, for weeks before leaving, we kept on the floor of our rooms, unzipped, with everything folded neatly.

Wendy's suitcase was filled with important items for an eight-year-old like toys, games and her favourite doll Barbara. She didn't leave much space for clothes, but she was planning on putting some things in Carla's suitcase, since Carla, a practical eleven-year-old, was only bringing the items she absolutely needed.

My sisters and I discussed how weird it was that I would be in California without them for a week, but Carla wanted to go to the wedding in Montreal, and it would be too much trouble for us to look after Wendy.

Everyone in our house was up way before the sunrise on that Sunday morning. My sisters waited patiently for me to finish in the washroom without the usual excessive pounding on the door.

It was a ritual for my father to make a special breakfast for us every Sunday. The delicious aroma of French toast sizzling in the pan permeated the house. Even though I was too young to drink coffee, I loved the smell of it bubbling in the electric percolator.

I was busting to get to the airport and could hardly eat. I licked the maple syrup off my fingers, gulped down the last bit of my milk, and ran to the bathroom one more time to check my hair. My mother had patiently combed out all of the knots, and I wanted to make sure it still looked perfect for the airplane.

I grabbed the Etch A Sketch from my room and stuffed it into my small bag, already filled with coloured pencils, a notepad, a book, candy, bubble gum and two homemade chocolate chip cookies tightly wrapped in Saran Wrap. I loved that I could draw something on the Etch A Sketch, shake it clean and then draw something else. Fascinating.

We picked up my grandparents on the way to the airport, and once we piled tightly into the station wagon, we were off. Everyone talking at once: my mother, father and grandfather in the front discussing the best route to take, while my sisters and I speculated about what it would be like on the airplane. Bubby was in the back with the three of us. She had a big plastic bag on her lap, filled with food. As if we didn't already know, she reminded us that she much preferred her own food, rather than eating the lousy food they would serve on the plane. As much as I loved her salami sandwiches and sour pickles, I really wanted to eat the airplane food, even if it was lousy. Mom had told me that it was like a little TV dinner with everything separated into sections. That sounded so fun.

When we got to the ticket counter, I could not have felt any prouder telling the lady that I was going on the plane to California. I didn't mention that it was my first time. She handed the three boarding passes to my dad, but I took the one with my name on it. I was old enough to carry my own boarding pass. My mom smiled at me as she gently pushed a few strands of hair away from my face.

Everyone walked us to the doorway that would lead to our gate. Then we had to say goodbye, because they weren't allowed to walk us all the way to the plane. We all hugged and hugged. My mom started crying, but that was nothing unusual for her. She cried so easily. She cried when she heard a sad song on the radio, when she watched movies, whenever she heard bad news, and every time she spoke to her best friend Elly. We were accustomed to seeing her cry.

One more hug and then Bubby, Zaida and I headed for the gate. For some reason, I looked back again with mixed emotions. The four of them smiled and waved. Our family had always done everything together. This felt strange, like a different kind of goodbye, but at the same time, it was very exciting.

WE HAD THREE seats together halfway towards the back. My grandparents let me have the window seat so I could look out. We were more crowded than I expected, but as I looked around I thought the plane was full of fascinating things. A button that turned on a spotlight, another one that called the stewardess, a little fan that could be moved in different directions, a table tray, seat belts, seats that reclined. I checked out everything.

I watched the safety demonstration with interest and intrigue. The stewardesses reminded me of the ladies on *Let's Make A Deal*, all smiley and pretty.

Take-off was exhilarating. I knew that we were going to fly in the air, but I hadn't realized that the plane would go so fast, speeding down the runway and zooming upwards. I wanted to remember every second of the thrilling feeling.

And I loved the meal served on the small plates, all wrapped up like a present! I even got to eat some of Bubby's meal, because she refused to try it. She was totally enjoying her picnic of sandwiches and pickles. Zaida must have been starving because he ate his entire airplane meal and the sandwich from home.

As I felt myself dozing off, I reminded my grandparents to wake me before the landing. I did not want to miss that. That had to be amazing.

CHAPTER 3

MY MOTHER WAS the second child in her family of six kids. My grandparents had eleven grandchildren, and Friday nights were usually spent at their house.

We could smell Bubby's cooking before we even walked in the door: hot fruit pies and freshly baked cookies on the counter, a mammoth pot of homemade chicken noodle soup bubbling on the stove and an oven packed with roasted chicken or beef brisket, meatballs, potato pudding, carrot pie and knishes. Those knishes were puffy, bite-sized mixtures of potatoes, fried onions and seasoned ground chicken surrounded by crushed corn flakes.

Since we weren't allowed to sit down at the huge dining table until everyone arrived, my sisters, cousins and I were always chased out of my grandmother's kitchen for stealing knishes from the oven. But we couldn't help ourselves. My grandmother pretended she was angry but she had a perpetual smirk on her face as she lovingly swatted us with a damp tea towel.

My Zaida's face glowed as he sat at the head of that dining room table surrounded by his children and grandchildren. A short, chubby, bald man, he had a moustache for a while but, after hearing his grandchildren complain about his scratchy kisses, shaved it off. He wore a suit, tie and starched white shirt every single day but, just like my dad, he never stayed neat for long. His shirt was always full of stains, mostly from the dirt he touched when he handled the fresh fruit and vegetables at his stand.

Zaida left the house every morning at four o'clock with his bagged lunch and worked until dinner time. My mother often remarked that he did not know how to say no and that customers took advantage of his good nature. He extended credit or, in some cases, let customers have produce for free. Maybe for a few, he'd admit, pointing out that he had more than enough money to put food on his table. How could he say no to these women who had so little? And that was that.

My Bubby never seemed to stop. She spent her days volunteering: helping out in a nursing home, knitting scarves, mittens and sweaters for a charity bazaar, or knocking on doors at clothing factories, collecting donations. She didn't drive a car, but managed to lug the heavy bags of clothing on the bus.

Bubby made her own sour pickles and always had multiple gallons of crunchy pickles loaded with garlic in the little storage room just outside the kitchen. She made way more in a month than the two of them could possibly eat in a whole year and was constantly giving a gallon to anyone who came over. The only stipulation was that the empty jar be returned so she could use it again.

The only time she would ever consider eating out was if she could go to McDonald's for fish filet. Otherwise, she claimed, restaurant food was ridiculously overpriced, overcooked and overrated. "For the same price," she told us, "I could feed everyone I know and all their relatives. And, at least, my food has some taste. This is dry and has no flavour."

She also played cards with "the ladies": a group of women who covered their faces in light beige powder, punctuated with a circle of rouge on each cheek. If we stopped by her house while one of her card games was on, Bubby would casually introduce us for the hundredth time. We loved listening to the conversations that took place as they dealt and played and discussed psychology, which they pronounced "saychology." Mrs. Wall's son was a "saychologist" so the card games doubled as "saychology workshops." But Mrs. Wall wasn't the only expert on the subject; the ladies offered their own saychology opinions, agreeing, disagreeing and debating anything and everything.

Bubby always needed her coffee or tea cup to be filled right to the top. "If I wanted half a cup, I'd have asked for half a cup." And she always made a point of using the washroom just before leaving someone's house. "Why should I pay for the flush at my house when I can use the toilet here?"

Despite their quirks—or perhaps because of them—my grandparents' home overflowed with food, love, laughter and contentment. Even their African Violets felt it. Scattered throughout their home were purple, pink and white flowers blossoming beautifully in their little pots, just like the vibrant family Bubby and Zaida had raised.

CHAPTER 4

CALIFORNIA WAS EXACTLY as I had imagined. My Auntie Shirley had rented a furnished apartment for us in the same building as hers, right in the heart of Los Angeles. Kids poured out of that enormous complex of what seemed liked hundreds of apartments backed onto a common concrete courtyard. Some kids threw basketballs into a hoop that hung lopsided off a wall, while others skipped with a long rope tied to the handle of the garbage room door. There always seemed to be dogs and cats running around, an intense game of hide-and-seek or hopscotch, little girls blowing bubbles and others busy dressing their Barbie dolls. It was a carnival without the rides.

Zaida was a fresh bagel fanatic and, since he didn't like his bagel toasted, he insisted on buying new ones every morning. Early each day, my grandfather and uncle went to the bakery and were back before the rest of us awoke. Of course Zaida couldn't just buy bagels, he had to get croissants, cheeses, smoked fish, olives, muffins, chocolate donuts. Breakfast each day was a gourmet feast.

Bubby complained that he bought too much food and that she could have easily scrambled some eggs or made us French toast, but for someone who grumbled about the food, she sure seemed to enjoy it.

Every afternoon, Bubby and Auntie Shirley busied themselves in the kitchen. By the time the food was ready, my cousins and I were back inside and had set the table for dinner. That apartment smelled delicious.

Zaida was in his glory. He didn't get to spend much time with my California cousins, and sitting down for dinner with them was how he got the most amount of pleasure, surrounded by his grandchildren.

After everything was cleaned up from dinner, Bubby, Auntie Shirley and I spent our time cleaning and organizing our summer apartment, which was just down the hall.

Every single piece of furniture was made of the same dark brown wood, full of scratches and chipped edges. The kitchen had a stained white table, topped with a plain glass vase jammed with red plastic flowers. The cupboards were sparsely stocked with mismatched dishes, glasses, cutlery, pots and pans. There was a can opener screwed to the side of the cabinet and a toaster on the counter. I pulled the plug out. My mother never let us keep our toaster plugged in unless we were using it. She said it was a fire hazard.

I wanted to clean the bathroom myself. I told my grandmother and aunt not to come in until I gave them permission. I assured them that when I was done, they would not believe their eyes. It would look brand new. I used Ajax and a big yellow sponge to scrub the matching avocado-coloured bathtub, toilet and sink. I even used Ajax on the edges of the floor, to remove the grime that seemed to have been collecting there forever. My aunt gave me a pair of rubber gloves, but they were huge and I couldn't grip the sponge properly. I finally took them off.

Some of the plastic shower curtain hooks were missing, and the door on the medicine cabinet was hard to open. You had to dig your fingers into the bottom of the mirrored door and pull, while pulling on the handle at the same time. There was nothing in there, but I cleaned the inside of it anyway.

Once I was done with the bathroom, and had received more than enough recognition for doing such a great job, I joined my grandmother and aunt in the kitchen. I decided to tackle the oven and stove with my trusty Ajax. My aunt told me that I shouldn't worry about cleaning the inside of the oven, but I didn't listen. My mother hated when the oven at our house was dirty, so I knew she'd want this one to be clean.

I swept the floors with the worn broom that I found in the cupboard, then went down the hall to my aunt's apartment and returned with a bucket, a mop and some Spic and Span. I loved sprinkling that green crystal-like powder into hot water, and watching it dissolve. If you watched closely, an array of colours would appear for a few seconds as they mixed with the steaming water.

It was almost midnight on Wednesday when we hung two big towels on the metal bar in the bathroom, put toilet paper on the holder stuck to the wall, and placed a fresh bar of soap in the bathtub. We were finally done. All we had left to do was to stock the kitchen with cereal, milk, eggs, cheese, jam, butter, ketchup and crackers for Wendy. She was addicted to crackers. My aunt said that we would get everything at the grocery store on Saturday, except for fresh bread, which we all agreed would be best to buy on Sunday.

ON THURSDAY EVENING, we watched television in my aunt's apartment, with the volume turned up way too high. The big television rested against the wall in the middle of the room with tall shelving units on either side. The shelves were filled with books, framed pictures, yellowed greeting cards, keys and a big jar of coins. There were two goldfish in a glass bowl next to a plastic green net and a container of fish food. Board games and puzzles, the lids sliding sloppily off the top of the boxes, crammed the bottom shelves of each unit.

There was hardly any space to move in that living room, since all seven of us were gathered in there, either on the couch or floor.

Bubby was knitting, Auntie Shirley was folding laundry, and I was ironing, the little adult homemaker that I was. As I placed a shirt on the end of the ironing board, attempting to flatten it as much as possible, the iron slipped and hit my leg, searing the skin, before it landed on the floor. I still have a scar on my leg from that burn. It hurt and I asked my aunt if I could please call my mother to tell her what had happened. Since it was a long distance call, she said no, it was too expensive. I didn't make a fuss, I knew that my aunt did not have much money. Besides, they would be coming in a few days; I could tell my mother about the burn when I saw her.

CHAPTER 5

I STOOD BAREFOOT on the beige carpet, barely awake, frozen in one spot, my skin clammy and sweaty, my breathing shallow and fast. They were screaming and crying. Raw, animal sounds came from my grandparents' bodies. They staggered, unsteady, pacing back and forth across the living room. Muttering. Withering to the ground. Tears muddied their faces. Everyone was going crazy. I crept over to my grandmother and crouched by her, wrapping my arms around her shaking frame. She leaned almost all of her weight into me. I thought she was going to knock me over. I stayed strong and held onto her but it didn't seem to comfort her at all. My arms dropped and I stood, backing away, gazing around the living room.

It was madness.

My aunt had her back to me. She was on the phone, whispering. Her hand shook and the tremors seemed to move through her body and down her spine in jerky movements. My uncle stood next to her, rubbing her back over and over again, her nightgown swirling under his hand. She hung up the phone and turned, her body swaying slightly as she leaned into my uncle.

"We have to pack our suitcases."

I was completely paralyzed.

A plane crash. Impossible. That happened to little planes in far away countries. Not in Canada. And not with my family on board.

Wake up. My dry lips formed the words. Nightmare. It had to be a nightmare. Whenever I had a nightmare, my mother came into my room. "It's okay. It's just a bad dream. Everything's fine." She would smooth my sweaty forehead and reassure me. Nightmares were not real. Even though they were scary and can seem so, they weren't real.

But the sun was starting to peek through the heavy drapes…Why wasn't my mother coming into my room to comfort me?

Standing there by myself, my uncle approached me and quietly told me to go and pack my things.

My aunt picked up the phone again, shaking and swaying, jerking and trembling. I heard her murmur to the people on the other end. All these long distance calls, one after another, but when I wanted to call my mother to tell her about the burn on my leg…. I turned and walked back into the bedroom.

My cousins helped us pack, throwing everything from the drawers into the suitcases, mixing up my clothes with my grandparents' things. There was no time for breakfast. We took the suitcases down to the car. My cousins stood on the sidewalk, silently staring, as we pulled away. No one even waved goodbye.

And no one said one word the entire drive to the airport. The car was silent without silence, because my grandparents were crying. My uncle concentrated on driving and my aunt just sat there, stunned. I looked out the window and didn't speak to anyone.

When we got to the ticket counter, there was an awkwardness about the way the Air Canada woman treated us. An uneasiness. Discomfort. It reminded me of the way people act around someone who has a contagious disease.

A man wearing an Air Canada shirt walked us to the gate. He offered to get my grandmother a wheelchair but she said no. I didn't blame him for offering. Pale and wobbly, with her hair standing out in tufts around her swollen eyes and red cheeks, she looked like a drooping flower.

Saying goodbye to my uncle was quick. No long and exciting farewells this time. The Air Canada man brought us right onto the plane and told us to sit in seats in the first class section, right at the front. Really comfortable seats with much more space than the ones we had on our way to California. My aunt was coming back to Montreal with us. That part suddenly struck me as weird. But I thought it was amazing that we got to sit in first class, and the stewardesses were unbelievably doting. They kept offering us things to make us feel comfortable, like pillows and blankets, magazines, food and drinks. I felt like a princess. When I told them that I thought the little teaspoon that came with my meal was cute, they said it was alright for me to keep it.

Bubby and Zaida acted strangely. Stuck to their seats, they were silent the entire flight. There, but not there. Zaida was sweating excessively, his eyes sunken and bloodshot. Bubby was restless, distracted and unfriendly. Her faced looked so tense that her eyebrows squished together. She was grinding her teeth and her lips looked dry. They were both jumpy and weary at the same time. The stewardesses kept offering them food, which they refused, and my aunt kept telling them to eat something, but they wouldn't change their minds. Bubby said she wasn't hungry, but I knew that she would have eaten if she had brought her own food on board. I thought she was grumpy and upset that she didn't have time at my aunt's to make her own sandwiches.

They stared into space and cried a lot. In fact, the whole time on the plane, it seemed as if everyone in first class was silent or whispering. The passengers, stewardesses, everyone. The same way that people act in hospital waiting rooms. I knew because I had been in one when one of my uncles had a brain tumour.

Or, maybe this was a rich and famous thing for people travelling in first class. So, when I talked to my aunt, my grandparents or the stewardesses, I also whispered.

WHEN WE LANDED for the stopover in Toronto, we were barraged by reporters and giant flashing cameras. They shoved microphones in our faces and the questions flew. "Did you have any family members on that doomed flight?" "How old are you?" "What are your names?" "Who did you lose in the plane crash?"

The Air Canada staff did their best to shield us. I thought the whole thing was kind of exciting, like we were celebrities. It was just like the paparazzi I had seen on TV. I didn't mind it at all. Besides, this was all just an awful nightmare and soon I would wake up. So why hadn't my mother come in yet?

We were ushered into empty corridors where our footsteps echoed, and everyone walked fast and spoke softly. There was that whispering again. They brought us back to the plane, to our first class seats, and we took off for Montreal.

When we exited the plane in Montreal, there were lots of security officers and Air Canada employees, who immediately herded us into a long, cold hallway, safely away from the slew of reporters.

And then I saw my father.

He stood at the end of the hallway with his older brother, Dave, and my cousin Mark. They each looked completely terrified, their faces twisted in pain and anxiety. The crying and hysterics started again. I had never, ever seen my father, uncle or cousin crying before.

My stomach began to bubble, my legs felt wobbly and I was finding it hard to breathe. It was like watching a scene from above. Like I wasn't really there. Then I started shaking and felt so unsteady that I had to lean on the concrete wall in order to stay upright.

Everything looked and felt real. Dreams can seem just like real life. But then you wake up and it's all over.

I was more than ready to wake up.

I barely remember heading to the parking lot, its blur of gray walls and multicoloured cars like pieces of a broken rainbow. My cousin Mark drove my dad and me in one car, and my uncle drove my grandparents and aunt. Silence. Not even a whisper. I was not used to sitting in a car with no one talking. Even when we travelled a short distance, my sisters and I chatted nonstop. It was unbearable. But there are no words when you've just found out that your family has been killed in a plane crash. Life as we knew it was extinguished. Gone.

Yes, the drive was in complete silence.

Now what do we do? What happens next? Do we go home and make dinner? What will our life be like now that I don't have a mother or sisters?

CHAPTER 6

THE KITCHEN WAS the nucleus of our home, and when the pale yellow Formica table with chrome edges wasn't being used for a meal, it served as a homework desk, an arts and crafts table or a place for reading the newspaper. Hung on the wall above the kitchen table were three pictures, framed in cheap plastic frames, with sayings that my mother loved: This house is blessed with family, friends, laughter and love; No matter where I serve my guests, it seems they like my kitchen best; and We are too blessed to be stressed.

Sitting down for breakfast and dinner every day as a family was non-negotiable in our house. In fact, we all looked forward to that family time together. And we could always count on Wendy to have us howling with laughter.

Everyone had their own regular seat at our kitchen table, which comfortably sat eight, and was much bigger than what our small kitchen should have had. Wendy's job was to set the table and most of the time, she would fold each napkin into a flower or butterfly. She was especially creative if we expected company.

My dad always sat at one end, and Wendy at the other. Originally, that was where her highchair fit, but when she graduated to a regular chair, she kept the spot. It was a perfect place because she had a clear view of everyone and could monitor our reactions to her comments, which of course just fuelled her comedy routine.

We all loved cooking with our mother, and together we served the food family style with platters and big bowls: baked chicken, homemade burgers and perfectly seasoned fish with fruity, tangy sauce, salad and steamed vegetables or rice. No matter what was cooking, dinnertime always smelled delicious.

Our kitchen was full of chatter and laughter. We each appreciated the mealtime as an opportunity to talk about our day, hear about everyone else's, and discuss any news or happenings. We never felt rushed and, while my sisters and I may have bickered at other times, we never did so during meals. Eating together around our table was our time for solidarity. It was sacred and cherished.

Everyone helped clear the table, put the leftovers away, and the ketchup back in the fridge. We had a bottle of ketchup on the table for pretty much every meal. Not that my mother wasn't a great cook, because she was. We just loved ketchup.

Wendy loved sweeping the floor. She moved gracefully for a skinny little kid with crazy long legs. She had huge green eyes, high cheekbones and tiny rosebud lips that perpetually smiled. She didn't do a very good job of sweeping, but she put on an inspired performance with the broom. A veritable one-person show featuring the broom as a microphone, magic wand, balance beam, cane, dance partner, limbo stick and pretty much anything except its actual purpose. Inevitably, one of us would sweep again, after she was done.

My dad always sat at the table long after the meal was finished, drinking his cup of tea in a clear glass mug, while the rest of us cleaned up. Sometimes he would read the newspaper, but most of the time he would just sip his tea, hum or whistle a song—he could whistle an entire song without stopping to take a breath—and watch us with genuine interest and pride.

EVEN THOUGH MY father's name was Saul, everyone called him Shloime. His claim to fame was his joke-telling because although he was not the best conversationalist, he had an amazing memory for jokes and stories.

He was a short, quite bald man who, in the cold weather, always wore a brown, gray or black hat with a brim. My sisters and I loved taking his hat off, touching his bald head, feeling the shiny, smooth skin and then spiking his few strands of hair.

He was the youngest child of four, and definitely the softest, most easygoing personality in a family of tough, opinionated parents and siblings. Actually, judgmental was the way I always described my father's family: always quick to judge people by their religious views, their apparent financial situation, their clothes, shoes, jobs, the cleanliness of their house, the behaviour of their kids, and on and on. My sisters and I were the youngest kids of all the cousins and, while we loved spending time with our older cousins, we had a different kind of fun. We played cards, board games and sat politely at the dining room table.

Whenever there was a "hot" issue or concern, where advice and opinions were flying, the expression I heard most from my father's side of the family was "You must lead with your head, and not with your heart." My mother's relatives said the exact opposite. I know that deep down my father's family was caring, but it was tough to feel completely comfortable or relaxed in their presence. Not like with my mother's family. They led with their hearts.

My mother used to tell me that when she met my father, he was more like his parents and siblings than we would ever believe. She showed him the kinder, gentler way of relating to people, and that going out of your way for others felt good. She taught him that measuring someone's worth by their money or appearance was wrong. You have to look into someone's heart and see their goodness. See their real personality. She meant it.

My father actually had a heart of gold, and when he thought something was funny, he giggled. I will never forget that giggle. So spontaneous and natural for him, yet I am quite sure that he never giggled before he met my mother. I doubt that giggling was allowed in his family.

Whenever we had nothing to do for a few hours, and my mother was busy, my father always seemed to find some unusual thing to do with us. As a little girl, I remember visits to the smelly fish markets where they piled what seemed like hundreds of fish on tables of ice. There were huge tanks packed to the brim; the poor animals couldn't move. Customers lined up to buy fish, wrapped in newspaper and tossed to them across the counter.

We figured that our dad was quite popular because he knew most of the customers and all of the men who worked in the market. Even though the place was crowded with people pushing and shoving, they were always happy to see Shloime.

If there was time, we would head down the street to the shop where chickens were slaughtered by an old man with a huge beard. He sat in a rickety wooden chair, blood everywhere, and one by one he would cut the throat of a chicken and wait for it to die. I couldn't believe my father brought three little girls to see that. It's a wonder that the whole experience didn't traumatize us.

My father rarely said no to any of us. If we needed a pencil, a notebook, even an eraser, he would stop on his way home from work to buy it. He and his older brother Dave were partners in the floor covering business, a small retail store called *Weinberg Brothers* that was started by their father. The three of them worked together for many years until my grandfather's sudden passing when I was six years old. His two sons continued the same routine of selling, ordering, receiving and shipping tiles, linoleum and flooring adhesives. They had a part-time bookkeeper and several installers. The employees always gravitated towards my dad, the friendlier of the two, the nicer boss. My uncle always said that he was too soft-hearted for his own good and that the employees took advantage of him.

Hearing this, even at a young age, I secretly thought it made perfect sense to treat people nicely, even if they were employees. But I would never dare share that opinion with my uncle. I knew that people liked my dad and he liked them. He was the first one to jump out of his chair to greet a customer. Within minutes of meeting, he would be cracking jokes, and then happily talking business.

My uncle was much more serious, stern and impatient. No one ever told him to his face but, behind his back, they all said that it was better for him to do the administrative stuff, the paperwork, and agreed that my dad should be the one to deal with the customers and staff.

My dad and his brother each had their own giant steel desk amidst the tightly packed inventory. Uncle Dave's desk was always tidy and organized, with his papers stacked neatly in one corner and his pencils all facing the same direction in a pencil holder. My father's desk had papers strewn about, along with dust, empty coffee cups, dirty teaspoons and remnants of pencil erasers.

They shared a metal pencil sharpener that was screwed onto the wall between their two desks. Black phones with extra-long, curly black cords were mounted throughout the store. The phones had dirt-stained buttons that lit up when someone was using one of the three phone lines.

Both my dad and my uncle wore white, short-sleeve shirts and ties to the store every day. My father left our house looking neat and tidy, a clean handkerchief in the pocket of his pants. But, within a short while, his shirt was dirty and only half-tucked into his pants, his handkerchief filthy from his frequent nose blowing. He kept a pencil tucked behind one ear and several pens in his breast pocket. Usually, one would leak and a blue ink stain seeped onto his shirt.

Unlike my dad, my uncle stayed perfectly clean and starched. He never kept a pencil behind his ear and had one pen neatly clipped to his shirt pocket. Never did I see an ink stain.

Deep down Uncle Dave was a caring man, but he came across as tough and strict. My sisters and I were actually a little fearful of him. When we went to the store, we behaved like perfect angels. But if Uncle Dave wasn't there, we had a blast. Packed with rolls of carpets and boxes of tiles, there were countless hiding spots. And there was an electric conveyor belt between the two floors, which was way better than any slide in any park. I think that my father looked for excuses to bring us to the store after hours, when he knew that his brother wouldn't be there.

And when he came home, no matter how tired he was, we would get him to sit and play cards with us, or watch a cartoon on the big black and white television set.

During the summer of 1969 when Carla and I were brides-maids and Wendy was the flower girl at our cousin's wedding, my father took picture after picture of us. We all had our hair done at the hairdresser and wore matching pink and white evening gowns. So excited about our updos, we insisted on leaving for camp that summer with our dishevelled hairdos, still full of bobby pins and hair spray.

My father was so proud of his three little girls. He never introduced us to anyone by our names. Never. He always referred to us with such pride, as number one, number two and number three.

And so it was, under our father's gaze, we never felt rushed to clean up the kitchen. We took our time. I actually enjoyed standing at the sink and washing the plates, pots, pans, utensils, and serving dishes. Someone would always dry with one of our striped dish towels, which gave the two of us, whoever it was, a chance to chat. Once everything was done, I would sprinkle Ajax all over the sink and scrub it until it was spotless. My mother always said that no matter how tired we are, we should never go to bed unless the kitchen is clean. That way you never have to wake up to a messy kitchen.

CHAPTER 7

The next morning, the darkness had disappeared. I looked around my room. Everything looked normal. I studied the picture painted on my white musical jewelry box, sitting on my dresser. It was a picture of a princess surrounded by butterflies.

The sun shone through the side of the blinds. My alarm clock ticked away. Tick tock. Tick tock. Feeling a whoosh of relief, I was convinced that the whole horrific episode was indeed a bad dream.

Except it wasn't a dream, because the minute I stepped out of my bedroom, the terrifying reality crushed me with the force of a tidal wave. As I crept along the shadowy hallway towards the kitchen, I felt the very air envelope me, stifling and thick. Like drowning, but out of the water.

Everyone was sitting in the kitchen drinking coffee. Red moist eyes. Their fists clutching dirty tissues. They just stared at me through the fog. Frozen, painful stares. Silence. My aunts, uncles and father.

What an awful realization.

For the next few days, I lived through an ongoing feeling of revulsion as we were plunged into a living hell. My stomach churned and my body felt like it wasn't attached to the rest of me, my limbs floating yet heavy. Muffled conversations like a relentless buzzing filled the house and, everywhere I looked, people carried on but it was as if I were watching them on TV. When I was awake I felt like a zombie, yet when I tried to sleep the pain was sharp, and my mind raced, constantly replaying the last few days in minute detail, trying to find a point where I could return to, where it was safe and calm and where the reality was that none of this had happened. But when I awoke, I knew otherwise. Our house was packed with relatives and friends…but my mother and sisters were missing.

As soon as everyone retired for the night, I went into the kitchen to finish cleaning it properly. I swept, wiped all of the counters, and scrubbed the sink with Ajax.

On the way to my room, I stood outside of my parent's closed bedroom door listening for the snoring I was accustomed to hearing. Instead I heard my dad quietly crying. I never went inside. I just couldn't.

So I went to bed and just lay there. I felt exhausted, drained and confused. No one came to sit at the edge of my bed to talk to me about my day. No one came to wake me to say goodnight. I went to find Tiger, Carla's cat, and brought her into my bed, but I had the hardest time falling asleep. Even cuddling Tiger, I still felt anxious, tossing and turning, worrying, thinking, and mostly crying softly under my pillow, weeping until sleep, albeit restless and interrupted, finally was inevitable.

IT WAS BECOMING clear to me that this nightmare was actually reality. Further proof was the endless media coverage about the plane crash. This was a terrible event that impacted people in Montreal, Toronto, California, and probably all of North America. And of course, Air Canada. Apparently, this was Air Canada's second major plane crash in seven years. The television played graphic details and pictures. The newspaper was full of articles and photos from the crash site. I knew because people were kind enough to inundate us with whatever newspaper clippings they could find about the plane crash. They brought them to our house, as if they were bringing us a gift. As if we needed to read more gory information, and add a little more salt to our wounds. There wasn't enough crying and hysterics without the black and white proof to enlighten us, describe the details, and enhance our mundane vocabulary with words like "pulverized bodies," "ravages of the disaster," "ghastly and distinguishing marks on bodies."

My little cousin Cindy was barely four years old and even at her young age, she knew that something terrible had happened to her Auntie Rita and her cousins Carla and Wendy. She threw an uncontrollable temper tantrum on our front lawn and adamantly refused to come into the house.

My Aunt Naomi, my mom's sister, was a complete mess. Join the crowd. She had been on a road trip when the crash occurred, and no one knew how to reach her. She was with a group of friends driving to Atlantic City when she heard about the plane crash on the radio. She had frantically searched for a pay phone at a rest stop on the highway, but by then she was pretty sure that she already knew. She spoke to my mother several times each week. She knew they were on that flight.

My Aunt Bernice, my mother's other sister fell to the ground in our living room, and everyone said she had fainted. Passed out. I thought we should call an ambulance for her but one of my other aunts said it wasn't necessary. Someone had a little bottle containing beige crystals and a strong-smelling liquid. They stuck it in front of her nose and she woke up. They called it smelling salts.

There was a lot of talk about having a funeral, but it seemed to be a controversial subject involving several Rabbis, and no one seemed to know what to do about it. This dispute added even more distress to the already horrific situation. The consensus seemed to be that we couldn't plan a funeral without the bodies, and so far they hadn't been able to identify any bodies. All I heard was that we'd have to wait. Wait for what?

In support of their efforts to identify the bodies, Air Canada sent over two unfriendly, official-looking men who walked into our house wearing dark suits, shiny black shoes and carrying briefcases. They didn't smile or say much until everyone else silently cleared out of the kitchen and my father and my Uncle Dave were sitting with them at the kitchen table. I peered in attentively from the hallway near the kitchen but I definitely did not want to walk in there and join them. These Air Canada employees were scary, a far cry from the sweet flight attendants we had met in first class. I couldn't wait for them to get out of our house.

Only one of the men spoke, and he did so in a serious and quiet voice. He said they needed some family photos and dental records, all of which he would return to us. And then he pulled out some pictures. At that point, my dad asked me and some of my aunts to come into the kitchen to look through the pictures and see what we might recognize. I walked in and sat down without saying a word. I had no idea what they were going to show us. I thought it was going to be pictures of dead bodies like the pictures in the newspapers. My heart just stopped, and then I thought I was going to vomit.

They placed the pile of pictures on the table. They were pictures of items. Clothing, jewellery, wallets, books, whatever they had found at the site. I quickly realized that while they couldn't identify their bodies, they wanted us to claim the stuff that had belonged to our family members who had perished.

Considering that 109 people had been on board, there wasn't that much to be claimed. Between the fire from the crash and explosion, the looters, yes there were looters, more appropriately referred to as vultures, caught going through the gore and debris, and then the mysterious disappearance of items already identified, not much was left. We all recognized and "officially identified" my mother's diamond engagement ring in one of the pictures and Wendy's doll in another, but, in the end, we never got the ring or the doll. They apologized profusely. They had no idea where either of them had gone.

THE NEXT MORNING, my poor grandfather was so distressed that he got on a big Greyhound bus headed for Toronto. I did not know how anyone knew that he was on his way, but someone found out and arranged for him to be taken off the bus and brought back to Montreal. He told us that he was going there to help find his precious daughter and granddaughters' bodies, so we could proceed with the funeral. Poor, sweet man. He was completely traumatized.

CHAPTER 8

OUR FAMILY LIVED in a small three bedroom bungalow in Cote St. Luc, a suburb just outside of Montreal. It was a real home in the true sense of the word. It was never quiet. Relatives, friends and neighbours visited all the time, the phone rang a lot and the radio was always on. It was a busy, noisy, happy place.

Since I was the oldest, I had my own bedroom. It had pale blue walls and dark blue, shaggy carpets. I had a white dresser with a mirror above it and a matching white desk which was in front of the window. My bedroom faced the street and I could sit and do my homework while looking outside to see if there was any action going on.

When my parents finished the basement, my father's flooring installers put a perfectly cut linoleum hopscotch game right into the tiles. We didn't get a television set until I was almost eight years old, but we never spent much time indoors anyway. Unless it was absolutely pouring rain or a horrendous snow storm, we played outside with the rest of the neighbourhood kids from the minute we got home from school until it was time for dinner. We ran through sprinklers, jumped in puddles, built snow forts and snowmen and threw snowballs at each other. We played hide and seek, kick the can, hopscotch, champ, and an intense game we invented called war. Happy and free. Never bored.

Our house was on a small dead-end court and it was rare for anyone to drive onto our street unless they lived there, were visiting or making a delivery. When a vehicle entered our street, the neighbourhood kids would stop whatever we were doing and swarm around the car to see who was driving, where they were going and what they were doing. We were like the neighbourhood safety and security patrol. Ironically, no one ever seemed to worry about our safety.

My best friends were my neighbours Jon and Shelley. Shelley lived next door and Jon lived right behind my house. The three of us were in the same grade and, every morning, we would walk the few blocks to school together. Then we would meet in the school yard to walk home for lunch, then back to school again for the afternoon. Four times a day, every single day.

WE DID NOT have much money and we never went on real hotel vacations, but we never felt deprived or that we were missing out on anything. My childhood was filled with warmth, security and family time.

For special occasions, like birthdays, our parents' anniversary, Mother's Day or Father's Day, Carla, Wendy and I would surprise our parents with breakfast in bed. Looking back, I'm sure they were anything but surprised considering the lengthy, noisy preparation procedure that involved clanking, banging and giggling in the kitchen.

I was the official egg cracker. My mother had taught me the art to cracking eggs without getting any shell into the bowl. The trick was to firmly hit the middle of the egg against the pointed end of the counter, so the egg cracked straight across the middle.

As soon as Carla was done slicing tomatoes and cucumbers into perfect circles, she would whip the eggs with a fork. She added salt, pepper and a tiny bit of milk to the mixture and whipped it over and over to get it perfectly bubbly. She had way more patience than I did. But nobody could do a more beautiful job of artistically placing the red and green veggie circles on a platter than Wendy.

Our specialty was called "little eggs." Carla used a miniature ladle to drop a small amount of the egg mixture into the frying pan. She could fit six "little eggs" into the pan each time, butter splattering everywhere amidst the crackling sounds of the eggs frying. They were ready to be flipped almost immediately and then she put them on a plate. Wendy then arranged them in the centre of the platter surrounded by the veggies.

WHILE WE WERE each totally focused on our individual responsibilities for creating this feast, we chatted nonstop.

"Lower the radio or they'll wake up."

"Tell me when the eggs are ready and I will turn on the toaster."

"Do you think I should put the ketchup into a little bowl, or just leave it in the bottle?"

As Wendy stood in front of the fridge, I wondered what she needed. "What are you looking for?"

"Something else to decorate the platter. Oh perfect. Purple grapes. I'll cut them into little pieces and sprinkle them on the eggs."

"That's gross. "

"No it's not."

"Don't cut them up. You're too young to use a knife. Leave them whole."

"You're not the boss of me."

"We better hurry up. Their coffee is getting cold."

"They are going to be so happy to wake up to such a beautiful breakfast."

"If the lilacs were blooming now, we could put those in a vase. Mommy loves the way they smell."

While the kitchen was a complete mess, the huge white tray on the kitchen table looked perfect. Two plates, two glasses of orange juice, two coffee mugs, milk and sugar, a bottle of ketchup, buttered toast, two forks, two teaspoons, salt, pepper, napkins folded like flowers, the platter of little eggs garnished with the cucumber and tomato circles, clusters of grapes, and a small vase with plastic flowers.

They always pretended to be fast asleep when we marched into their room with the tray. It overflowed with food, and we overflowed with love and pride.

I WAS SIXTEEN months older than Carla, but we were only a year apart in school. Some people thought Carla and I were twins because we looked the same age. We shared ski school, summer camp, and after-school programs. We rode our bikes together, took piano lessons and sang a duet at several local charity events, belting out the words as if we were professional entertainers.

Carla was an avid reader and an accomplished student. The shelves in the bedroom she shared with Wendy were overflowing with books. She treasured her books which she bought every time she had extra money. She loved to play the piano and do her needlepoint pictures. As long as there was an animal in the picture, she was happy to work on it. She kept the tiny rolls of wool all organized in a shoe box, and whatever she was currently working on was neatly rolled up and pinned together with the needle.

Wendy, on the other hand, had enough energy for all three of us. Since she loved to keep moving, she learned how to skip rope very young. She kept her skipping rope in her schoolbag and skipped on the way to and from school, and during recess. She skipped in our living room, our basement, our backyard and in front of our house. She knew every skipping game there was and was definitely the skipping champion in the neighbourhood. We used to tease her that she was skipping in her sleep, reciting her favourite skipping games over and over again.

Teddy bear, teddy bear, turn around
Teddy bear, teddy bear, touch the ground.

Miss Mary Mack, Mack, Mack,
All dressed in black, black, black,
With silver buttons, buttons, buttons,
All down her back, back, back

Unlike rambunctious Wendy loaded with volumes of personality, Carla was gentle, level-headed and intuitive. Her dream was to be a doctor who would undoubtedly find cures for terrible diseases. One of our favourite things to do was take the city bus to the SPCA, the Society for Prevention of Cruelty to Animals. We loved visiting the animals awaiting new homes. Most of the time the staff let us sit on the floor and play with a litter of puppies or kittens. If they were in the mood, they let us take a few of the dogs into the outdoor fenced-in area so we could run and play with them.

One day Carla found a tiny multi-coloured kitten in my grandmother's backyard. She named her Tiger, and together they spent hours every day on the couch, as she nourished her soul with books. She took meticulous care of Tiger, and it was clear to everyone in our family that Tiger was her cat. For several weeks before the scheduled trip to California, Carla was busy writing out detailed instructions and schedules about caring for Tiger and all of her needs. Carla was only eleven at the time, yet she was mature and responsible well beyond her years.

Although Carla, Wendy
and I were close in age, we were
as different as could be in looks
and personalities. I was tall, a
bit chubby, with light brown
curly hair that I kept shoulder
length. Carla was average height
and slim, with straight brown
hair that was so long it would
reach the top of her butt when
it was wet. We always joked that
Wendy was adopted because she was tinier than any of us.

I was enormously interested in everything the adults did or talked about. I loved and needed positive recognition, and was happy to do whatever it took to help others. At ten years old, I was already volunteering with my grandmother at a nursing home. The place smelled from disinfectant and urine, and the constant blare of the television barely drowned the distant moaning. The patients were wrinkled and white-haired with glazed looks on their faces. I thought their clothes looked way too big for them, as I strolled past the wheelchairs lined up in the hallways. With blankets over their knees, the residents sat hunched over and motionless, or half-stood, gripping their walkers. Despite everything, I got the biggest kick out of these old people, particularly the ones who were demented. I knew how to get them and the staff to laugh, I gave rides up and down the halls in their wheelchairs, and I would listen to their nonsensical stories for hours at a time.

When I turned twelve, I was finally old enough to wear an official pink and white candy-striper uniform. I convinced Shelley to come with me to the nursing home. She came once. To this day, she still tells me how much she hated the whole experience. She was terrified when I showed her the door to the morgue, explaining that the dead bodies were stored in there. She complained that the vile smell of the place made her sick to her stomach, as did having to feed the patients and watch them dribble the food down their chins.

Quite to the contrary, I adored helping patients and found it particularly rewarding. I still actually giggle at the images I have of Shelley's obvious disgust in the whole experience.

CHAPTER 9

THE HOUSE HAD transformed from a place of laughter, safety and comfort to one of total despair. Everyone was either silent, or sobbing. Whirling in a terrifying and insane new world, and desperate for some privacy, I locked myself and Tiger in the bathroom every chance I got. That's where I was when I heard the wail coming from the backyard. A horrible, unforgettable sound. I stood on the edge of the bathtub so I could reach the window high up above the bathtub, and look outside. It was my father making that sound. The only thing that came out of my mouth was "*oh my God.*" His whole body seemed to be in complete spasm as he leaned on his brother. And he continued to wail.

That was not the last time I heard that horrendous sound. For months afterwards, I would hear him wailing in the middle of the night. I often wondered if he was doing it in his sleep, or if he was awake. I was always too frightened to go and find out. Instead, I pulled the pillow tight around my head, muffling the awful noise that exploded through the silence of the night like a blasting bomb. My own little bomb shelter.

Now, out in the yard, they told my father that they had identified Wendy's body. Our little Wendy. Hyper and funny. Our family entertainer. Eight years old.

THE NEXT DAY we had a funeral for Wendy. There must have been hundreds and hundreds of people packed into the chapel. The crowded room was full of men dressed in suits, and grave-looking women in their black clothes and pale lips, their big, dark sunglasses hiding their red eyes. I couldn't believe that with that number of people, no one uttered a word. The only sounds in the huge room were crying, sniffling and coughing.

We sat in a separate section reserved for the immediate family. There were prayers and eulogy speeches, but I was far more focused on the box that was sitting at the front of the chapel. I could not take my eyes off of it. It wasn't one of those nice coffins that you saw on television. Instead, it was a plywood box, unpainted, just sitting there. All by itself. No one went near it. And it seemed to be nailed closed. Obviously they didn't want us to open that box. I didn't know what a "pulverized body" meant, but I knew it had to be terrible. I had heard people talking in the backyard about identifying body parts. They said that all you needed in order to have a funeral was one part of the body. An arm, a leg, even a finger.

I did not want to think about body parts. I did not want to think about Wendy being hurt, or cut, or burned. I remembered the burn on my leg from just a few days earlier, and how much it had hurt. I didn't want to imagine Wendy in pain or in any way other than my cute little sister dancing around the living room or sweeping the kitchen or sitting in the bathroom while we cut her bangs too short. Wendy was our little wind-up toy. From the minute she woke up every day, she was happy and busy, singing her favourite song *Doe A Deer* and then graduating to *Sugar Sugar*. She let us dress her in funny clothes, style her straight and shiny brown hair, cover her in make-up, and do pretty much anything else we wanted to have fun with her. Being a skinny, flexible little kid meant that we could hide Wendy in small places and she'd stay as still and quiet as a mouse, for as long as it took to find her. My thoughts drifted to the image of her delight in being found during a game of hide and seek. She had never minded those small, dark hiding spots. She never hesitated to sit under a pile of dirty laundry waiting to be discovered. And when she was, she'd pop up like a jack-in-the-box, scurrying out and ready for the next round.

At the conclusion of the service, everyone stood in preparation for leaving the chapel and heading to the cemetery. My father and I were the first ones to lead the procession behind that plywood coffin. That horrible box. My grandparents were right behind us with many family members, everyone holding tightly onto each other. I wanted to walk slowly. My father wanted to stay as close to the box as possible. He pulled me forward. Almost close enough to touch it. I didn't know why we had to walk faster, and so close to it. I didn't want to. It was a plain old box. And I instinctively knew that no one was going to walk ahead of us. Yet he kept pulling me ahead. I wondered why.

There was a big black limousine waiting for us outside the chapel to drive us to the cemetery. Once again, we sat in complete silence, looking out of the window, driving away from the city to the cemetery. I felt numb. Emotionless. All I could think about was that the inside of the limousine smelled like morning breath, as if my father and grandparents had forgotten to brush their teeth that morning.

When we got out of the limo, there was an endless line-up of cars pulling in behind us. It was an excessively hot day in the middle of summer, with no breeze and the sun beating down on the hushed, enormous cemetery.

We followed the men who carried the plywood box. All you could hear were people crying and the crunch of gravel as they walked on the path towards the giant hole with piles of dirt all around it. They walked a few steps. They stopped. They said a prayer in Hebrew. They walked a few more steps. They prayed. They walked. Stop. Pray. Walk. Like a game of follow the leader.

I figured that the guys who dug the hole got too hot and had to go take a break, since they left their shovels standing upright in the mountain of dirt. It reminded me of the big holes we used to dig in the sand when we went to the beach. Then one of us would jump in and everyone would pile the sand all around us, leaving only a head sticking out. People would walk by and laugh at the head popping out of the sand.

No one was laughing today.

The sobbing got much louder and my grandmother moaned and thrashed her arms. My uncles hugged her tightly. The people who held the big plywood box placed it on some straps on top of the hole. Sniffling and sobbing, praying and wailing. My Auntie Bernice fainted so someone waved the smelling salts under her nose. I couldn't believe that my uncle had actually even thought to have a little bottle of that stuff in his jacket pocket.

The big box was slowly lowered into the hole. When it was at the bottom, the cemetery workers pulled the straps out of the hole. I knew they were the workers because they weren't wearing a dark suit. Just t-shirts, jeans and big dirty boots covered in mud. Their skin was tanned and their hands dirty. They didn't look at anyone or say anything.

Then people took turns shovelling dirt into the hole. Taking the shovel from the pile of dirt, shovelling some earth into the hole, and then sticking the shovel back into the pile. Person after person. Silently, with no eye contact. The only sounds were the earth hitting the box, and loud weeping.

I stepped away. I didn't want a turn. In fact, I wanted nothing to do with what I thought was a horrible ritual of everyone participating in burying the box. I looked around at the little gardens in front of the other graves and thought that the flowers looked so pretty, so manicured, so beautifully cared for.

We went back to our house, to the sobbing house. A house filled with sorrow, shock and disbelief. Now they called it the Shiva house. That's what Jewish people do right after a funeral. They sit Shiva, usually for about a week following the funeral. The men pray twice a day. The immediate family members, the mourners, are not allowed to do anything except sit in low, uncomfortable chairs. People send meals to the house, catered meals on fancy catering platters. The mirrors have to be covered to remind people that their appearance is not important. And people can drop by any time they want, to pay their respects, to help serve food, to clean up from a meal. Basically to do something to make themselves feel useful and somehow helpful to the grieving family. So people kept coming over, telling us how sorry they were. Sombre head shaking. Weeping. Clicking their tongues sympathetically. Someone saying something right out of a Hallmark card, others nodding in agreement. Staring at us, speechless, awkward, upset.

Some people were eager to tell us their stories about their terrible losses. To prove to us that they shared our pain. They understood how much misery we were in. That impulse to say "me too." Someone had just gotten up from sitting Shiva themselves, after losing their elderly parent. They felt our pain. Someone knew of someone else who recently lost a child. They felt our pain. Someone had a third cousin once removed who lost a mother at a young age. They felt our pain.

In my mind, they couldn't possibly feel our pain. Nothing compared to us losing three family members in a plane crash.

These people made me sick. Really, was our Shiva house the place to come and tell us, the mourners, these morbid stories? There were times when we, my family members, the mourners, consoled these people coming to pay their respects to us, telling them how sorry we were to hear about their loss.

I spent as much time as possible locked in the bathroom with Tiger, sitting on the floor with her, petting her soft fur, and flipping through the magazines and Archie comic books we kept in a big white wicker basket next to the toilet. I counted the white square tiles. I measured the floor with my feet, with my hands, with my fingers. I scrubbed the tub with Ajax and used Windex to clean the mirror and the chrome faucets.

People kept knocking on the door, asking if I was okay. I told them I was fine and would be out in a minute. Eventually they stopped bothering me.

Whether my eyes were opened or closed, I couldn't stop the terrifying flashbacks of that plywood box.

CHAPTER 10

WHEN MY MOTHER was pregnant with Wendy, my parents decided that we should have a live-in babysitter so that my mom could go back to work. My mother was a bookkeeper for a giant granite quarry. She had a brown wooden desk in a small office area at the front end of the quarry where hundreds of skids sat, stacked with massive slabs of stone. She had to keep the office door closed most of the time in order to block out some of the noise and activity from the busy shipping and loading areas.

When we were older, I always called her at work the minute I got home from school and she always answered the phone in a serious business voice. Sometimes, she had to call me back because she was busy but usually she could chat and I would tell her about my day and find out what was for supper. By the time she got home, we were done with homework and outside playing. She always honked the horn when she pulled into our driveway. She was excited to be home. Happy to see us.

Back when my mother was pregnant with Wendy, Julie had answered the ad in the local newspaper, having just arrived in Montreal from St. Lucia.

When Wendy was born, Julie carried her around as if she was her mother. She fed her, burped her, kissed her, hugged her, rocked her. When Wendy was old enough to sit by herself, she let us bring her in the bath with us. When Wendy started to talk, she couldn't say "Julie" so she called her "Deedee" over and over again.

My mother and Julie were almost the same age and they got along well from the moment they met. My mother adored Julie, and always said that she completely trusted her, and how lucky we were to have her living in our house.

From the moment that Julie moved into our house, she made herself comfortable in the kitchen, preparing and cooking traditional West Indian food. Her stew and "dumplins" were an instant hit and became a regular part of our family's dinner menu.

She also boiled disgustingly smelly fish and, although the odour lingered in the house for days, my parents never said a word to her about it, and never asked her to stop. My sisters and I on the other hand, made a huge deal about it, dramatically holding our noses, moaning about the strong smell and covering our mouths with masks made out of dish towels.

Since our complaints were ignored, we gave up on our mission to ban boiled fish. It was a small price to pay for the love Julie so readily doled out.

Julie was part of our family. If you needed a hug, she wrapped you so tightly in her arms you could barely breathe. She ate with us, did homework with us, got angry if we didn't listen to her, laughed with us, hugged us, loved us. And we loved her.

She didn't have a bone of nonsense about her. If she didn't like something or someone, she said what was on her mind. No fuss. No politics. She was just a down to earth, bold and sincere human being. An honest to goodness angel.

Julie referred to my mother as "mommy" and to my dad as "Mr. Applebaum." The real Mr. Applebaum had once phoned and left a message with her for my dad, and she thought it was the funniest name she had ever heard. From that day on, she renamed my dad.

Deedee stayed with us for almost six years and, when Wendy went to school full days, Deedee moved out. She found a job in a retail store and lived with a few friends in an apartment, but she missed living with us, and we missed her. She still came to Friday night dinners at my grandparents' house, and didn't miss any holiday, birthday or other special occasion. She called us on the phone and dropped by during the week for supper. We went to see her at her apartment, and stopped by the store where she was working. Deedee promised Wendy that when she had children, she would move in and help her with her kids. That always made Wendy smile.

CHAPTER 11

THE WEATHER WAS scorching, and people stood around outside, all day, all evening. The house was so hot and sticky that even the electric fans plugged in all over did little to cool it down.

Each day it would start over again. The police officers came every day, apparently for traffic control. Our once quiet street, and several streets around us, now resembled a jam-packed parking lot. The entire city of Montreal was talking about this tragedy and even people who didn't know us, drove by to have a look at the house and maybe get a glimpse of the family. In fact, my bedroom was in the front of the house, and for a long time, probably for months afterwards, I used to tell my father that cars would stop in front of our house and people would just stare. As if we were freaks in a freak show.

A FEW DAYS later, they identified what they referred to as "the remains" of my thirty-nine-year-old mother, Rita, and my eleven-year-old sister, Carla. Remains. What did that mean?

We did the horrible funeral thing again. This time with two big plywood boxes and a much larger pile of dirt right next to where they had buried the other big plywood box. It looked like a double-sized hole. The single hole had already been filled to the top with dirt. No flowers. Just dirt.

Sobbing, praying, wailing, shovelling the dirt into the hole. It seemed as if everyone took a turn. Except me. I still didn't want to have a turn.

I decided right then that I would come back and plant purple lilacs on my mother and sisters' graves, since purple lilacs were my mother's favourite flowers. I didn't see any graves with lilacs. I loved my plan.

ACCORDING TO JEWISH custom, we had to start the week of Shiva all over again. At this point, I was exhausted, confused and totally sick of having people constantly at our house. Everyone seemed to be telling us what to do, how to do it, what to eat, when to eat, what to wear, when to sleep, what to say, what not to say. People actually debated about what was best for Saul and Lynda. They talked about us as if we weren't in the room.

And all of these people, some of whom I never even knew existed, kept showing up at our house. People who had known my mother, people who knew my aunts or uncles, my sisters' teachers, neighbours, acquaintances. An assortment of people who had heard about the tragedy and had decided to come and pay their respects. While they had come to express their condolences, most of them could barely get the words out, struck with dumb awkwardness.

And then there were the lawyers. Lawyers who offered us the opportunity to have them handle our lawsuit against Air Canada. Our new best friends. Some were subtle about it, others were pretty aggressive. My aunts and uncles called them ambulance chasers. The consensus amongst my relatives was that they were disgusting to come to a Shiva house looking for business.

The endless parade of people coming and going ended when the Shiva was officially over. As much as I had hated the constant crowd, I wasn't at all prepared for this emptiness. Dead silence. Loud silence. Deafening silence.

WITHIN A FEW days, one dapper looking lawyer sent his pretty wife over with a tuna casserole for us. She was all sweetness and bubbly, concerned about me and my father, even offering to take me shopping for school. I was starting high school in September and, now that I didn't have a mother, someone would have to make sure I got what I needed. Why not a complete stranger, whose husband happens to be a lawyer, who really wants to handle our case?

My father was not very happy with me and with the way I spoke to our new lawyer's wife. I didn't know that he had already decided to use her husband as our lawyer. I didn't know anything about lawyers or what they would be doing for us, but still, there was something about that well turned-out lawyer and his fancy wife that just didn't sit right with me. I couldn't pinpoint the reason, but I thought that choosing him to help us was a big mistake.

And besides, who wanted to eat a tuna casserole? My mother cooked real food for us. She didn't mix a can of tuna into some overcooked noodles. I told Mrs. Bubbly lawyer's wife that she could take her tuna casserole back home, and that I was already completely organized for school.

CHAPTER 12

D ESPITE THE FACT that she worked full time and spent endless hours doing volunteer work, my mother found time to produce delicious meals and mouth-watering desserts. She moved around the kitchen with ease, grabbing ingredients, reaching for bowls, stirring, tossing, whipping, blending, and either humming a tune or chatting away. My mother made it all look effortless. She cleaned up as she cooked so there was never a pile of things to be washed. She was neat, organized and in control.

It seemed as if there was always someone at our house for a cooking lesson, or maybe they were just looking for an excuse to spend time with her.

People adored my mother. She was a great listener—always giving advice. Sometimes, when I drifted close to the kitchen I would hear her.

"Everything happens for a reason. I really believe that. You'll see. It will all work out."

"I will be right by your side to support you. Call me any time, day or night. I mean it."

Her favourite line was "Life is too short to let nonsense bother you."

She looked for the good in people and, as a result, seemed to bring out the best in them. She always said that the more you give of yourself, the more joy you will get back in your own life.

When my mother's close friend delivered a baby with Down Syndrome, which in those days was referred to as mentally retarded, my mother found her new mission in life. She was determined to help the families in Montreal dealing with "retarded" children. She gathered a group of over twenty women and together they formed a Chapter of the "Montreal Association of the Mentally Retarded" or as it became popularly referred to as the M.A.M.R. Under my mother's leadership, these women met on a regular basis organizing fundraising activities and events. As the elected President of the M.A.M.R, my mother received a round gold pin which she proudly wore every day.

There was a school in Montreal specifically for children who were then referred to as "mentally retarded." When my mother organized a Saturday night dance for the students, we all helped. We spent the afternoon moving tables and chairs into the school's gymnasium, decorating the room with balloons and streamers, carefully arranging cookies and squares on big platters, and pouring fruit juice into a huge punch bowl. As the children arrived, the lights dimmed and music blasted out of the record player.

Carla and I danced with the kids the entire evening. We caught my mother crying and she said they were tears of joy and pride as she watched us "dance in their shoes."

I sat in on every minute of every M.A.M.R. meeting that took place at our house. In addition to planning fund-raising activities, the women talked about getting support services for the families of retarded children. What they did was pretty progressive stuff for the 1960s. I was determined to do something equally important when I grew up.

My mother was genuinely happy, and didn't want or need much for herself. Wearing Madame Rochas perfume and colouring her hair on a regular basis were the two things she did for herself. She rarely wore makeup and didn't care about keeping up with clothing styles. She talked about wanting to lose weight, but didn't let dieting control her life. My dad always used to tell us that the reason he married her was because whenever they went on a date to a restaurant, she always finished her meal. And then he would giggle.

She often hummed her favourite song, *Sunrise Sunset*. She loved when Carla and I would serenade her, with Carla's lovely piano playing and my overly confident singing skills. Wendy couldn't sit still long enough to sit on the piano bench and sing; instead she would perform a creative dance routine, totally off step to the beat. She was such an actress.

Sunrise, sunset
Sunrise, sunset
Swiftly flow the days
Seedlings turn overnight to sunflowers

Blossoming even as we gaze
Sunrise, sunset
Sunrise, sunset
Swiftly fly the years
One season following another
Laden with happiness and tears

Having our mother stretched out at the edge of each of our beds talking about our day, was the way my sisters and I fell asleep every night. She didn't have to say much because we always had loads to tell her during this special time together. We were completely honest with her, telling her our deepest, darkest secrets, because she never judged. I always got to stay up the latest, so my mother spent the most amount of time with me. It was one of the benefits of being the oldest daughter.

If she had to go out for an evening, she would wake each of us when she got home. She never forgot to do her rounds, even if it was just for a minute, no matter how late it was. We might have had something we were waiting to tell her. And she confessed that she always slept much better after she said goodnight to us.

My mother and I had some special rituals of our own. I was still young enough at that point in life that I couldn't or wouldn't see any faults at all in my mom. I was madly in love with her. She was my mentor, my confidante, my best friend in the whole world.

Sometimes I got to stay up late and watch a movie with my mother on the black and white television set she had in her bedroom. I remember peeking out from under the covers as we watched one of our favourites, Alfred Hitchcock's *The Birds*. Watching that scary movie with her filled me with a mixture of terror and comfort, the kind that only a mother can provide. As I clung to my mother in fear and love, she used to tell me that you can't stop watching a movie just because you're scared. You have to find the courage within you to stay tuned for the whole thing.

The Birds had an unusual ending. It just ended untraditionally. My mother always said that it was purposely made that way so that people could imagine or create their own ending to the story. We would lay there together, long after the movie was over, with my dad snoring away in the bed with us, making up different endings. "It can end whatever way we want it to end. It's merely a continuation of their lives. It's up to them to make their life as joyful and meaningful as possible. Or, maybe, there is life after death so there's never really an ending for anyone." In light of all the possibilities, most of the time, the ending we gave it was always a happy one.

Aside from making you choose your own ending, your own journey, my mother believed that *The Birds* had another important message about life. It was never give up, even if you're scared to death.

When the *TV Guide* listed *The Wizard of Oz, Mary Poppins, The Sound of Music* or *Heidi,* my sisters joined us and stayed up late to watch. That bed certainly was crowded with the five of us lying in it, glued to the television set. Our dad never managed to stay awake for a whole movie but, before he fell asleep, he always said that he was in his glory surrounded by all his girls.

"Shhhh, Daddy, we're watching."

CHAPTER 13

M Y AUNTS HAD formed a committee, representing both sides of the family. The "let's decide what's best for Saul and Lynda" committee. A combination of those who lead with their head, and those who lead with their heart. Oil and water.

I didn't want a committee making decisions for us. I fully appreciated everything my aunts did for us, but I longed for my mother, to see her face, smell her perfume, talk to her, hug her. I missed having my mother take care of everything in what always seemed like an effortless, positive way.

Hiring a full-time housekeeper who could cook, clean and take care of me and my father, became a mission for the committee. They held the back-to-back interviews in the living room of our house. I sat in the room with everyone, but I didn't say much. I was waiting for a gust of wind to blow the candidates out of the house and for Mary Poppins and her umbrella to float down from the ceiling.

Four of my aunts fired nonstop questions at these nervous-looking women, each applicant claiming to have the skills necessary to do the job. Of course my dad's side of the family wanted to be sure the woman was strict, organized and professional. My aunts on my mom's side wanted someone who was kind-hearted, compassionate and sensitive.

I watched as a steady stream of applicants for the job came and went, until my aunts could agree on who to hire.

"Lunatics" is the word that comes to mind when I think of only a few of our several housekeepers who actually made it past the interview stage. Mrs. Diano insisted that I refer to her as "Misses" in order to show her the respect she deserved. That impressed my dad's side of the family. She may have interviewed well but, once she moved in, she was a different person. She carried with her and slept with, at all times, a large butcher knife, explaining to me that she'd been around the block, she knew men and she didn't trust them. And she certainly wasn't taking any chances in a house with a lonely, newly widowed man. I ratted her out to the committee. Bye bye Mrs. Diano.

Then there was Mrs. Buckley. She was a short, chubby woman who kept her hair pulled tightly in a bun, and always wore an apron. She was extremely vocal about the health and digestion risks associated with having a glass of water, or any other beverage, while eating food. She also argued with me, insisting that I sit down at the kitchen table to eat my meals. I had lied and told her that my mother always let me stand at the counter and eat. The truth was that I couldn't sit at that big kitchen table, in my regular seat, or in anyone else's seat for that matter. It was just too painful, too difficult for me. Instead, I stood at the counter, or brought my food into my bedroom and ate at my desk.

Mrs. Buckley was so crazy she refused to do laundry more than once a week because touching the damp clothing could cause Arthritis. She could never do it when it was cold or rainy outside, as that would certainly, at the very minimum, cause the flu. Whenever I was out of the house, she would forbid our cat, Tiger, from coming upstairs, keeping her locked in the basement because she carried diseases. I notified the committee. Bye bye Mrs. Buckley.

And so it went. We went through about six of them, and then Julie, aka Deedee, finally stepped in to save the day. Thank God. My dad and I couldn't get to her apartment fast enough to fill his station wagon with her clothes and whatever other items she could fit in the car. I told her that she could boil her smelly fish every single day, I wouldn't care. I was just relieved to have her back with us.

I was hungry for some of that good, old fashioned St. Lucia love that Deedee was blessed with giving.

There are some people on earth who are actually angels. They come into your life when you need their help, in those times of darkness, carrying you when you need to be held, guiding, comforting, understanding, teaching. Honest-to-goodness angels.

Deedee, our angel.

WE ALL STRUGGLED to try and find a new normal. As if that was at all possible. One minute you thought that maybe, just maybe, you were going to be okay and the next minute you were overcome with anguish. Paralyzed. Out of nowhere would come a fresh flood of terror. A panic attack. Like a time bomb, ticking away silently and then exploding with a loud boom. Flashbacks where painful memories and pictures burst unwanted into your mind, suddenly, searingly. Replaying the horrors over and over. The phone call. The big plywood boxes. Follow the leader. The shovel stuck in the pile of dirt. The women with no lipstick and dark sunglasses. The pictures from the newspapers. Those scary men from Air Canada. Flashbacks that were like a dripping faucet that didn't shut off no matter how tightly you turned the handle. Impossible to ignore. Unstoppable. Drip. Drip. Drip.

My heart would start pounding and I felt myself breathing fast. Too fast. Gulping for air. I was sure I was having a heart attack. I would find myself clutching my head, squeezing my eyes shut until it hurt, trying to stop the worries. Trying anything, just to block them out. I turned to distraction. Find something, anything, to think about that would replace the monsters that were suffocating me. Clean the house. Organize a drawer or closet. Empty the book shelves, wipe off all the dust, and then line the books all up on the shelves again. Perfectly lined up. In order of height. Maybe even divided by subject or theme. More to think about. More of a distraction.

That's how it goes when you're in the whirlwind of a crisis. One minute you're coping. The next minute you're a wreck.

THE COMMITTEE THOUGHT it would be best for us to get rid of all of the personal items that belonged to my mother and sisters. They didn't think it was healthy that we still kept their toothbrushes in the cup by the bathroom sink, Wendy's pink bubble bath on the edge of the tub, my mother's big bottle of *Madame Rochas* perfume, their clothes in the closets and dresser drawers, their shoes, their boots, their mementos. I heard of their plans to pack everything up and donate it all to the M.A.M.R. second-hand store that my mother had worked hard to support. I begged them not to. Not yet.

I needed more time. I wanted their things around. I wanted to touch them, to smell them. The truth was that I needed to pretend that they were still alive, and would be coming home soon. Maybe they had survived and were walking around with amnesia.

The committee won. I came home to find their closets and drawers empty. Only Julie's and my toothbrushes in the cup. No pink bubble bath. They even took Carla's and Wendy's bikes out of the garage. I guess they didn't know that sometimes Carla and I would trade bikes, just for the fun of it. Now I could only ride my own bike.

Julie told me that she had spent the whole day with my aunts, packing up all of the items and loading everything into their cars. She said that she had kept some of Wendy's dolls and stuffed animals on the bed as decorations for the room. My aunts let her keep Wendy's pink flower girl dress, and she showed me that she had saved the bottle of my mother's perfume for me.

If this was supposed to be the healthy alternative. I would have preferred to stay unhealthy. The house felt enormous. I could have sworn that my voice echoed when I talked. None of the rooms looked the same any more. I didn't know where to go or what to do.

By the end of the summer and once I started grade eight, which according to the Montreal school system was my first year in high school, we had somewhat of a routine. My father, Julie and I had a comfortable relationship, although none of us spent too much time at home. We never talked about it, but I knew that we all hated the deafening silence of the house. The emptiness. The indescribable sadness, loneliness and pain. People tried hard to be nice to us. So we spent lots of time at other people's houses. Family members, friends, new friends who invited us over for dinner, neighbours, anywhere but home.

Our "home" had become a house. A place to store our clothes. A place to sleep. A place where we could hide in our rooms and cry.

CHAPTER 14

A LMOST EVERY YEAR, our family went up north to spend a few weeks in the "country." My mother and a few of her friends found this group of low budget, dilapidated rental country houses located just an hour north of Montreal. I remember it as a mouse-infested, rickety, musty-smelling shack with old dishes, dented pots and pans, ancient furniture and linoleum floors that curled at the seams and creaked when you walked on them. There were cobwebs everywhere and curly brown flypaper hanging from the ceiling. It did a supreme job of catching flies but you had to be careful that your hair didn't get caught in it. We just loved that place.

Using every possible inch of space, everyone packed up their cars with food, clothes, towels, fishing rods, bikes, inflatable rafts, board games, flashlights and bedding. Then off to the cottages we all went, in a big convoy.

It was understood that all of the kids stayed together and looked out for each other. We were summer sisters and brothers and we all treasured those weeks. We ate all our meals together, swam in the lake, climbed trees, caught frogs, picked wild blueberries and raspberries, rode our bikes on the bumpy dirt roads and just hung out. Free and happy. There was an old beat up row boat, that no one seemed to own, tied to the dock and, of course, we never hesitated to use it. As long as we bailed out the water the whole time, it stayed afloat. At least once a day, we piled into that green relic, with surely more passengers than was allowed or safe, and away we went. Some of us would fish while others would lean back and sun bathe. There had to be one person to row and, of course, someone to constantly fill up the old, rusty apple juice can with water from the floor of the boat and dump it overboard. No life jackets. No rules. No restrictions. And not a worry in the world.

The dads would each drive up on Friday evenings and stay until Monday morning. Their arrival generated excitement and mayhem. As soon as we heard the first car pull onto the dirt road, every single kid dashed over, usually barefoot and screaming, to greet the dad, regardless of whose dad it may have been. We knew that they always had something delicious for all of us kids—donuts, cookies, ice cream or chocolate cake. The various desserts on Friday nights were always extra special.

On Saturday or Sunday mornings, often on both, my dad and I went fishing, just the two of us. No one else was ever down at the lake and I liked being the first people awake. It felt special, important. On those early mornings, with the sun just rising, the lake was totally still, shimmering like a mirror. It was usually chilly, and the air was sweet with morning fog. The gentle symphony of birds chirping, frogs croaking and leaves rustling accompanied us as we strolled down to the dock carrying a metal pail, two fishing rods, a white Styrofoam container of fresh, plump worms and a string with hooks that my dad used to tie the fish and hang them over the side of the boat. My dad would whistle while we walked, gravel crunching underfoot. He was a good whistler and when I wasn't busy guessing the song or trying to whistle along with him, I updated him on all he'd missed.

"We caught so many frogs this week that we had to use pails from everyone's house. Don't worry. We let them all go. We didn't want them to die."

"We only had to take two cars into town to buy groceries because we fit seven people in each car. We were squished in there like sardines. Crammed in like they do in the circus car."

"We found an abandoned house on the road near the old church. For sure no one lives there and the windows are all boarded up. We broke in by crawling through a small window that wasn't even locked. It's full of cobwebs and dust every where. It was so much fun. So cool. We're going to go back next week."

"Tiger loves it up here. Every morning we find a dead mouse or bird in front of the house. Mommy says she is bringing us presents. It's so gross."

My dad listened, smiled...and, of course, he giggled.

Once in the rowboat with our rods in the water, waiting for a bite, my father never whistled. He said it would scare away the fish. The only sounds were the squeal of the oars, the creaking of the benches, and the water splashing against the boat. We would giggle together as he watched me put a worm on the hook. My dad used to tell me that the fish couldn't resist my worms because I put them on the hook perfectly. We always caught some fish. Mostly perch. We would bring our catch up to the cottage, clean the fish on newspaper spread out over the table and have them frying in the pan with butter splattering all over the stove by the time everyone was up and ready for breakfast. A ritual. Our ritual. Mine and my dad's.

CHAPTER 15

IT WAS THE doorbell. It had a different ring than usual, more of a buzzer sound. Cold and unfriendly. When I opened the door, a person stood there holding a huge box. A plywood box, unpainted, nailed closed. A mysterious and horrifying box.

I thought he was a man, but he had no face so I didn't know for sure. He extended his arms to hand me the box but I backed away. I didn't want it. He pushed it closer to me. He said I had to take it.

Everyone was standing behind me, in dark clothes, sunglasses, crying. My father, my grandparents, my aunts, uncles, cousins, friends. Except for my mother and sisters. They weren't there. No one was speaking. They were just leaning on each other, some of them quietly weeping, most of them sobbing uncontrollably.

The man put the ominous box in my arms and turned and walked away. It was very light. It felt like there was hardly anything in there. I put it down on the floor, trying to decide what to do with it. Should I open it? Should I leave it nailed closed? Should I bury it? Where was the big hole with the dirt piled all around it? Where were the cemetery workers, all sweaty with their dirty hands and big muddy boots?

Everyone just stared at me. Sombre head shaking. Waiting for me to decide what to do. Someone handed me a tool, a long piece of metal with a sharp edge. I guess I could use it to pry open the box. But the Air Canada people would be angry. They said we had to keep it sealed.

I have to know what's in the box, but I don't want to see it. It could be a finger, or an arm, or a leg. I was so scared. They all looked at me. And waited. No one spoke.

I woke up and crawled into bed with Deedee.

DEEDEE WAS THE only one who knew about my nightmares. Waking up in the morning and finding me in her bed was her number one clue. I told her all of the gory details about that horrifying plywood box, the man with no face, the mystery of what is sealed inside…and she would hold me until I was calm. As real and vivid as they were, Julie promised that it was only been a bad dream. Everything would be okay.

Reassuring. Comforting.

If I didn't want to talk about the graphic details, I didn't have to. She already knew. I didn't tell anyone else. When the nightmares woke me, I crawled into her bed, and that was it. No big discussion about it, no need for therapy. It was just a bad dream. Everything will be okay.

PART TWO:

Absence

CHAPTER 1

WENDY'S BIRTHDAY CAME first, just a few weeks after the plane crash. The days leading up to, and then getting through that day, were sheer torture. How could August 1st come and go without us having a birthday party for our little Wendy? She was supposed to turn nine. And instead, she was dead.

Birthdays had always been a big deal in our house. My mother invited lots of people over and baked several cakes, not just one. We cherished the traditions of turning out the lights and singing, accompanied by Carla on the piano, our family's operatic version of Happy Birthday. In that previous life we were always celebrating the good stuff with a house full of extended family.

When the dreaded day finally arrived, no one talked about it, even when they called us on the phone. Not a word. Not me, my dad, my grand-parents, aunts, uncles, cousins. No one. We all knew what day it was, but there was nothing to say. What can you say?

I walked around that whole day in a complete fog. I was awake but I felt like I was watching from somewhere outside of my own body. There, but not really there. I watched people go about their day. Strangers. Acting normally. Laughing. Driving cars. Eating. Just carrying on with their lives. But nothing was normal. None of it seemed right. It was Wendy's birthday and she wasn't here any more. Didn't they know?

Clearly, the whole world already forgot about our tragedy and every-one had moved on. We were yesterday's news.

I couldn't let the day go by without doing something to acknow-ledge Wendy's birthday, even if I had to do so alone. Maybe I was losing my mind, because I knew in my head that she was gone so there was no birthday to celebrate, but in my heart, which ached for her and for Carla and my mom, and the happy daddy that I had up until a few weeks ago, I decided to have my own private little birthday celebration in her room. Just me and Tiger. I went in there with Tiger in my arms, closed the door and sat on Wendy's bed. Her dolls and stuffed animals were all lined up neatly in front of her pillow. The only one missing was her favourite doll, which she had named Barbara, and that was the only doll that she took with her whenever she slept away from home. In fact, Barbara had been

The Montreal Star

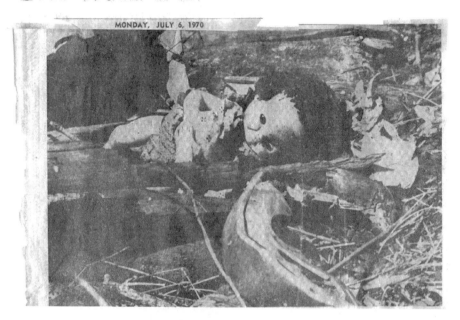

MONDAY, JULY 6, 1970

identified by Air Canada a few days before Wendy's "pulverized remains" were found. A picture of Barbara had even made it to the front page of the newspaper.

I brought her little china tea set to the bed, lined up the stuffed animals in a semi-circle, facing me, with Tiger purring lazily amongst them, and together we sang Happy Birthday to Wendy in our quietest voices. Then we ate invisible cake and drank invisible tea together, at what I imagined had to have been the loneliest birthday party that had ever taken place.

I must have cried myself to sleep right there on Wendy's bed, because I woke up several hours later to my father gently shaking me and telling me to go and sleep in my own bed. I left the birthday party and went to my room. Not a word was mentioned about it the next day. Nothing.

Same story in September, when we had to somehow get through both Carla's and my mother's birthdays. On September 16th, Carla was supposed to celebrate her twelfth birthday. My mother would have turned forty on September 23rd.

Dreaded anticipation. Horrific days. But not a word mentioned. No acknowledgment. No discussion. No private birthday parties with invisible cake or tea. Just the unspoken understanding that we are all aware, but there is no way we can talk to each other about it. That would be impossible.

On top of it all, my father was turning forty-five in November. I was at a complete loss as to how we were going to deal with his birthday. No idea. The thought of it was actually terrifying to me.

For my father's fortieth, my mother had made him a fabulous surprise party. Since it was close to Halloween, everyone came in costume. My mother had gone all out and even rented costumes for our immediate family. My father was a king, my mother a queen, and the three of us were jesters. She splurged on a flashy king's crown with big red stones. So typical of my mother. She always brought out the best in him, made him look good and feel great about himself. She always found a way to make him feel like he was a King.

But life does go on, along with the arrival of birthdays for those people who are still alive. Those birthdays can't be ignored. They also can't be celebrated with the same excitement. Fake enthusiasm is allowed. Gifts are fine. Guilt is inevitable. Even choosing a card and deciding how to sign it is difficult. Making a wish and then blowing out the candles...*I wish my mother and sisters were still alive. I wish my father didn't have to suffer so much. I wish I could be happy again.* It's probably better to just have a cake and forget the wishes or the candles. Somehow, at the very least, the birthday has to be acknowledged.

Rule number one after the death of a member, or multiple members of your family, is that birthdays for everyone, dead or alive, now include a heavy heart, weighed down with emotions that are not listed anywhere in the happy birthday cards. A birthday can be dealt with in a variety of ways. You can ignore it, pretending that it is just an ordinary day. That would be denial. You can acknowledge it and maybe even admit to the terrible sadness you feel about the person no longer there to celebrate their own birthday. As for the guilt you feel for remaining alive, and the grief, pity, anger, sadness, sorrow...these birthday feelings will probably return year after year.

Dear Diary,

Birthdays as we knew them are gone for good. Now we have new rules. New traditions. And plenty of new emotions. We had to follow the new rules for Daddy's birthday, so tonight we were invited to Uncle Dave and Auntie Riva's house. Everyone from the Weinberg side of the family was there. I was surrounded by so many people, but I felt alone. Lonely. Hard to describe. Empty. Alone. Scared.

We ate dinner. We talked about nothing. Auntie Riva brought out a small chocolate cake. It had one candle. There was no singing or smiling. Not even the fake kind. Thank God no one suggested that he make a wish. He blew out the candle, we ate the cake. He opened his gifts. A wallet. A sweater. A book. We went home. The end.

Sunrise Sunset. Sunrise Sunset.

CHAPTER 2

I HUNG OUT with friends as much as possible. Even though I knew that I could talk to Donna or Barbara about absolutely anything, I much preferred our intense conversations about normal teenage stuff like boys, friends and school. I wanted life to be ordinary, whatever that was. The last thing I wanted to do was feel sorry for myself, panic or feel anxious, mope around or be depressed.

I had already spent plenty of time thinking about what had happened, reliving the nightmare over and over, feeling stuck in that dark place. Alone. Scared. Miserable. Cold. I hated it there. Sudden anxious and irritable feelings. Memories and images that popped up out of nowhere. Whenever I found myself slipping into that black tunnel, I distracted myself with normal things. Do not panic, I told myself. Instead, try cleaning the house. Organizing closets. Ironing. Riding my bike. Cooking. Baking. Keeping busy. Always busy.

I waffled between normal and psycho. I had a real life and a life in my head. Like living in two different worlds.

That wonderful break from reality was like a mini-vacation. When I was really desperate for a way to calm down, I pretended that the plane crash had never occurred and that life was just the same as it was before July 5th, 1970. When I was by myself, I talked to them, my mother and sisters, pretending they were with me. I closed my eyes and pictured them. I took myself back to those moments when our whole family sat at our kitchen table, laughing, eating, cleaning up together. I clung to the memories that were calming and comforting. Pretending. Dreaming. Wishing.

I imagined my mom sitting on my bed at night, leaning towards me, listening, speaking quietly. I particularly loved when I could imagine hearing them speak…my mother's soft, soothing voice, Carla's calm and logical way of saying things, and Wendy's nonstop, enthusiastic chatter.

EACH DAY AT sundown, as the daylight dimmed, a queasiness started to come over me. Nights were not a good time. Thoughts and details crowded my mind. Worry, despair, loneliness. The darkness scared me.

THE BEST THING about Donna and Barbara was that they treated me in an everyday way. That was the way I wanted, and needed, to appear and to be treated. They were comfortable around me, unlike so many of the kids I knew at school. We didn't have those awkward moments where the conversation ended abruptly because they worried about having said something in front of me that might upset me. They could talk about their mothers or siblings. They could even complain about them. I was well aware of their typical, happy families, and they were well aware of my situation. But really, none of that mattered when talking about our crushes or gossiping about the sluts in our grade.

When I wasn't with them, I always managed to find somewhere to go after school so I wouldn't have to walk into that silent house. I suffered from conflicting desires. While I wanted to be exactly like everybody else, I also wanted to be special enough that people invited me to spend time at their homes, to join them for meals at their noisy, normal tables. It was a small gesture that meant so much. I was enormously relieved when I knew I didn't yet have to go back to my empty house.

Of course, wherever I was, I knew that the parents would always offer to drive me home. It was obvious that they felt sorry for me and my father, but no one ever said anything about it. They didn't have to. Unlike with Donna and Barbara, any subject that in any way related to death, mothers, sisters, mourning, loss, whatever, was completely avoided. If someone inadvertently mentioned something that they thought would make me uncomfortable, the subject was quickly changed. But only after a few seconds of total silence. Seconds that felt like minutes. Uncomfortable for everyone.

My situation was complicated. Unusual. Unfamiliar. I knew it. I accepted it. I felt isolated. I felt as if I was the only person in the world who had lost a mother and two sisters. The only person in the world whose father was a walking zombie. I was different and most people didn't know how to act around me. Too bad they didn't know what I really wanted. I wanted life to feel as ordinary as it could. Most of all, I wanted to be happy and to get on with my life.

WHEN I WASN'T invited to someone's home, I kept moving and stayed busy on my own. I found things to do and places to go. Often, I was next door with my dear friends Jon and Shelley. Shelley, Jon and I spent hours and hours together, mostly sitting and talking on the floor in Shelley's room. It helped to talk to people also going through a tough time. When the weather was nice, the three of us would climb up to the highest branches possible in the big willow tree behind Shelley's house. We talked. We didn't talk. Either way, we were content being together.

Shelley's parents were divorced, which was highly unusual in those days. Her mother was an eccentric woman, completely incapable of mothering. To say the least, she had a lot of issues so Shelley was really the mother in that house, responsible for her two younger brothers, three dogs, a monkey, birds and a tank filled with tropical fish.

Jon's mother had died when Jon was three years old. She had a brain hemorrhage just hours after giving birth to Jon's younger brother. His grandmother had moved in with the family to help look after the three children.

Jon's dad had remarried a few years later. Combined, there were six kids in his family. There were always bathroom line-ups in that small house, which was packed with eight people, bunk beds, and a huge kitchen table.

We had an unspoken understanding between the three of us about being unusual. Different than most of the kids we knew, who had regular families. But no matter what, we never felt sorry for ourselves or for each other. It was never a case of "misery loves company." Quite to the contrary. We kept each other up. Optimistic. Determined. We ate bags of chips, baked cookies, we laughed, we did homework together, and we could just be silent together. The three of us were destined to be neighbours. Soul siblings. And we were grateful to have each other. We had each been through a lot, yet we knew how important it was to find the good in any situation. We knew it was important to look for the rainbows in every storm. We talked a lot about that—finding rainbows.

Dear Diary,
I am not kidding when I say that I stay away from home as much as possible. I dread being alone in this house. I hear noises and I'm scared. Even when Daddy's here I feel so alone 'cuz he's not really here. Besides I never know what state he will be in. I just hate being here so I just come here to sleep. And anyways I don't sleep very well. Almost every night I am woken up in the middle of the night by that horrible sound Daddy makes when he's crying. I can't stand it. I pull my pillow over my ears to block out the sounds. My life sucks.

CHAPTER 3

I WAS NOT at all prepared for my parents'
wedding anniversary. My mother always teased
my dad about forgetting it. I guess I had hoped
that this time, this year, he really would forget
the date, so that it would be somewhat bearable.
That was definitely not the case.

As I had done every morning since the accident, I went looking for my father the minute
I woke up. Usually he was in his bathroom
with the door closed. I would knock, say good
morning, ask him if he slept okay, hear the usual
yes even though I knew that he hadn't because I
had heard him either crying or wandering aimlessly around the house during the night, and
then I would get washed and dressed.

But on this day, his bathroom door was
open. When I called his name, I heard a faint
response coming from the dining room. I found
him sitting at the dining room table, slumped over, weeping quietly, with
their wedding album open on the table. He looked up at me with his
bloodshot eyes and an expression on his face of sheer agony. A face dis-
playing a horrible combination of desperation, sadness and anguish.

I leaned over him from the back of the chair, draped my arms around
his neck, and together we cried and cried. No words were spoken. My
tears poured onto his shiny, bald head, but he didn't move. He couldn't. I
couldn't. As if we were both frozen in pain. Stunned.

I don't know how long we stayed locked together in that painful
acknowledgement of loss, hurt, loneliness. It could have been seconds,
moments, or an hour.

I looked up and saw Julie standing at the doorway, watching, quietly
crying. Helpless. Immobilized. I pulled away from my father and walked
directly to my room. I got dressed and ready for school. I grabbed an apple
from the fridge and quietly walked out the door. Shelley and Jon were
waiting to walk to school with me. I put a smile on my face and off we went.

None of us ever said a word about it. It was much easier to just pretend it never happened.

EVERYTHING IN MY life was different. New and scary. And I was in my first year of high school. The school was huge, a melting pot for about eight elementary schools. Most of the kids had no idea who I was or what I was dealing with. I hid it well. When panic seeped into my thoughts without any warning, I locked myself in a bathroom cubicle, crying, hyperventilating, quickly sliding into my fantasy world, waiting for the fear to subside. For the most part, I was just another grade eight student wearing jeans and an oversized t-shirt, hustling to class, hanging around my locker, lining up in the cafeteria for a greasy hamburger, and trying to look comfortable and confident. Truth be told, I was insecure, anxious and worried. I felt anonymous and vulnerable. There were clearly defined cliques, and my friends and I were unofficially ranked by our fellow eighth graders as cool, average or nerdy. I'm pretty sure I was average.

It was made clear to us grade eight students that we were the newest members of the high school tribe, the babies, the rookies. The older kids ruled the school but not in a big sister or big brother way. They weren't protective or helpful. I found the whole atmosphere intimidating and unfriendly. The panic attacks and freaking out in the bathroom stall didn't help. One day a group of older girls walked in and heard me crying. "Hey! Take a chill pill in there." And they all started laughing. I froze. I didn't come out until I was positive that they were gone.

Dear Diary,

Today there was an open house at my high school where everyone was invited to bring their parents to meet the teachers and see the school. I will never go to one of those again. I used to love going to school open houses with Mommy. I never should have gone with Daddy. He didn't know what to do or what to say on his own without Mommy there to talk for both of them. I felt everyone's eyes on us the whole time, staring at us. The teachers acted so weird.

I want Mommy back. I want her back so badly.

CHAPTER 4

I KEPT BUSY but I was not really okay. I felt like I was treading water in the deep end, and the only way I could keep from drowning was by finding things to do. I guess my dad felt the same way. I couldn't remember the last time we ate a meal or watched TV together in our house. He always managed to find somewhere to go, only returning home when it was already dark. Seeing customers, going to synagogue, dropping by his brother's or sisters' houses…anything except coming home. Each of us kept busy, hanging onto hectic schedules like life jackets.

I quickly became consumed by projects that would divert my thoughts. I enthusiastically got involved in school fundraising activities and local volunteer projects. I always had something on the go. I made plans and to-do lists. I wrote everything down on a calendar and made sure there were never any blank spaces.

I continued to volunteer at a local nursing home, proudly sporting my pink and white striped uniform, which they only gave to the teen volunteers who completed the volunteer training program and could then call themselves candy-stripers. I didn't exactly need any special training since all I was doing was feeding the patients, chatting with them, and doing whatever jobs the staff gave me to do.

I had regular babysitting jobs especially on Saturday nights, and was booked weeks in advance. Saturday nights in my house were one of my favourite times with my sisters. Before my parents went out and while they got ready to leave, the three of us had supper together. It was never the same kind of food we ate every other night, because we were allowed to make whatever we wanted. Sometimes we would pretend to be chefs in a fancy restaurant and, after choosing recipes from one of my mother's ridiculous number of cookbooks, we would prepare a gourmet feast. Our parents always said that our dinner was definitely going to be much better than the one they were going to have with their friends, either in a restaurant or at someone else's house.

If there was something special on TV and we didn't have time to do the whole elegant dinner meal, we would just boil noodles and then mix them with a jar of spaghetti sauce and some slices of orange cheese.

No matter what we prepared, my dad would always be ready before my mom, so he'd come into the kitchen for what he called "a little taste," "an appetizer." We knew he was sneaking it, because my mom would get mad at him for eating before they went out for dinner. If she walked into the kitchen, he would quickly pass his plate to one of us, so he wouldn't get caught. Funny how our giggling never gave it away.

Making sure I had babysitting jobs on Saturday nights was critical to me. I was probably the only babysitter who, after putting the kids to bed, cleaned the entire kitchen, scrubbed the sink with Ajax, and organized all the toys and books. It wasn't about being obsessive compulsive; I loved pleasing these people who were nice to me. Truthfully, I couldn't sit still. I was fidgety and panicky when faced with the thought of being in a silent house. Often I was tempted to wake the kids so I could play with them. Instead, I turned up the volume on the television, or vacuumed the living room, or both. Of course, by throwing in my cleaning lady services, I made way more money with my babysitting jobs than any of my friends. Win win.

One of my favourite places to babysit was at my Uncle Issie's house. My mother had been particularly connected to her older brother, so we spent a lot of time with their family. Their two daughters were almost like sisters to me and my sisters. My sisters and I had loved babysitting for Fern and Cindy, playing with them, taking them to the park, organizing their birthday parties, dressing them up for Halloween, and anything else we could do with them. Their house was like our second home.

Dear Diary,
I can't stand being at home. Every time I walk in that house, I feel like I'm walking into a deserted building. I keep thinking about how we should have a big VACANCY sign that is lit up in neon lights, just like they do in those old motels on the side of a dark dirt road in an abandoned town.

I love spending time at Auntie Nicky and Uncle Issie's house. The guest bedroom is now officially my room, and I am their weekend babysitter. I am spending so much time there, it is actually starting to feel like my home. And I like to pretend that Fern and Cindy are my little sisters. I want that so badly. I miss Carla and Wendy terribly.

CHAPTER 5

O UR LAWYER'S JET black hair was always perfectly combed and he had a cocky expression on his face. Smug ambulance chaser. We had to provide him with a variety of personal information as he apparently built a case against Air Canada. He asked for permission to obtain copies of Carla's and Wendy's previous report cards, to support the "future loss of income" for each of them.

My father and I had to attend a meeting with our lawyer, which took place in a luxurious conference room at his office. The reception desk was manned by a pretty woman in a colourful dress and high heels that clicked on the floor when she walked. She escorted us into the meeting. Everyone else had already arrived, and had papers, fancy pens and files spread out in front of them. They stood up when we walked in.

This was the first important business meeting I had ever attended. I was so anxious to look grown up and mature, that it took me all morning to pick out my outfit. I tried on practically everything in my closet, finally settling on a navy skirt and white blouse.

My father introduced himself as Saul Weinberg, and then introduced me as his daughter, Lynda. That stung. He used to introduce me as "number one" but now I was the only one. I had to bite the inside of my cheeks to stop myself from bursting into tears. I realized right at that moment that my dad would never again call me his "number one."

I was no longer part of a nuclear family. We were just a dad and a daughter. I was no longer the older sister. I was no one's sister. I was no longer number one.

We sat on burgundy upholstered chairs around a gleaming, cherry wood table. In the centre of the table was a large tray with a silver jug of ice water, glasses and tea cups all perfectly lined up, coffee, tea, sugar, cream, teaspoons, cocktail napkins and assorted tea biscuits.

They all looked very serious and quiet, looking around the room as if no one knew exactly what to say. People cleared their throats, examined their fingernails, looked at their watches, flipped through papers without actually reading anything.

Once the secretary was done pouring drinks, she sat down and our lawyer began speaking. He thanked everyone for coming and introduced us to the four official-looking men who were representatives of Air Canada and an insurance company.

The men spoke one at a time, asking us questions that seemed rather personal and intrusive, and jotting down notes. Questions about my mother's job, her relationship with her parents and her involvement in helping them with their financial matters, other responsibilities she had assumed in her volunteer work, Carla and Wendy's academic abilities and challenges, their personalities and their interests.

They were intimidating and businesslike, leaving me feeling as if we had somehow done something wrong. My father sat there looking utterly blank. Glazed. Transfixed. I felt a tight pressing in my chest and with my bottom lip trembling uncontrollably, I blurted out "Carla was very smart. She got all As in school. She was going to be a doctor."

The room was silent, that stark type of silence, and everyone suddenly looked uneasy. One of the men with penetrating eyes authoritatively responded.

"I think we ought to stick to the agenda."

I felt so stupid for opening my mouth. I couldn't help it. Blinking hard, my eyes stinging, the tears rushed out, pouring down my face. But no one seemed to notice anyways—or, at least they pretended not to notice. I just wanted to get out of there as quickly as possible. For the remainder of the meeting, I sat there without making a sound, anxiously nibbling at my finger nails.

I imagined that was what it felt like to be sent to the Principal's office. I had never been in there, but I had walked by it enough times to see kids who'd been sent by their teacher for misbehaving.

But this was different, we'd done nothing wrong. It just bewildered and angered me that these Air Canada and insurance suits were talking about my family members like random, anonymous and irrelevant individuals. I assumed that for Air Canada, the plane crash and our important meeting were all strictly business. The only Air Canada employees who ever showed us any compassion or understanding had been the doting flight attendants on the day of the crash. Aside from the day the officials came over to our house with pictures of items retrieved from the site, and this official meeting, as far as I knew, we never heard from Air Canada again.

I often overheard my relatives saying that they must have been instructed to keep their distance from the families of the victims. They went on and on that the Air Canada decision-makers and lawyers were concerned that follow-up calls or visits to monitor and support the families would potentially translate into more dollars that would have to be spent by them. There was no concern for or even an awareness of the magnitude of our loss, and the struggles we faced as we tried to cope with the neverending fallout of such a horrific tragedy.

I overheard these countless discussions and arguments amongst the committee, which had now grown to include my uncles, about our lawyer and the airline's apparent rush to settle this case. They felt that the amount of the proposed settlement was grossly and obviously insufficient. They wanted me and my father to seek professional help and advice to determine the immediate and long term effects of the tragedy. They felt that the paltry sum offered as a settlement would not even compensate for my mother's lack of income and the cost of housekeepers, let alone the understated and underestimated emotional damage and ongoing therapy.

The committee felt that my father was being pressured and rushed, and railroaded into an unfavourable and pathetic settlement. They wanted him to insist on slowing things down and waiting for some of the other victims' cases to be settled. But my father didn't listen to my aunts and uncles. First of all, he was so vulnerable and distraught that he certainly didn't have the backbone or energy to insist on anything. And while he was intimidated and overwhelmed by the whole legal system, he trusted this lawyer. I didn't understand a lot of what was said, but I knew that my relatives did not trust the lawyer. I may have been young, but I agreed with them. I intuitively felt that he was a self-serving, phoney and heartless man.

I tried to talk to my father about all of this at home. It was like talking to a mannequin. He gave me that vacant look, with tearful eyes and slumped shoulders. He looked so beaten. So defeated. I didn't pursue it.

Despite everything, I was determined, and felt destined to live a happy life. I believed that it was no mistake that I was not on the plane with my mother and sisters. I had to believe that. For whatever reason, I was supposed to be alive. I had things to do. There were people who needed me. I didn't know exactly who they were or what I was supposed to be doing, but I just knew that I was alive for a reason.

What I wanted to know was how I was supposed to get through the rest of my life without my mother and sisters. And how could I go on and have a happy life with my own father suffering so intensely?

There were so many unanswered questions. What is a fair financial settlement for the loss of family members? My father, the daddy that I knew, had died that day too. Abandoned me, just shut off, like a tap. He was so emotionally destroyed, distraught and unstable that he was unable to function as a parent, to provide any fatherly support, guidance or direction, or be of any useful, reasonably expected assistance to me at all.

Essentially, I lost everyone in my immediate family. What monetary value do you put on the "official" death of a mother and two sisters, and the "unofficial" death of a father? The death of a man's soul. How much is all of that worth? What price do you put on a mother's goodnight time together, tight hugs and kisses? How much is it worth to have your mother and sisters at your fourteenth birthday? How much compensation takes the pain away from having a birthday without them? What dollar amount equals your mother taking care of you when you are sick? What about getting your period for the first time? Would a large cheque put an end to that wounded wailing sound coming from my father's room?

How much money could diminish the pain of watching my father and grandparents each in a state of hopeless sadness, continuously collapsing deeper into despair?

There wasn't enough money in the whole world to compensate us for what we lost, and for what we were dealing with now in the midst of all this personal trauma. No amount of money could numb the pain.

What I desperately needed was for my father to pick himself up and move forward. I needed him to stop his blood-chilling wailing in the middle of the night, and to hear him whistle again. Maybe even giggle once in a while. And I needed some reassurance, some promise, that the difficulties would go away as I got older. That I wouldn't always feel cheated out of having my parents and sisters with me for the day-to-day and significant events in my life. A promise that no one could possibly make.

Instead my father agreed to settle our case soon afterwards, and we ended up with what the committee continued to refer to as a ridiculously low and unfair settlement.

FILE CLOSED.

Dear God,

Let's make a deal. I don't want the money from Air Canada. I won't ask for anything again in my whole life, I will help people who are sick or mentally retarded. I will listen to my teachers and I will do everything I am told to do. I will even become religious. Just give me back my family even for just a few more years. Even just for one day. Please God.

CHAPTER 6

MY AUNTIE NAOMI called me from New York at least once every single day. She never worried about the long distance bills. But she did worry about me, and with that booming personality of hers, she never hesitated to express her opinions. She told me that if I don't talk about the accident and I keep it all inside, I will have a nervous breakdown when I grow up.

"You can't keep it all bottled up. You have to have a good cry."

"I do talk about it. You don't have to worry. You worry too much."

She was not at all convinced.

"Do me a favour." She always said that. "Let me make arrangements for you to go and talk to someone. I'll pay for it. Humour me."

I knew that she was just concerned about me. I also knew that she was talking about a Shrink.

Dear Diary,

I actually went to see a Shrink today, mostly to make Auntie Naomi happy and get her off my back. She was very nice, asked me a lot of questions, and after the whole session, she pretty much told me that I was fine. She said that my aunt worries about me. NO KIDDING. I admitted to her that I have my moments, but I do talk to people about my feelings. Just not my dad or my aunt. I told her that my dad is the one who should be talking to her, because he is always very sad. She agreed with me.

We talked about how mommy always told me that even the scary movies can have a happy ending, and that you have to search within yourself for courage and strength to keep watching. Whatever you do, you don't stop watching at the scary parts. I told her that I can be brave because I know that the "story" continues on and on, and there can be a happy ending.

I think she's right that I'm fine, or maybe I just know how to act in front of a Shrink.

CHAPTER 7

M Y FATHER WAS a complete lost soul. To add to his desolate state, his mother, my grandmother, was diagnosed with terminal cancer. She was deteriorating rapidly, transforming from a healthy, robust and opinionated woman to a frail, thin patient. It was inconceivable that my father, in his completely helpless state, now had to watch his mother weaken and suffer in pain.

She soon passed away and, once again, my father was sitting Shiva. Thank goodness they sat at my Uncle Dave's house, but we still had to deal with that whole Shiva scene: the crowded house, people telling us how sorry they were, hearing about their losses, and that sombre head shaking that people do when they feel sorry for you. I hated that.

It was heart wrenching to look at my father. Beaten. Weak. Talk about overloading a human being with more heartbreak than he could possibly handle. The whole situation just defied the definition of "enough."

He went to synagogue as often as possible, finding some comfort there. When he wasn't at synagogue, he was either at work, with one or some of his siblings, or in his room, sobbing. He tried to put on a happy face for me, but I knew. I did the same for him.

MY FATHER BUILT himself an emotional fortress with no openings for any discussion about my mother and sisters. I wanted to talk about them, but he wouldn't. Or he couldn't. So we didn't.

It took him a long time to finally talk to me about anything related to the plane crash. We were driving to visit friends of my parents who lived in Toronto and playing a game where we kept track of the excessive number of dead animals on the highway. Whoever spotted the road kill first got a point. I kept score on a piece of paper.

We had this whole discussion about the dead animals: what they do with them when they pick them up off the highway, how many days they would be laying there, dead, whether or not the drivers know that they killed an animal, the pros and cons of dodging an animal running out onto the road, and a debate about other animals trying to eat the carcasses.

I finally brought up the subject I had been aching to talk about. I wanted my dad to tell me about the day of the plane crash. To talk to me about them. The airport. Their goodbyes. His feelings. Something. Anything. Just talk about it.

He told me three things.

One. They almost missed the flight because my mother had found a bottle of prescription pills in the airport washroom. She did not want to head towards the gate until she was sure that someone at the ticket counter would make sure to find the person who had lost their pills. My dad said he had been annoyed with her for worrying so much about this stranger, that she risked the three of them missing the flight. Typical of my mother to go out of her way for a complete stranger. My father was sure to remind me that my mother was like that. She would do things for others at the expense of herself. And my poor father was obviously feeling guilty for telling her not to worry about the pills, he would take care of it, and then rushing them to get on that plane. Rushing them on to that doomed flight.

Two. The number seven was very significant. They were sitting in row seven, it was the seventh month, the seventh day of the week, it was 1970, the plane left Montreal in the seventh hour, it crashed seven miles from the airport, and there had been another Air Canada plane crash seven years earlier. Seven.

Three. This third issue was obviously haunting him, causing him the kind of pain that doesn't subside with pain meds. Soul pain. Apparently he had found out, somehow, that while the plane was in trouble for about three minutes, everyone on board knew they were actually going to crash for sixteen seconds. My father was convinced that the pilot had announced sixteen seconds before the plane crashed, that there was nothing more he could do. That meant that for sixteen seconds they were aware and terrified, plummeting to their death, bracing themselves, taking those last few breaths of air, knowing they were going to crash. My father timed sixteen seconds on his watch to show me how sixteen seconds can feel like forever, especially with impending doom.

He also wanted to be sure I understood that they didn't really die instantly, even though everyone said they did, because it actually took sixteen seconds. And then he was sure to point out that sixteen, or one plus six, equals seven.

I remember asking him if he thought that the oxygen masks had "dropped automatically" and if everyone was wearing one. If they were, did that mean they were hopeful until the very last second? He had no answers.

We barely said a word to each other for the remainder of the drive. That was a lot of information to digest.

Sixteen seconds resonated with me for the longest time. Time seems to stand still when you're counting to sixteen. I found myself timing things to see how much I could do in sixteen seconds. And every time people talked about the timing in races, I would think about those sixteen seconds. Running, swimming, biking, horse racing, car racing, skiing, plummeting from the sky and crashing a plane.

Dear Diary,
Daddy FINALLY talked to me about the plane crash and now I wish he hadn't. I have enough things on my mind and now the number seven is scaring me so much. The thought of any connection to the number seven spooks me to death. And I never realized that 16 seconds is SOOOOOOOOOO long.

CHAPTER 8

M Y MOTHER RAN our household seamlessly. She was the centre of our home and kept everything under control, kept us all grounded. When she died, I lost that feeling of security. That feeling that everything was fine.

My mom was also the paperwork person in our family. A bookkeeper. She was organized and kept impeccable records. My dad never did paperwork. He was not a paperwork kind of guy. He was a salesman. A people person. But suddenly he seemed bombarded with paperwork, always sitting at the dining room table doing paperwork.

One day, when I came home from school, I noticed the dining room covered in stacks of papers. No one was home so I left my bag at the front door and approached the table. It was a mass of white sheets, gray type, and my father's messy handwriting. I reached out and tentatively picked up a type-written page:

1 package cottage cheese

5 pieces of smoked carp

24 cherry blossoms

2 cases of May West

Jewellery (diamond engagement ring, 14k gold wedding band, gold bangle bracelet, earrings with opals, watch, necklace of 2 strands of cultured pearls)

It was a detailed list of the personal effects and jewellery my mother had carried on board the flight. I dropped it as if it burned my fingers, but frantically started rifling through the others.

I found questionnaires.

One hundred and eighteen pages of *Interrogatories*, 116 questions. One hundred and sixteen personal and seemingly irrelevant questions (from the attorneys for McDonnell Douglas and Air Canada) that my father had to complete:

How tall are you?

What is your weight?

Describe each physical or mental disorder, infirmity, illness or abnormality with which you are now afflicted?

Was decedent afflicted with any physical or mental disorder, infirmity, illness or abnormality at the time of or immediately before the accident? If so, give a full description of each, including the inclusive dates.

What hobbies, sports, games, cultural, vocational and other interests did you share with decedent or enjoy in common with him?

How many hours per day did you regularly spend with decedent in the last 5 years of his life?

What was the frequency and duration of quarrels between you and decedent during the last 5 years of his life?

On top of losing his wife and two daughters, my father was forced to fill in forms, make lists and answer ridiculous, lengthy questions. My poor father. I never knew.

There was an agreement with the lawyer providing him with $33^1/_3$% of all amounts received in the lawsuit. If it had to go to trial, that lawyer was going to keep 40% (plus he made sure that my dad paid for all court costs and expenses).

I discovered more words to add to my vocabulary: *Proof of Loss, Estate Tax Return, Coroner's Inquest, depositions, witnesses, testimony, counsel, disbursements, quantum of damages, depose the heirs, wrongful death.*

In my dad's handwriting, I found lists of expenses:

Death notices

Funeral home

Cemetery plots

Long distance bills

Monuments

Carving, lettering on monuments

Annual maintenance of plots

Accounting fees for winding up of estates

Legal fees for winding up of estates

As I CONTINUED to read, tears dripping all over the papers, blurring the words, I came across legal documents with language I barely understood:

"...My calculations on projection of the value of mother replacement services.—housekeeper services with 2 days off; babysitter services for 22 hours/ week; gardening services.

The mother as a cook, dietician, dishwasher, governess, general housekeeper and in the preparation of the children's meals. The housekeeper does not do heavy laundry such as sheets, towels, etc. which are sent to the laundry.

I have said above that the loss for each child with respect to the counsels of her parents is distinct from the loss of love and affection provided by them. Thus love is lost forever; but guidance, teaching, parental correction, etcetera, provided by a parent, cannot be expected to continue to an appreciable extent beyond a certain age of the child in question."

Then came the form letter from the claims department of Air Canada. A form letter. Generic. Standard. The same letter they would send to someone who lost their luggage.

How could they? How dare they? With a moan, I collapsed to the floor, pages clutched in my hands, the pressing tightness in my chest releasing as each sob filled the empty space and my mind swirled.

That's where Deedee found me: coat on, curled up with my fists clenched around crumpled sheets, dried tears and snot staining my cheeks, eyes closed tight and dreaming of another day, another time.

Dear Diary,
Until today I never really thought about the Sunday morning phone call. Like who called Daddy to tell him that the plane crashed? I wonder what they said.

"Hello Mr. Weinberg. I'm calling to tell you that your wife and two daughters were on the plane that crashed and we don't think anyone survived. Have a nice day."

I hope it wasn't like that. I'll NEVER ask Daddy.

AIR CANADA ✺

Files: 703-89
      703-90
      703-91

P.O. Box 8107,
Montreal 101, Que.

July 14, 1970.

Mr. Saul Weinberg,
5767 Mc Murray St.,
Cote St. Luc, Que.

Dear Sir:

According to the information available to us, your name
appears as the person to be contacted with respect to
the death of Mrs. S. Rita Weinberg, Miss Carla Weinberg,
and Miss Wendy Weinberg in the accident which occurred
at Toronto, on July 5, 1970.

I have been instructed by Air Canada to communicate with
you in order to determine who may be entitled to
compensation and the amount recoverable under our filed
tariffs.

In order that Air Canada may give immediate attention to
this matter, will you please provide me with the following
information:

1.   Names of all dependants including
     children.

2.   The relationship of each dependant
     to the deceased persons.

3.   The age and date of birth of each
     dependant.

4.   Residence address for each dependant.

5.   Occupation of each dependant.

6.   The ages and dates of birth of the
     deceased persons.

7.   The date and place of marriage of
     Mrs. S. Rita Weinberg.

.../2

- 2 -

8. The occupation of the deceased
    persons.

9. The average earnings of the deceased
    persons.

10. Other income of the deceased persons
    apart from earnings, e.g., pensions
    or investment income.

11. Names and addresses of the executor
    of the estates of the deceased
    persons.

Air Canada is prepared to consider making a cash advance
to anyone entitled to compensation who is suffering
immediate financial hardship as a result of this accident.
In that event, please give details in addition to the
information requested above.

One of our representatives will communicate with you
soon, if this has not already been done.

In answering this letter, please advise the name, address
and telephone number of the family representative to
whom future communications should be made.

Yours truly,

Roger Lyr,
Manager - General Claims.

RC/nl

CHAPTER 9

M Y POOR FATHER was a mess. And I felt completely helpless to do any-thing about it. The more I thought about it, the more I would feel overtaken by anguish, panic and terror.

I was also worried about my heartbroken Bubby and Zaida, so I spent as much time as I could with them. They had dark shadows under their eyes and were having a terrible time coping. They had a picture of my mother blown up to poster size. They hung it over their living room couch.

They had aged years since the accident, and stopped doing many of the things they used to enjoy. My grandmother stopped getting dressed and instead was staying in her "duster" all day. Her routine went from one that was busy and active with volunteer work, playing cards and studying saychology with the ladies, to spending days sitting around on the couch watching television in a silent stupor, and still knitting, thank God. As often as possible, they went to the cemetery to visit the graves. I went with them a few times, but it ripped my heart out to watch them fall apart right in front of my eyes. My grandmother literally crumbled to her knees and withered to the ground as she sobbed, muttering things I couldn't even understand. Excruciating to watch. So hard to be there with them.

The only conversation that ever seemed to give them any comfort was when we talked about my mother and sisters' souls living on.

In the late sixties, my parents friends' son Brian died at age thirteen of a brain hemorrhage. That was our family's first experience with the sudden death of someone close to us. Brian had been a blonde, good looking boy who was a couple of years older than me. He was friendly and popular, and I had always been proud to tell people that he was my "cousin."

I swear, my mother cried all the time about Brian's death. She was devas-tated. She watched in horror as her dear friends suffered, losing their precious son. She was supportive and loving to them in a way that only my mother could be. With her complete heart and soul. With everything she had.

As time went on, I listened to many discussions between my mother and her distraught friend about life after death, consoling her dear friend with an unquestioning belief that Brian would always be around, even if he wasn't here in person. My mother said that there was some sort of life after death. She talked a lot about her late grandmother who apparently visited on a regular basis with messages and signs from "the other side."

My mother and grandmother had similar discussions. They both believed that the spirit lives on, no matter what happens to the physical body. They talked, comfortably, about the signs they got from relatives and friends who had passed, as ongoing proof that these people were still around.

I gave my grandparents examples of when I knew my mother and sisters were with me, times when I felt their presence, smelled them, and even saw them. My grandparents were the only people in my life who I would talk to about this stuff. I didn't know if anyone else would understand, or even believe me. I was worried that people would think I was insane. But somehow, I knew and trusted that my grandparents would understand. And they would believe me.

Not only did they believe me, but they received signs and messages as well. My grandmother told me about an experience she had on the bus, where she just knew that my mother was right there, next to her. She looked up and saw a woman staring at her with the exact same eyes as my mother. And often when she lit her Sabbath candles, she closed her eyes and felt them touching her on the shoulder.

We shared these private and comforting experiences with each other as often as we could. Moments that made us cry and smile at the same time. Proof that they were still with us. I just knew that Carla was sending me messages through her cat, Tiger. I would walk by Tiger lying dreamily on the couch and stop dead in my tracks to hear her purring and watch as her fur was literally being petted. Wendy's favourite song would be playing on the radio at exactly the same time as I was cuddling one of her many favourite stuffed animals. And my mother was there day and night, in so many different ways. I smelled her perfume, I heard her humming as I felt a breeze in the room, and the best was when she visited me in my dreams. My dreams at night, while sleeping, and my daydreams. I loved escaping into my daydreams, where she was with me as vividly and clearly as if she were still alive.

I did my best to take care of my father and my grandparents, the three people most important to me. I tried cooking the Friday night dinners and having my grandparents over to join me and my father. They came a few times. We ate at that big kitchen table, just the four of us. I stopped doing it. It wasn't working out well. It was just too hard, too painful for all of us to sit at that table which had gone from a happy place to a sad and depressing one.

I made them take me shopping, just to get them out of their house. And I would always be sure to get an invitation for my grandparents to come with us when we were invited anywhere for dinner. Everyone was always happy to have them, to do something, anything to help these badly suffering, kind souls.

I worried so much about them that I brought dimes with me to school so I could call my grandmother from the school pay phone in the middle of the day. I tried to encourage her to go out and collect clothes for the bazaar, but she always seemed to have excuses about why she couldn't go.

One of my favourite things was to bring my friends, particularly Barbara or Donna, over to their house. I knew that with my friends there, she would get off the couch and cook something for us. And we would find a way to make them smile.

Dear Diary,
Bubby has stopped making pickles. She even threw out all of the empty gallon jars. Zaida still goes to work every day, but he no longer has that sparkle in his eyes. He always seems so sad. He doesn't even have treats for me in his jacket pocket. I guess that he lost his favourite daughter and his sweet little granddaughters, and he just can't deal with it. Believe me, I understand.

CHAPTER 10

I FELT JUMPY at school. Irritable, forgetful and guarded. Distracted and unable to concentrate. Horrible thoughts crept into my head. Fear. Anxiety.

While I had been a good student in the past, with all this daydreaming and panic attacks, I was having a hard time academically. My cousins Mark and Sara, on my father's side, were both teachers. Thank goodness, because I doubt I would have passed grade eight without their help. Maybe I would have because the teachers felt sorry for me. But, I wanted good marks, and I wanted to do well in school, legitimately. So they tutored me in most of my grade eight subjects, and I ended up doing well. That was important to me.

ONE SATURDAY AFTERNOON I found a big brown envelope in the drawer in my father's night table, stuffed with newspaper clippings about the plane crash. I never knew that my father had saved them. I sat on his bed and read some of the articles. I had forgotten much of the gory details. Repressed them. I felt sick to my stomach as I read the words over and over, as if it were the first time I was reading them. And seeing the pictures again, particularly the one of Barbara, Wendy's precious doll, was agony.

I tried hard to stay positive about life, grasping at the good stuff and determined to get through all of this misery, but stumbling across that envelope was like being yanked back in time.

That evening when I tried to talk to my father about the articles, he told me that he had saved them for me in case I ever wanted to read them. He told me to take the envelope and keep it in my room. And then he walked away from me. That was the end of the discussion.

That night I had another bad dream but the dreadful details and raw terror lingered long after I awoke.

THAT PLYWOOD BOX continued to haunt me day and night, but this night-mare was different from the others. This time, when the man with no face handed me the big plywood box, it was heavy. Very heavy. He helped me put it on the floor and then he left. I was alone in the silent house.

There were no nails keeping the box sealed shut. I lifted the lid slowly and peered inside. It was dark in the box and I couldn't see anything. It smelled awful, like smelling salts. I had to step back because the odour was so strong. I waited sixteen seconds to get used to the smell. Then I stepped closer to the box and looked inside. There was a body in there, a whole body. Not just an arm, or a leg or a finger. I didn't recognize the body. It just stared at me with a vacant look. Like a mannequin. Like someone who had died but didn't really die.

It was breathing, taking regular breaths in and out. But it didn't smile. It didn't cry. It was just breathing.

I turned around and saw that everyone was there, standing behind me, in dark clothes, sunglasses, and crying. My father, my grandparents, my aunts, uncles, cousins, friends. Except for my mother and sisters. They weren't there. No one spoke. They just stood there, leaning on each other, sombre head shaking, watching me.

I didn't know what to do with the box. I didn't want to pull the lid back down because the body in there was breathing. It would suffocate. But I couldn't leave the big box in the middle of the floor. It was right in front of the door. I wouldn't be able to get in and out of the house. And it was too heavy to move.

I asked my relatives for advice. I wanted them to tell me what to do, but they just stared at me. No one answered. Their lips never moved. I didn't know if I should lead with my head, or with my heart. Nothing made sense. So I left it there. With the lid opened. In front of the door. With the body in it, still breathing, but not talking or laughing or crying. Not whistling or humming or giggling. Just existing. I decided that I would just have to step over the box when I had to get in or out of the house.

Dear Diary,
It's the middle of the night. I can't stay in bed anymore. I'm having these bad dreams all the time and I wake up scared and all sweaty. They are so real. Mommy always came into my room when I was having a bad dream. She knew what to say to make me feel better.

Now I tell myself that it was just a bad dream. I try to make myself feel better but when I go back to sleep, the bad dream continues where it left off. I feel so alone. I am so lucky to have Tiger. I love cuddling with her. She understands me. She's lonely too. Her purring calms me. It blocks out the silence. When she stops purring, I rub the back of her ears and she starts again.

CHAPTER 11

EVERY YEAR, MOTHER'S Day arrives after a long, cold winter. There is a lot of hype leading up to the traditional day. Television and radio advertising, displays in stores, special brunches and dinners at restaurants. Mother's Day lingo everywhere about mom's making sacrifices, being the comforter, the encourager, a teacher, a nurse, a chauffeur, a friend. Choose her gift carefully. Let her know she is special, pamper her, touch her heart.

There was no escaping Mother's Day. Nobody ever forgets about Mother's Day. No way of pretending that it was just an ordinary day. Unavoidable. My mother was a dedicated mother. A devoted wife. A precious daughter. Her absence was profound. Unlike birthdays, denial was not an option. Yet acknowledging or celebrating even with my grandmother was definitely out of the question.

Needless to say, getting through the day, for me, my father, my grandparents, my aunts, my cousins, was torture. It was like a fresh burn on your skin. Seeping and raw. A day where we gathered silently in my aunt's house, weeping, apathetic eating, cleaning up, wandering, waiting for the day to end. A day packed with intense sorrow.

FATHER'S DAY HAD its own issues, different of course from Mother's Day. My father wasn't a husband any more. He was still a father, my father, but now his father status was reduced from three to one. My grandfather desperately missed fathering my mom, and grandfathering my little sisters.

I thought about all of this way too much, analyzing it, agonizing about it. It was too bad that Mother's Day and Father's Day were so close to one another. And that both were close to my May 10th birthday and to July 5th. Everything all at once. It was a lot to think about. A lot to handle.

I wanted to make the day feel special for my father, for my grandfather, for me. I wanted it to be a little bit normal. But nothing was normal any more.

Julie and I tried to recreate what my mother had always done for Father's Day. A barbecue for our relatives. Hamburgers and hot dogs. Potato chips in baskets. Bottles of soft drinks. My mother's famous corn bread, florentines and lemon cake. Auntie Riva's apple pie.

They all came over. The house was busy. The delicious smell of the barbecue a comforting familiarity. Everyone said they were proud of me for organizing such a nice Father's Day for my dad, my grandfather, my uncles. I liked when people were proud of me. And most of all, I needed to keep busy and distracted. A crowded house full of loving relatives can be a great distraction. Feeling a tinge of relief, I acknowledged that my father and grandfather actually seemed to be a tiny bit happy that day.

Dear Diary,
Father's Day was much easier than Mother's Day. But I still had a stomach ache all day. And I can't get rid of that alone feeling, no matter how many people are around me. I wonder if I ever will....

June 1971

CHAPTER 12

Dear Diary,

Today is July 5th, 1971 the one year anniversary of the plane crash. An anniversary is supposed to be a celebration about a happy event, not for something terrible. There are no Hallmark cards in the stores for this kind of anniversary.

The Montreal Star was packed with pages of memorials in the same section as the birth and death notices. I brought the paper into my room and closed the door, so I could read all of the beautiful poems about how much people miss my mother and sisters. I stayed in my room for the whole afternoon, crying and crying. Daddy didn't come in at all. It was better that way. I just wanted to be alone.

A whole year has gone by. It's been a really terrible year.

Sunrise, sunset
Sunrise, sunset
Swiftly fly the years
One season following another
Laden with happiness and tears…

CHAPTER 13

D RUGS AND CIGARETTES were the hot topic at school. People were either for or against them, and the division amongst everyone was obvious. The "bad" kids hung out in front of the school smoking, skipping classes and acting as if they were way cooler than the rest of us. They laughed at us because we were so not cool. And I had no interest whatsoever in any of them or in the way they chose to live. I was pretty surprised by some of the people I knew who had decided to switch to that side of the tracks. People who I had thought were sensible and knew better.

One day I was invited to a party at a girl's house, and was told to bring a bottle of pills from our medicine cabinet. Anything would be fine. I was shocked. I didn't go.

This girl had been such a "good girl" until her father was killed in a car accident. Ever since then, she was different. But I couldn't figure out what was different about her. Now I knew. And I understood, probably more than most kids, that she was falling apart because of what had happened. She wasn't strong enough to hold herself up and make wise choices. So she was self-destructive, succumbing to the pressure of drugs and bad decisions. And the escape from reality that the drugs must have given her.

She didn't know my secret escape plan. My ability to daydream into the future. My happy future. Making up my own ending to the story. And my conscious decision to just be patient.

I thought about talking to her, telling her about my ability to secretly escape from difficult times. But I didn't do it. I didn't have the guts. I thought she might laugh at me, or tell me that what I was doing was ridiculous. I couldn't take that chance. So I didn't tell her. I didn't tell anyone. I just hung onto the comfort and hope in knowing that we have choices. We always have choices.

My scrapbook was my other ideal escape from reality. I loved getting lost in my world of magazines, finding messages, poems or quotes that seemed meaningful and true. They were about love, friendship, gratitude, happiness, peace, karma, serendipity. Authors unknown, but words that resonated with me. I cut them out and glued them into my precious scrap-book. The magazines always had pictures of people who looked so happy. I was drawn to those pictures. Pictures without sadness.

The glue made the pages lumpy. Just like my life had been. But I wasn't going to focus on the lumps. The messages and pictures were comforting, beautiful, and always there for me. All I had to do was flip through that scrapbook over and over again.

Dear Diary,

I love looking through my scrapbook and reading the poems and stories. When I do, I feel so much better. My favourites…

Every day of your life is a gift from God. Don't squander it. Don't waste it by being upset with anyone. Don't let it slip away by feeling sorry for yourself. Be grateful for this precious gift of life and spend it by being as happy and as thankful as you possibly can. Let your mind dwell on the good things which have happened to you. Let gratitude be your attitude. Think of your assets, and don't let anyone else spoil your day for you. Enjoy every day of your life to the fullest. Realize that you can add to the joy of each day by making someone else happy.

- *When life gives you lemons, make lemonade.*
- *Every cloud has a silver lining.*
- *Most people have far more courage than they realize.*
- *Never give up on your dreams.*

CHAPTER 14

THAT SUMMER, AT the mature age of fourteen I discovered boys. On Friday and Saturday nights, groups of us average boys and girls would gather at someone's house. We had crushes on boys and were obsessed with mouthwash. God forbid any of us should ever have bad breath.

There was one boy who I had a big crush on. He was so cute. I almost fainted when he asked me to go to a Sunday afternoon movie with him. I brushed my teeth four times that morning, and gargled at least half a bottle of Listerine.

Sitting next to him in that theatre, with his arm around me and leaning on each other made it impossible to concentrate on the movie. I had heard that people neck in movie theatres and I just knew that my first kiss was looming. About half way through the movie, he pulled me closer to him and came in for the kill. With our heads tilted in opposite directions, eyes closed and lips open, we started necking. My heart was pounding and it all seemed perfect. Our lips locked and he didn't even let the bar dividing our seats become an issue, although it had to have been jabbing him in the ribs as he practically lay on it to reach me. We necked until the movie was over and when we peeled away from each other, I realized that my leg was soaking wet. So much for the first kiss being a romantic event. I was totally grossed out by what I thought was pee.

We didn't utter a word to each other until the bus had stopped at the corner of my street. I thanked him for the movie and quickly stepped off the bus. And then I burst into tears. I had never heard of someone peeing in the middle of necking. I was grossed out, embarrassed and mortified. I would have told my mother. I certainly could never tell my father and I wasn't about to tell my friends. I had no idea what to do.

When Auntie Naomi called that evening, I blurted the whole thing out to her. When she stopped laughing long enough to speak, she explained that he had "ejaculated" on me.

I never spoke to him again.

BUT I WASN'T the only one dating. After waiting the respectful amount of time of approximately one year after my mother died, women started calling our house, inviting my father to all kinds of social events. Some of them had known my mother, and others were just random women who had been given my dad's phone number. When he did get dressed up to go out, he never seemed to be excited about the whole dating scene. It was almost like he was forcing himself to go.

After a few of his social outings my father revealed that he was shocked by the aggressive behaviour of these women. I told him that I felt the same way about horny, fourteen-year-old boys.

Dear Diary,

Tonight Daddy went on another date but he came home shortly after he had left. When I asked him why he was back so soon, he just mumbled a response that made no sense to me at all. I was not giving up on that one. And when I pushed him for an answer, he told me that the woman wanted to go straight to a motel with him and he wasn't interested.

No wonder he ran back home. That is so gross. Doubly gross.

CHAPTER 15

JUST OVER A year after the accident, my father was introduced to a woman named Sonia. She was originally from Poland, and while she and her family remained in Europe during the War, they were thankfully spared the devastation that most Jewish people experienced. She was married in Poland at a young age and, together with her parents and siblings, the young couple immigrated to Montreal. Sonia and her husband established themselves quickly, had two children, a successful electronics business, and a big house in a beautiful Montreal neighbourhood.

When my father met her, Sonia was also a recent widow whose husband had died of a heart attack, and had left her with a hefty bank account. Her daughter Esther was living in Israel with her new husband, Jacob, and her son Harry was getting ready to go off to University. Harvard or MIT were his top choices.

I had never really known anyone like Sonia. She was an attractive woman who was always dressed in expensive clothes and flashy jewellery. She didn't drive a car. She didn't work. She shopped in expensive boutiques. She had a big fancy house full of what looked like ornate, costly furniture which she proudly informed me was all imported from Europe. She also said that her rugs were from the Orient and that the massive crystal chandelier over her dining room table was so heavy, she had to have it professionally hung. There were pricey-looking statues and knickknacks on her fancy gold and glass end tables. Her living room was bigger than our whole house. To me, her house looked like a museum or a smaller version of Granny and Jed's house in the show *The Beverly Hillbillies*. Everything looked fragile and expensive. I was afraid to touch any of it.

I THOUGHT THAT Sonia was the complete opposite of my mother. Except for the fact that she was also an amazing cook. If we weren't eating at her house, she sent food, beautifully packaged of course, home with my father. Packaging things beautifully was easy for Sonia. Actually, I quickly realized that she was all about the packaging.

Sonia took me shopping in boutiques, small stores I never even knew existed. She wanted me to throw out my jeans and only wear designer pants. She bought me beautiful shoes to replace my running shoes and construction boots. I wasn't a tomboy, I just loved wearing comfortable, casual clothes.

I was accustomed to everyone calling my dad Shloime, but for some reason Sonia called him Saul. And Saul's wardrobe and his entire look changed completely. My plain and simple father was now sporting designer clothes. And a toupee. He was looking very well-packaged. Who was this man?

Sonia was subtle about it, but it was clear to me that she did not like my father's family, and particularly Uncle Dave and Auntie Riva. Nor did she have anything nice to say about my mother's side of the family. She was not on speaking terms with one of her own brothers, and she didn't like most of my father's friends. In fact, as time went on, I realized that there weren't too many people that she did like. Well certainly not the "plain and simple" folks. She was impressed by people who had money or, as she put it, people who were "loaded." Cars, houses, clothes and jewellery were the criteria for being rated high on the Sonia meter. We didn't have a lot of those people in our lives.

Within a few months of dating, they announced their engagement. The thought of my father being happy, and of us having a normal family again seemed like a step in the right direction. Even though I wasn't convinced that my dad was all that blissful, and I was far from crazy about Sonia, I assumed that as time went on, he'd find happiness. And since I didn't remember ever hearing him giggle again, since that haunting day in July, I thought that maybe he'd even start giggling again. Maybe even telling jokes.

I decided that this definitely could be a good thing.

I even suggested that they adopt a toddler, so they could have a child together. Truthfully, I did not want to be the only child at home. I intuitively knew that there would be way too much time to focus on me and my life. I desperately wanted them to have a distraction. Not because I wasn't a good kid, because I was. But I realized early on that Sonia was controlling and critical. After almost two years of running my own show, I was not in the mood to be micromanaged. And besides, I really did want a sibling.

They were not at all interested. They spent all their time planning their wedding and mapping out their future together. Well, Sonia was doing the mapping. My father was going along with whatever Sonia wanted.

Dear Diary,
It seems like the business is slowly going down the toilet. I overheard Daddy and Uncle Dave talking about closing the store. But I am quite sure that Sonia doesn't know anything about this. Daddy found a woman who takes care of him, feeds and dresses him well. He isn't about to tell her any bad news about his financial situation. I think that she is the kind of person who would break up with him if she knew that he was having money or business problems. He's probably afraid to lose her.

CHAPTER 16

I KNEW MY father well and, as his wedding date approached, it seemed to me that he still didn't have any will to *really* live. To have fun again. To tell jokes. To giggle. He just kind of went through the motions of life each day, on his same path of hopelessness and despair, just as he had the day before. Tick-tock. Tick-tock.

The one thing he did without any hesitation was attend funerals. My father read the obituaries in the newspaper religiously, every single day. He knew so many people who had passed away: someone from the community, from synagogue, someone's parent, a previous customer, an old school mate. Even if he barely knew the person, he went to pay his respects at the funeral.

We were so different, me and my dad, when it came to funerals. I went when I absolutely had to, but I found every excuse possible to avoid going to that funeral home. The distinct smell of it, the silence, the whispering, the sombre head shaking. The mystery box otherwise known as the coffin. I couldn't stand the thought of being there. My memories were just too painful to revisit.

Cemeteries were even worse. I couldn't help feeling such overwhelming despair when I walked into one. That pile of earth by an empty hole, the shovel standing upright waiting for people to take turns shovelling dirt, the sounds of people walking on the gravel. I couldn't shake the images I had of my grandmother shrivelling to the ground as if that brought her closer to the plywood boxes buried deep below the beautiful granite stones. Big, plywood boxes nailed closed, concealing their remains, whatever that was. A finger, an arm, a leg. Who knows.

HE NEVER MENTIONED my mother or my sisters. If I brought up their names, he changed the subject. He said he was happy about starting a new life, but he sure didn't seem like he meant it. I always sensed a deep sadness and emptiness about him. Vacant staring. A trance. Like he was lost in the woods, wondering which way to go.

Two people living through the same situation, and we each made different choices. I chose a direction and walked, trying to find my way, doing what I had to do in order to survive. But my father, quite to the contrary, just walked slowly in circles. Around and around. Aimlessly. Struggling.

It seemed as if the only way he could move forward at all, was if he erased his previous life. As if his life had been drawn on an Etch A Sketch and he could just shake it clean and draw himself a new life when he felt like forgetting it all. Just like he did right in front of me with their wedding album. He walked into the garage and tossed it into the garbage can. I was stunned. Who throws out a wedding album? They weren't divorced. It was a beautiful album with pictures of both their families. I told him that I wanted it, but he said that we did not need to keep it. He said that since we don't need it, it's better to throw it out and forget it.

Just throw the past in the garbage.

I later retrieved the heavy white and gold album from the garbage, brought it into my room, closed the door and sat on my bed slowly looking through the pictures, each one protected by thick plastic.

Everyone looked so joyful, so beautiful, so proud. My mother was such a pretty bride in her long white gown with a train that seemed to flow for several feet behind her. My dad looked as handsome and dapper as a movie star with his tuxedo. My grandparents appeared young and carefree, especially compared to how they looked now, which was old, worn out and terribly sad.

I wrapped it in an old sheet and hid it in my closet. I needed it and I would treasure it forever.

Then I quietly went down to the basement with an empty box and filled it with some items my mother had kept in the basement closet. Before my father had a chance to throw all of that in the garbage as well.

I went back into my room and looked through the box filled with *Dear Abby* columns, engagement and wedding announcements, some of her high school diaries, the baby bracelet from when I was born, and a bundle of cards. Cards from me, my sisters and my dad. My bed was so crowded with everything, that I had to move onto the floor. I sat on my blue shaggy carpet surrounded by the colourful cards, like a lone boat drifting on a lake strewn with fallen leaves. And the tears just flowed. I couldn't stop them. The cards that my sisters and I had created, with construction paper, doilies and crayons, now took on a whole different meaning. The once sweet words carefully handwritten on the cards now stung with pain.

To a wonderful mom, so sweet and kind
You're the best mom anyone could find
I love you a lot and I'm thanking you
For a wonderful year thru and thru

and . . .

To a mom who's kind at heart
Sweet inside & outside
You give us love
Like nobody else would
When you are around us, we feel safe,
And we know we are in no danger at all
Except for a kiss from you
We are sending you some of our love
And with it we are sending you a present
Which took us a long time to find
So use it in good health or else for next year
We won't take so long to pick out your gift.
We love you Mom.

Luv and kisses,
Your sweet daughters and husband
Lynda, Carla, Wendy W, Saul

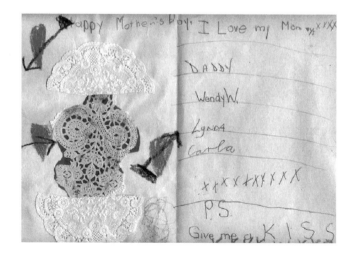

I sobbed my eyes out when I saw how the cards were signed with *Wendy W,* as if we wouldn't know which Wendy she was.

There were beautiful store-bought cards from my dad, for Valentine's Day and their wedding anniversary. I definitely had to hide those from my father, or for sure he would have destroyed them.

I came across a newspaper clipping of a poem about sisters. I remembered when my mother found that poem and showed it to us before putting it in the box. She loved that poem.

I packed everything back into the box, and climbed on a chair in my bedroom closet to put it on the top shelf, high up and out of view. Stuffed with so many painful reminders of his life now gone, I knew he would throw out the entire box.

Dear Diary,

Reading the cards I found in the basement made me feel so lonely all over again. Sometimes I just don't know what to do to make myself feel better. I hate being sad—but I want to remember. Tiger is so sweet. It's like she knows I'm upset. She jumps up on my bed and snuggles with me.

The cards were really beautiful, especially the ones we made. Mommy loved those the best. She always said that actions speak louder than words. That people can say a lot but what they do is what really counts. I know I do a lot of good things for other people. I am so proud that I come from a family that was sincere and meant what they said to others. I think Mommy would be proud of me.

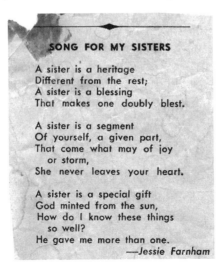

SONG FOR MY SISTERS

A sister is a heritage
Different from the rest;
A sister is a blessing
That makes one doubly blest.

A sister is a segment
Of yourself, a given part,
That come what may of joy
    or storm,
She never leaves your heart.

A sister is a special gift
God minted from the sun,
How do I know these things
    so well?
He gave me more than one.
                    —Jessie Farnham

CHAPTER 17

My father and Sonia had decided that they would sell both of their houses and buy one together. Our house sold immediately, but not Sonia's. My aunts and uncles told me that the reason it sold fast was because my father practically gave it away. Along with just about everything in it. All of the things my parents had collected throughout their years together. Treasured together. Sonia didn't want any of it around, and certainly not any of my mother's things. Our furniture was "not her taste." Except for the crystal bowls and the beautiful set of Rosenthal fine china that my parents had received from all of their siblings for their tenth anniversary. Sonia really liked those Rosenthal dishes. Service for twelve. Very expensive.

So now we were moving into Sonia's house, temporarily. After the wedding of course. And after they came back from their honeymoon in Spain.

My mother never got to go on fancy trips to Europe. I couldn't believe that my father was suddenly rich enough to pay for such an expensive honeymoon. Especially after paying for the wedding.

When I talked to Auntie Nicky about this, she went up to her room and came back down with a cloth bag that was tied on the end with what looked like a silky shoelace. Inside the bag was a white beaded evening purse with some pastel coloured beads on it and a gold clasp. She told me that she had been keeping this purse for me because it was something special to my mother, and it came with an interesting story. About a year before the accident, my aunt was shopping with my mother for an evening purse that she wanted to wear to Mark and Sara's wedding. Apparently my mother just loved this particular purse, but was reluctant to spend that much money. The salesman told her that she should buy the purse, because if she doesn't spend the money, the second wife will.

His "second wife" theory had gotten to her and she bought the purse. In fact, they had both walked away and agreed that he was a smart man and probably correct about his theory.

My aunt said that his comment had stuck with her ever since, and when she was going through my mother's closets, she found the purse and kept it for me. She had just been waiting for the right moment to give it to me.

I brought that purse home and sat down on my bed with the purse carefully placed next to me. I ran my fingers across the tiny beads and pictured my mother and father all dressed up for the wedding. She was wearing her off-white dressy suit with gold trim on a band along the base of the top. Her gold shoes peaked out of the bottom of the long skirt, and her hair was done with curls on the side and the rest up in a beautiful silver clip. Because it was such a special occasion, she was wearing eye makeup and lipstick. My dad was wearing a tuxedo and a bow tie. In her hand, she proudly clutched this purse.

I gently placed the purse back into the bag and tucked it into one of my drawers. For me, it was a fragile treasure.

Dear Diary,

Today is October 22, 1972. My father and Sonia got married today. I hope Daddy will be happy again. Sonia is so different than Mommy was, but he seems to like her. She is very pretty and a really good cook. I felt happy and sad at the same time. I want to have a normal life again. I want to have a mother. Hopefully this will be the answer to my dreams. I have to trust Daddy when he says she's a good person and will be a good mother to me, but it's still so weird to see him with another woman, especially when I see him kissing her.

The wedding was nice. Pleasant. People weren't dancing, just talking a lot. They are leaving for Spain tomorrow....

CHAPTER 18

Ididn't have to wait for my alarm clock to go off on that unforgettable Wednesday morning. When I heard Carla screaming, I immediately sat up in bed. It was still dark.

"Tiger gave birth. We have four kittens. Come see them. Everyone, come see them."

Our house instantly came alive. Lights turned on and we practically knocked each other over racing to the basement. Within seconds, we were all down in the basement gathered around the couch, gawking in awe at this litter of tiny kittens that looked more like hairless rodents.

We stared in silence. This was the most beautiful sight to watch. Tiger was lying down and concentrating on licking them, as these tiny little creatures struggled to suck on her nipples.

I had barely opened my eyes and in a heartbeat, at age ten, I had witnessed a miracle.

"I am not going to school today."

"Neither am I."

"Me three."

Sonia did not like cats or dogs. She thought it was disgusting that Tiger slept in my bed, and she certainly did not like Tiger at all. Within a short time of living in Sonia's house, she made it clear that the cat had to go. Despite my pleading and promises to confine Tiger, her litter box, food and water bowls all to my room, the decision  was made. No discussion. No debate. I was learning that Sonia always got her way.

I formed my own committee, and I was on a mission to find a good home for Tiger. I couldn't give her to just anyone. She was Carla's cat and I wanted to be sure she would be going to a good home. I called animal hospitals and shelters, asking if I could hang a notice to help locate a loving family to adopt her.

I only got a few phone calls in response to my ads, but one woman sounded very sweet on the phone as she responded to my numerous questions and concerns.

The following weekend, my father and I packed up Tiger's litter box, bowls and all her favourite toys, and brought her to the woman's house. We didn't say one word to each other in the car.

Dear Diary,

I haven't stopped crying since daddy and I got home from dropping Tiger off at that nice lady's house. She was so friendly and kind, I am sure she will take good care of Tiger. I explained that Tiger had already been through a hard time because she missed Carla so much. The lady promised me she would give her lots of attention and love. I hope Carla's not mad at me. It wasn't my decision to give her away. Sonia forced me. I had no choice.

CHAPTER 19

B Y JANUARY, MY father and his brother were closing the business, could not agree on the financial issues and, as a result, were no longer on speaking terms. An entire lifetime relationship had seemingly come to an end.

I overheard my father and Sonia endlessly defending their position as the victims in the business's financial battle. The ones who had been taken advantage of and had ultimately lost the most amount of money.

They were so angry at my aunt and uncle that they forbid me from seeing anyone on my father's side of the family. Well, Sonia set the law and my father went along. That was his character now. He was a puppet who just wanted to please his new wife. Even at fifteen, I understood his weakness. I didn't like it, but I just couldn't challenge him. He had suffered so much and was still so fragile. So pathetic.

Having endured my own losses, I wasn't about to stop seeing my cousins, or my aunts and uncles. Nothing could stop me. I appreciated all of them. Their support. Their love. Their friendship. When most of the teens I knew snuck out to smoke or drink, I slipped out to spend time with my relatives.

My cousins Mark and Sara had recently had their first baby, and I couldn't get enough of him. Mark used to pick me up a block away from my house, bring me to his apartment where I could help look after little Jeffrey, and then drop me off again at that same secret location. Ridiculous to have to lie to my father and Sonia about wanting to spend time with my new little cousin. Beyond ridiculous.

In fact, I did whatever I had to do in order to stay in touch with all of my relatives. Extended family takes on a different meaning when you've lost your immediate family. I was grateful to have grandparents, aunts, uncles and cousins. With my whole heart and soul, I appreciated them and everything they did for me, way more than any words could describe. I was not about to take any of these wonderful people for granted.

AT HOME, I struggled to survive. Whenever I was feeling anxious or unhappy, I slid back into that daydream state where I was content. If Alice in Wonderland could hop into the rabbit hole, I could dig deep to that spot inside. It was like a well that I could tap into any time I needed to generate positive feelings and replenish my thirst for joy. No matter where I was, I could bring myself to that place in time, before the crash, where it was all good, where it was just all good.

At least, temporarily.

Truthfully, daydreaming was a bit like taking a pill. It didn't get rid of the pain, but it did a good job of masking it. The only problem was, like a pill, the effect wore off. Back to reality.

I HAVE NEVER been religious in any traditional sense of the word but I have always been a spiritual person. My mother used to tell me that I was an old soul. That I looked at situations and people in a wise, knowing way. I just knew and understood that there was some explanation or reason for just about everything. Things always happen for a reason. People come into your life for a reason. People are no longer in your life for a reason. Even bad situations have some sort of a lesson associated with them—an opportunity to learn and grow. Trust fate and destiny. And most of all, believe in angels. Angels on the other side and angels here in physical bodies.

There's a bright side to everything. There has to be. My mother constantly taught us to look for the good.

She had a little game that she liked to play to show us that even when people are miserable, you can lift their spirits and help them snap out of their nasty state. She loved to prove that her theory was true, so she used every opportunity to demonstrate shifting someone's mood from grumpy or sad to something better. If salespeople seemed upset, watch this, she'd say, and she would smile and joke around with them, until they broke down and eventually had to smile. It worked every time.

Well, it worked with strangers. So far, it didn't work that well with me and Sonia.

Dear Diary,
Sonia is so different now that we are all living in the same house. She was much nicer to me before they got married. She is so moody and I don't think she likes me. I don't know why. I'm still the same person. She doesn't like when I dress in jeans and t-shirts, but that's what I like to wear. She asked me if my mother

raised me to be a boy, because I dress like a boy. That's the second time she has bad-mouthed my mother and the way I was raised. If she ever says anything bad again about my mother, I swear I will run away and go live at Auntie Nicky's house.

I miss the daddy I had.

For daddy's sake, I'll keep trying to get her to like me.

She is turning everyone against each other and making daddy mad at Auntie Riva and Uncle Dave too. Everything is just not going very well at all. I keep wishing this was all a nightmare and it would end already. I miss Mommy, Carla and Wendy so so so so so so so so so much!

CHAPTER 20

WHILE I WAS a young teenager with an indomitable will, I was hardly the picture of self-confidence. Quite the contrary, I was a bundle of insecurities. My entire life had drastically changed, I ached for my mother and sisters, and I prayed that my father would get stronger and be more like he was before the plane crash. To add to everything, I was faced with the usual friends and boy drama that, for a fifteen-year-old, felt like the weight of the world.

Having heard my friends talk about confiding in their mothers, I thought I would give it a shot with Sonia. I had been feeling particularly upset about a dispute amongst a few of my school friends, and I was debating a confrontation with them. After wrestling all evening with the pros and cons of interfering, the next morning, when Sonia and I were in the kitchen together, I decided to ask for her advice.

I should have known better. She was one of those people who seemed to gloat at another's misery. Many times I witnessed the fake concerned look she got when something bad happened to someone else; in reality she seemed to be enjoying herself.

I had recently started to drink coffee and felt very grown up filling a mug with coffee, putting in a package of artificial sweetener, some milk, and stirring it with a teaspoon. I casually mentioned the issue, prefacing it with the strict confidentiality of this highly sensitive situation, and wondering about her opinion.

While there was really no right or wrong answer, my issue with her was that the moment I left for school, she apparently called some of the mothers whose daughters were involved and discussed the situation with them. That of course caused the entire issue to escalate to something way bigger. I was beside myself. I felt betrayed and furious.

How does a fifteen-year-old confront a stepmother about basic trust and honesty? And how does a fifteen-year-old respond when told by the stepmother that she is overreacting and making a big deal out of nothing?

I could not wait for my father to get home that evening so I could tell him how his wife had lied to me, had unnecessarily and maliciously fuelled a fire, and that now she refused to take any responsibility for having interfered and gossiped about something that was important to me. But she got to him first. And by the time I tried to talk to him about it, he told me that he didn't want to be in the middle of an issue between Sonia and me.

Dear Diary,
I will NEVER trust Sonia again. She is a terrible stepmother, because a nice step-mother would keep her promises. She promised me she would keep a secret and she didn't keep her word. Now my friends are mad at me for telling her. She is such a liar and so phony. I hate her.

CHAPTER 21

According to Auntie Naomi, her sister in California was consumed with guilt. It was her son's Bar Mitzvah that everyone was coming to attend and, despite all logic, she felt responsible. Auntie Naomi exaggerated a lot so I wasn't sure that my Auntie Shirley was as bad as Auntie Naomi said she was, but just in case I decided to go and visit. My dad said it was fine, especially since I told him that she needed my help. I also wanted her to know that I was okay. And that I didn't blame her.

It was settled. I was going back to California, by plane, by myself.

I fully admitted to everyone, that I was terrified of flying and, even though they told me that lightning doesn't strike twice, I worried that my plane would crash too. I dreaded the phone ringing early in the morning with bad news and felt terrible about leaving my father and grandparents. In fact, my entire world no longer felt safe.

On the way to the airport, my dad and I didn't say a word. I knew that if I was worried, he was twice as worried. It was better not to talk about it.

We stood together in line at the Air Canada ticket counter with everyone else, a private rant playing out in my head.

"Don't all you people know what happened to my family? How come you let me sit in first class on the day of the crash and now I am just like everyone else? You may have closed the file, but I didn't. I couldn't. Don't I deserve any kind of special treatment? Whatever you do, don't let me sit in seat seven."

My family doctor had given me a prescription for a tranquilizer called Valium, which he said I should take about a half hour before flying. I swallowed the pill with some water from the water fountain at the airport. And then my dad walked me as close to the gate as possible.

Saying goodbye felt surreal. I thought my heart would fly out of my chest it was beating so hard. My hands were clammy. What was I doing? I was terrified of flying and I was getting on a plane.

Scared and uneasy, I walked away from my dad barely able to swallow, my throat tight. Turning and waving, I caught him wiping tears from his face with his handkerchief. He sure had changed from a man who was always joking, to someone who was often crying, and mostly lost in another world.

Once on board, I took my seat, put on my seat belt, and pulled out the papers in the flap in front of my seat. I read the entire safety manual, in both English and French. I didn't know how to pronounce a lot of the words in French, but I felt better knowing that I had thoroughly familiarized myself with everything I needed to know about safety on an airplane.

Soon the Valium began to work, and my body relaxed as I paid careful attention to the stewardess doing the safety demonstration. "…in the unlikely event of an emergency…"

As the plane took off, I held my breath, white-knuckles gripping the armrest so tightly my hands hurt. Once everything seemed secure, I started to doze off, only to be awoken by shaking and vibrating. I glanced nervously at the other passengers, but no one seemed too concerned. I decided that we probably weren't crashing. Just to be sure, I pressed the call button and when the stewardess came to my seat, I asked her why the plane was so wobbly. She had been busy serving food and was obviously pissed off that I had interrupted her. "It's just turbulence," she said abruptly, one fake-smile away from a full-out eye roll. I really didn't know what that meant, but I thanked her, even though she didn't hear me. She had already turned and was back to serving the little TV dinner meals.

By the time we were ready to land, the Valium must have worn off. I was certain things were bad; it was too bumpy, too noisy. Was that rain? I never should have done this. What was I thinking? I knew I had to do something to take control and get through this landing without making a scene right there on the airplane. I forced myself to think of something that felt good, something that was peaceful and beautiful. I thought of a rainbow, so beautiful, so perfect. I decided that flying gave me an opportunity to be closer to rainbows and, if I looked out the window, I might even be able to see the top of one that was just waiting for a rainy day so it could come out and show off its beautiful colours and perfect shape. Maybe we were somewhere over a rainbow. I started to sing, in my head, the song from the *Wizard of Oz*. I also made a mental note for future plane rides to take another Valium about an hour before landing. I didn't ever want to go through this torture again.

Dear Diary,
Auntie Shirley and her family moved into a new house, but we drove by the apartment complex. It was so weird to see it. I wanted to go into that clean, organized apartment that was supposed to be our home for one month. I wonder if anyone else used it that summer.

The whole time I was there, no one said one word about the accident, or about my family. Maybe they just didn't know what to say. Or maybe it is just too hard for them to talk about it. At least I know that Auntie Shirley is fine. She was better than I thought she was going to be, so that's good.

CHAPTER 22

MEANWHILE, BACK AT the ranch, the honeymoon was definitely over. My fantasy about having a real family again was not working out exactly the way I had imagined. I was in grade ten, leaving for school in my Sonia clothes and changing into my jeans and construction boots once I got there. I had a whole supply of clothes in my locker.

We moved into our new house, the fresh-start house. Full of Sonia's *Beverly Hillbillies* fancy furniture mind you. She got busy renovating and spending more money than I ever imagined possible.

I was curious about all this money flying around, since I had never seen my mother, or either of my parents for that matter, spend money so freely. My father sold tiles and linoleum to commercial customers who knew him from before. He worked from home, had a car full of samples, and he didn't have to worry about any overhead. But I knew that he couldn't be making too much money.

I was also wondering if both my father and Sonia had paid equally for the new house, how they were dividing expenses, who was paying for the fancy restaurants we now ate in, and basically how we lived this luxurious life. This was all unusual for me and knowing that Sonia's husband had left her and her kids with a lot of money, I wanted to know if she was contributing to the pot. Well that line of questioning opened a huge can of worms. My father told Sonia that I had been asking money-related questions, and she just flipped. The overriding message in their long lecture, with primarily Sonia barking at me, was to mind my own business, and to never question them again about money. Never.

Sonia's son, Harry, was at MIT in Boston, coming home during school breaks and holidays. Occasionally we would drive to Boston to spend a few days with Harry. Me, my father and Sonia. Those were fun car rides. Polar opposite to the pre-plane-crash station wagon trips we had taken with everyone packed into the car, eating my grandmother's salami sandwiches and sour pickles. Now, I sat by myself in the back seat and daydreamed. Fantasized. My own little magic trick. I would simply imagine myself somewhere else. Years ahead, when I would be happily married, with a hoard of kids, and living in a big house full of noise, laughter, radios blaring, televisions, visitors, good food, celebrations, overflowing closets and lots of pets. A dog, a cat, a bird, the more, the merrier. My dreams. Vivid dreams. Where I got lost for hours. I was planning the rest of my life. Conjuring up the scenes of my movie called *Life*.

One thing I knew for sure was that they all involved happiness.

BEFORE LONG, SONIA announced that her daughter and son-in-law, Esther and Jacob, would be moving back to Montreal from Israel. And guess where they would be living? With us! It actually sounded kind of good to me. They weren't my age, but they would give Sonia something else to focus on besides me. Boy, was I wrong.

We got their room and private bathroom all set up. They settled in quickly with jobs and a routine, followed Sonia's lead, referred to my dad as Saul and treated me fine. Nothing special. Nothing bad. Having them living in our house seemed to be working out okay. That was in the beginning. It was the honeymoon period for all of us.

"Lynda, set the table for dinner. Esther and Jacob will be home soon.... Lynda, take the garbage out.... Lynda, clean up the kitchen. Esther's tired from working all day.... You spend too much time on the phone.... Don't wear those clothes.... Why are you going out with that boy?... Why are you always going out?.... Why don't you stay home more often?"

Oh yes, the honeymoon was over.

Family dinners with this family were so different than they had been with my parents and sisters. Time at this family table was not a time of solidarity, or encouragement, or respite. And as famished as I was for the food, the luscious roasts and casseroles and home-made bread, my appetite for peace, harmony, recognition and joy was far greater. The strained and unhappy atmosphere in this kitchen was hardly going to satisfy that sort of hunger.

Everyone had their own regular seat at the table in the brand new, renovated kitchen. My dad sat at one end, and Sonia at the other. There were no colourful place cards and even though Sonia bought expensive napkins, they were never put on the table folded into flowers or butterflies.

While we rarely had any company for dinner, if we did, we had to eat in the dining room. Sonia refused to allow company to eat in the kitchen.

Sonia was an excellent cook and never asked for any help in the kitchen during the preparation of a meal. The food was always presented on fancy platters that we passed around the table. Conversation was either malicious gossip about someone, negative, nasty comments, or some superficial discussion. For the most part, I ate in silence.

I did my best to sit there politely for as long as possible, but the minute everyone was done eating, I would begin clearing the table, rinsing the dishes, loading the dishwasher, and putting the leftovers into Sonia's Tupperware containers with matching lids.

I actually hated standing at that sink and washing the pots, pans and platters. Sonia's daughter Esther was always willing to dry, so we focused on what we were doing and finished cleaning up pretty quickly. I didn't give up on my ritual of scrubbing the sink with Ajax. And I especially appreciated the speed with which I could sweep the floor with the electric broom, so that I could get out of that kitchen.

My dad still liked to sit at the table long after the meal was done, drinking his cup of tea from a glass mug. Sometimes he would read the newspaper, but most of the time he would just quietly sip his tea and stare vacantly into space, as if his thoughts were as far away from that kitchen as possible.

Dear Diary,
My new name might as well be Cinderella. It's like I'm their slave. I don't feel loved. I don't feel like I belong. I'm scared to say things. I feel like everything I say or do will be criticized. Even though Daddy's here, he's traded me in for them. I don't get it. I'm his real daughter. Why?

CHAPTER 23

WHO WANTS TO be home with constant criticism and bullying? I couldn't stand the dirty looks, the sarcasm, the vicious moods, and obvious exclusion. It was taking a huge toll on my self-confidence, and I found myself questioning my value as a person, my abilities, my self-esteem. I was desperate for approval, positive feedback, support and acceptance. Since I was treated well at everyone else's house, why spend time at home? So I didn't. And it drove Sonia crazy. Her own son admitted to me that the reason he went away to school was to get away from her constant criticism. That was like music to my ears. This wasn't personal. She did it to her own son. But I was not her real daughter, and she was not my real mother. We didn't have that unspoken, unconditional love that you have with a real mother–daughter relationship. She was the evil step-mother and I was the useless Cinderella. We started hating each other. A lot. Silent treatment. Dirty looks. Closed doors. Slamming doors. And guess who was in the middle? As if he hadn't been through enough, now my father was caught between the only two people he had left in his life.

Well, not exactly. Since I was part of that past life that he could no longer cope with thinking about, he chose Sonia. I guess he also knew that we did have that unconditional, unspoken love and security that a father and daughter have. His relationship with Sonia was anything but unconditional. It was completely conditional. Conditional upon providing her with all the material things she wanted. Designer clothes, accessories, shoes. Second wife stuff. Conditional upon agreeing with her. He didn't dare take my side on any issue, support or defend me. He was way too terrified of losing her. He could never have coped with any more loss. That was for sure.

I understood. I hated it. And I wanted him to take my side. But deep down, I knew he couldn't.

When she wasn't on my case about something or someone, Sonia and I did our best to tolerate each other. Fake niceness. But there was always an underlying tension between us: suspicion and a nasty, exhausting undercurrent.

She had certainly managed to create a two team feeling in the house, Sonia's team verses Lynda's team. It was not unusual for me to walk into a room where the conversation between Sonia and her daughter Esther, or both Esther and Jacob, came to an abrupt end. I knew they had been talking about me, bitching, complaining, finding something they didn't like about me. I refused to let them know how much that hurt me. I acted like I didn't know or didn't care. I certainly didn't want to give them the satisfaction of knowing that inside I was terribly hurt by their totally unjustified criticism and disapproval of me.

Sonia did the same thing with anyone outside of our house who would listen and join her "team." She even had the audacity to try and turn my best friend Donna against me, obviously underestimating Donna's awareness of the situation and unquestionable loyalty to our friendship.

She did succeed however with a few of my parent's "best friends" who after hearing her non-stop complaining about how hard she had tried to mother me, and all I did was cause her grief, finally joined her team. I didn't even bother trying to tell them my side of the endless stories and issues. It didn't matter. As Bubby told me over and over again in her ongoing saychology lectures, *"Just be yourself, continue to be good, to do good, and don't be distracted by Sonia from your purpose in life."*

Pausing by their bedroom, I heard Sonia talking to my father about me and how difficult it was for her to be a mother to me.

"She's keeping secrets. I don't like some of her friends. I don't know if she is doing her school work or taking school seriously enough. I don't believe that she actually goes to the library. Don't be naïve, Saul. I am convinced she is trying drugs."

I was dying to bust into the room and challenge her claims that were totally untrue. But instead, I went to my room and closed my door, frustrated and angry, often crying myself to sleep.

Dear Diary,

I heard Sonia tell daddy that I am taking drugs. I have never tried drugs and I never will. She just wants me to get into trouble, but daddy would never believe her. And I do take school seriously. I got such a good mark on my science test, and my math teacher says I am really good at math. I never skip classes and I don't hang out near the lockers where the druggy kids stay. Mommy would have been so proud of me that I am such a good kid.

I am just waiting for the day that Sonia, the meanie is going to tell my father to find another home for me, just like she did with Tiger. Maybe that is a good idea. I hate living in this house.

CHAPTER 24

I WAS DOING well in school, amazingly, and working two part time jobs. I washed hair and swept the floor of the beauty shop on Saturdays, and waited tables at a busy coffee shop restaurant two evenings a week. I did my school work at the library and basically stayed away from home, and from Sonia, as much as possible. We did have our occasional times where we actually got along, in that we were civilized with one another. Very occasional. Temporary. It was the kind where you walked on eggshells, pretended. Where you faked it well. For the sake of my father.

Sonia didn't like a lot of people, but she did like my two close friends, Donna and Barbara. Thank God. In fact, she liked Donna so much, she told her she wanted her as a daughter-in-law. Donna and I cracked up about that, behind her back of course. Donna had no interest in Sonia's son Harry, and she definitely didn't want Sonia as a mother-in-law. We loved theatrically role playing Sonia and her lucky daughter-in-law, whoever that might be. But we knew for sure that it would not be Donna.

Harry moved back to Montreal after graduating from MIT. He had been accepted to McGill medical school and would be living downtown in his own apartment. I knew that he was way too clever to move back into the house of horrors.

AT THE SAME time, my father told me that he was opening a new floor covering store. A big store. With carpets, area rugs, linoleum, and tiles. The store would be opened six days a week. And he seemed excited with this new venture. Life for my father was finally looking brighter. What a relief.

I told him I would help out in the store as much as possible. I loved the idea of being at the store with my dad, away from Sonia, and helping him build his dream. I was still serious about school, and I couldn't manage three part-time jobs. I quit the hair washing job so I could work with my dad on Saturdays. Those were nice times for us. He was animated when he made a sale, he joked around with the customers, and he reorganized the displays. In my mind, this store was the best therapy for him.

Not much had changed between me and Sonia. We were just so completely different. It was obvious to me that behind her facade of beautiful clothes, stylish hairdos and expensive furniture, was an unhappy, selfish, manipulative and dishonest woman. I didn't care about any of that packaging, but the biggest difference was that it wouldn't even dawn on me to try to change her. Yet she was determined to change me. She had her own values and ideas about what was important, and I had mine. So our battles continued. She criticized, she judged, she complained, and she gave me that passive aggressive silent treatment. No matter how many times I told them that they should be grateful that I was a "good" teen, they found something to complain about. Well, she did. And he supported her.

We tried family therapy and but that didn't last long. Sonia refused to go back, after sitting there with a sulky scowl, looking at her watch, flinching with annoyance. When the therapist tried to draw her in, she gave a remote shrug confirming her lack of interest in the whole thing. After a session of her examining her fingernails and making impatient clicking sounds, she claimed that it was a waste of money. Suddenly she was concerned about spending money. She also insisted that the therapist was siding with me. She referred to her as "your therapist". Ridiculous. So I went on my own. I was seventeen years old, doing well in school, enjoying my social life, and excited about the future. After a few sessions, I stopped seeing her. She made me feel much better, but I wanted to go out with my friends, go to parties, go shopping, meet people, have fun. I wanted to be a teenage girl. I didn't want to go over and over all of the garbage that I was dealing with. I couldn't change any of it. The therapist certainly had no influence on the mess we were in. I preferred to stay away from home as much as possible, and have fun with my friends. Their moms and dads loved me. My aunts, uncles and cousins loved me. I knew that there couldn't be any truth to the constant criticism of everything I did, and the ongoing allegations about me being a bad person.

I CONTINUED TO work at the coffee shop and also at my dad's store. Even at work, the customers loved me. I made great tips as a server. And I was skilful at selling flooring and carpeting.

I had graduated high school and had just started college, known in Montreal as CEGEP. It was the required stepping stone between High School and University. My dad told me that he had hired a really nice seventeen-year-old boy to work part-time in the store. In fact, he was exactly one month older than me. He was the nephew of one of my mom and dad's best friends, Rose and Herman, and he had recently been orphaned and left with an older, mentally challenged brother. And my dad thought this guy was just wonderful. He was a hard worker, quiet, focused, trustworthy, and he could twirl a basketball with one finger.

Dear Diary,
The store has been so good for Daddy. He seems a little bit happy when he's there. I love watching him joke around with customers. And he really likes this guy he just hired. He keeps telling me he can't wait for me to meet him. Maybe things are starting to look up.

PART THREE:

Difference

CHAPTER 1

O N A BALMY, clear Florida morning in November, 1957, Ruth went about her daily routine. Four-year-old Mitchell always woke up the minute he heard his little brother, Barry, crying in his crib. Ruth rushed into Barry's room and his blubbering instantly stopped, replaced by a gummy smile and gurgled, excited sounds. Mitchell watched quietly with his thumb stuck in his mouth, as his mother changed Barry's diaper, chatting easily with both boys.

"Should we go to the park today, boys? We can bring our pails and shovels and play in the big sandbox. You two can go on the swings and I will push you so high-up to the sky."

Barry had just started sitting in a high chair, and Ruth gave him a teething biscuit to gnaw on while she prepared oatmeal for the boys. Toothless, gumming away and drooling, Barry was squealing with delight at Ruth's words. As if he understood everything she was saying. Mitchell stood and watched. He didn't utter a word.

As the oatmeal bubbled away on the stove, Ruth lowered the flame, sprinkled in some brown sugar, and watched as it melted into the steaming cereal. Hyman walked in and kissed his wife. Everyone who knew them called them a sexy couple.

Ruth took the pot off the stove and plugged in the electric percolator. She dropped two pieces of toast into the toaster, smiling at her husband and children. She always told her husband how lucky she was to have her three handsome men.

Ruth Alpert grew up in Newark, New Jersey in the 1930s. She was an attractive woman, with a lovely personality that blended both modesty and confidence. Her parents, Samuel and Fanny Alpert, were American born, quiet and caring people. Samuel was a mechanical engineer, which was a rare yet major accomplishment for those days.

She had two brothers, but was particularly close with the youngest, Len. They were more like best friends than siblings.

Ruth met her husband, Hyman Fishman, while on vacation at a popular singles resort near Lake George, New York. They dated for several months, never doubting that they were destined to be together.

Ruth was delighted about the engagement ring that Hyman had surprised her with. She could barely contain her excitement when she introduced her brother Len to Hyman, the quiet, handsome and very sweet man she was going to marry. Hyman and Len hit it off immediately.

The Fishman's were thrilled that Hyman had met such a wonderful woman, so kind, and madly in love with Hyman. Since Ruth's family, the Alperts, lived in New Jersey, the couple married there. Hyman's best friend Ruby was their best man. Every one of Hyman's siblings, and his mother Annie, attended the wedding.

After a few months of marriage, they moved to Miami, Florida because Hyman had a skin condition which was further exacerbated by cold weather, and his doctor told him that exposure to the sun and warmth would potentially be helpful.

Hyman got a job as a salesman at a furniture and appliance store, where people immediately trusted and liked him. Ruth was a homemaker, spending her days either out in the beautiful Florida weather, or at home cleaning, doing laundry or baking. While she was a marvellous cook, she had quite a sweet tooth and loved baking, skilfully creating cookies, squares, and rich desserts. They were a happy couple who lived in a quiet neighbourhood with many other young families. They had a nice group of friends, many of whom had kids, and on the weekends everyone gathered in someone's backyard for a huge barbecue.

Shortly after Ruth gave birth to their son, Mitchell, she began to notice that Mitchell was not developing normally. They quickly realized that he was different from the other babies his same age.

Mitchell's thumb was red and blistered from his perpetual thumb sucking. While it seemed as if the other kids had a vocabulary of several hundred words, Mitchell barely spoke. When he did, it was difficult to understand anything he was saying. He had trouble building a tower of blocks while the other kids built what seemed to be giant towers. He couldn't put on his shoes, jump with both feet, peddle a bicycle. He didn't know his colours and he couldn't catch a ball.

There were other warning signs. He had no concept of danger, like a hot stove or a moving car. He would focus on objects rather than interacting with other kids. He was easily frustrated. Clumsy. He couldn't drink from a cup without spilling it all over himself.

Everything was a struggle. He had trouble feeding himself with a spoon or fork, so Ruth let him eat with his fingers.

Despite it all, Ruth dealt with Mitchell in the most loving and accepting way. He was special. He needed more help and that's what she was there for. She mothered him with unconditional love, yet she worried. He wasn't growing or developing like the other kids his age. Would he always struggle? Would he make friends? Would she always have the patience to help him?

When Ruth became pregnant with her second son, Barry, her only hope was that he would be normal and healthy. Having a three year old son with obvious developmental delays had taken its toll on her and Hyman. And in the 1950s, the professionals certainly didn't have the knowledge or resources to provide Ruth and Hyman with many options.

Every time Ruth brought Barry to the Paediatrician, she was relieved to hear that he was developing perfectly. He was smiling, amusing himself in his crib, recognizing her and Hyman. He was sitting in his high chair at seven months old, which was much sooner than Mitchell learned to sit.

And that's where Barry was sitting when his father came home to find his wife dead on the kitchen floor, with both his kids crying hysterically.

Along with the ambulance and police, were concerned friends and neighbours who remained in the house with the boys so Hyman could go in the ambulance with Ruth. But it was too late. There wasn't anything the paramedics could do. They rode silently, the paramedics busying themselves with nothing as they watched Hyman gripping the cold hand of his precious wife, tears streaming down his face.

After sitting in the hospital waiting room for what felt like forever, the doctor came to find Hyman. Heart failure. That was the only explanation he could give. There were no signs of any injury or any drugs. They were required by law to perform an autopsy, but for now it seemed apparent that her heart had just stopped.

Thirty-two years old. Beautiful, young wife and mother of two. Shocking. Unbelievable.

Hyman left the hospital with a plastic bag containing the clothes that Ruth had been wearing, her diamond engagement ring and gold wedding band, and the tiny gold heart necklace that he had bought her for their fifth wedding anniversary.

Mitchell's fourth birthday party was planned for that following weekend. No one ever picked up the choo-choo-train birthday cake that Ruth had preordered.

Hyman eventually admitted to Barry that he had relived that horrendous nightmare with uncontrollable flashbacks over and over again, for the rest of his life.

RUTH ALPERT FISHMAN
April 1925 – November 1957

Beloved wife, mother, daughter, sister, niece, cousin, sister-in-law, friend,
who in the bloom of her youth and of health
was in a moment summoned by the wisdom of God
from the cares of this world to the hopes and expectations of a better.

Two helpless children, pledges of mutual affection, the objects of her tenderest
anxiety and most watchful care alike, deplore her untimely fate.

CHAPTER 2

HYMAN WAS ONE of the middle siblings in a family of ten kids. He was quiet, caring and exceptionally handsome. His parents were born and lived in Europe before immigrating to Canada. Amazingly, all ten kids got along extremely well and took care of one another. With so many siblings, it could have easily been the opposite but the Fishman family were fortunate to be close and caring.

They were a poor family, living in Montreal in an old house with three bedrooms and one bathroom. Their father, Morris Harry, was a buttonhole maker, which in those days was a specialized skill that required use of a particular sewing machine. He worked long days for a large men's clothing manufacturer. When the company moved its plant to Sherbrooke, Quebec, Morris Harry rented a room in that small town and came home only on the weekends.

Their mother, Annie, was a short, large-bosomed woman, with thin hair, false teeth, and severe eczema. Despite her physical issues, Annie was strong and loving. She seemed to wear the same dress and apron every day, spending all of her time cooking in her kitchen. Though they lacked money, there was never a shortage of food.

Morris Harry looked elderly and worn out when he died in his sixties. He had been the king of the castle, the man to whom they all looked up and worshipped. But Annie and her children resumed their usual routine right after they got up from sitting Shiva. Annie's attitude about life was clear and simple: do what you have to do, and don't complain. There was no time for grieving. Life goes on, chores still have to be done, and food has to be put on the table.

When Ruth died, Hyman had no choice but to move back to his home town of Montreal with his boys. His whole family lived there, and he couldn't manage on his own. His mother Annie was alive and still quite energetic for a woman of her age. She insisted that Hyman and the boys move in with her. Grandma Annie said she would look after the boys while Hyman went to work. His sisters and sister-in-laws would all help. Even if it meant that the boys would be cared for by anyone and everyone, Hyman would not have to manage on his own. He had the Fishman family.

Ruth's parents and brothers visited Hyman and the boys in Montreal as often as possible. The shock and devastation of Ruth's death had taken its toll on the Alpert family. Ruth's mother had a particularly difficult time seeing her grandchildren and son-in-law struggling to get on with their new life. She was a tiny little woman with a gentle kindness and warmth, but she knew that Hyman was not coping well and was worried about him. He looked exhausted, frightened and sad. She understood. She felt the same way. She lost a huge part of herself when she lost her only daughter.

Len had lost his sister and best friend. But he knew that the best thing to do for Hyman and the boys was to be positive and optimistic about the future. Even if he didn't feel it, he would fake it for their sake. Ruth wouldn't have expected him to be any other way.

Hyman was grateful to have so much family support, but he missed Ruth terribly, his heart aching for the woman he had adored. The mother of his children. People were constantly offering to introduce him to single women, but he refused to date. He was completely committed to taking care of his boys. He worried himself sick about them, and the last thing he needed was to complicate his life with a new woman. No way.

He felt guilty having to depend on his elderly mother. Annie never complained, but Hyman knew that it was hard for her. Barry was an active, busy little boy, and Mitchell was, to say the least, difficult. He had to be watched constantly or he got himself into trouble. He was delayed in both his fine and gross motor skills, his speech and his judgment. And he could never be left alone with Barry, not even for a second. But Hyman had no choice about living with his mother. He had to wait at least until both boys were in school full time before he could manage without her constant help.

Finally, after a few years, Hyman had no choice. His mother was ill and it was time for him and the boys to move into their own place. He rented a one bedroom apartment in a impoverished part of Montreal. That was all he could afford. The boys shared the bedroom and he slept on a sofa bed in the living room. Hyman's job as a salesman for a men's clothing line

didn't pay very well, but it gave him the flexibility to be home for the boys at lunch time, and early enough at the end of the day to help them with homework and prepare dinner. Dinners consisted of frozen fish sticks, TV dinners, boiled hot dogs, and his specialty: salmon patties. He mixed a can of salmon with bread crumbs, an egg and some ketchup. After forming it into patties he would fry them in a frying pan with butter. Warm up a can of peas or corn, and there's dinner. For a special treat, and when he was just too exhausted to worry about dinner, they ate at Harvey's, a chain of fast-food hamburger restaurants. They would each order their own burger and share an order of fries between the three of them, but they could never afford to have a soft drink. Unless it was a special occasion, like one of their birthdays.

Mitchell was struggling terribly in school. He was way behind the other kids in every way: academically, socially, physically and emotionally. And the students were bullies in the truest sense of the word. Not a day went by that Mitchell didn't come home and tell his father that the kids at school were mean to him. Hyman was beside himself with worry about what to do. His family members were already doing so much, he didn't want to burden them. He kept it all to himself, and did everything to try and help Mitchell catch up. He read with him, and told Mitchell that he should just ignore the kids. Good old advice like "Sticks and stones will break your bones, but words will never harm you." The reality was that they weren't only humiliating and embarrassing Mitchell with cruel words, they threw things at him and took things from him, and played vicious pranks. In the classroom. In the school yard. In the hallways. In the bathrooms. Torture. Every single day.

Mitchell had a hard time controlling himself, and as soon as he discovered his strength, particularly when his temper flared and he was furious, Mitchell turned on these bullies. Fully attacked: punching, kicking, pinning them down. Completely out of control, but at least they left him alone.

DESPITE EVERYTHING, BARRY was bright, athletic, friendly and, although quiet, a relatively happy child. Barry was modest about his accomplishments. No matter how excited he was about making a team or getting a good mark, he never talked about it at home. He couldn't. He felt too guilty boasting, feeling proud about something, or expecting recognition, when Mitchell's life was so troubled.

Barry didn't really have a childhood. Seeing how tough life was for his father, he felt pressured to be "easy". He did not want to add to his father's stress so he never asked for guidance or direction. He saw how tough it was for Mitchell to find any joy in his life, and his Dad was often distraught and unhappy. Barry's issues, good or bad, seemed trivial.

When Barry brought home his report cards, he was casual about them. And Hyman was careful to not let Mitchell hear him tell Barry how proud he was. But Mitchell didn't have to hear the words. He knew. He knew that Barry was doing well in everything. He knew that Barry had friends and was smart, and that their dad was proud of him. In Mitchell's mind, their father was not proud of Mitchell. He was ashamed of the stupid things that Mitchell said, he was embarrassed by Mitchell's behaviour and he was frustrated by all of the challenges that Mitchell faced.

When Mitchell talked, he repeated his words over and over, obsessively mumbling. He suggested multiple choice options for anything he was struggling to understand, and couldn't grasp any abstract concepts or vague explanations. He wanted a plain and simple reason for absolutely everything. Black or white.

Eating with Mitchell was an experience like no other. He knocked over glasses when they were full. He couldn't hold the fork and knife properly, food always fell over the edge of his plate, and inevitably something would fly across the table when he was trying to cut it. Knowing that his father would be upset about the mess would make him even more nervous and upset. So things would get worse.

Mitchell broke everything. He dropped things, he twisted the on and off buttons too tightly, he pushed and pulled on things with too much force. He was in a perpetual state of nervousness, impatience, frustration, jealousy, remorse, anger, humiliation.

Yet, Mitchell was neither fish nor foul. He was not delayed enough to be oblivious to the differences between him and Barry, or everyone else for that matter, like his cousins, the kids at school, people on television, people everywhere. Instead, he was close enough to being normal to see others and compare himself, knowing that he wasn't the same. He was right on the fence between normal and delayed. He wanted to be better at doing things, but couldn't. He wanted to be as tall as Barry, but he was short. He wanted lots of friends. He had one. He wanted to be smart, but he wondered if the kids at school were right and he was retarded.

Mitchell constantly compared himself to his brother, and felt inferior to him in every single way. He knew he was supposed to love his brother and he did but, in many ways, he hated him. He constantly vacillated between the two emotions and whenever they got into an argument, Mitchell would revert to the one thing he knew he could do better than Barry. Fight. And he would use every bit of strength he had to beat up his younger brother.

Then he would feel guilty. Apologizing over and over again. Justifying what he had done by telling Barry he had provoked him. Apologizing. Justifying. Apologizing. Justifying.

Mitchell did have one friend at school: his best friend Sammy. Completely different from each other, but both quite delayed, Mitchell and Sammy hung out together at recess and lunch time. The kids in the school had a field day with those two, mocking and tormenting them every chance they got. But Mitchell and Sammy did their best to ignore the kids. At least they had each other. Until Sammy died of a medical complication. Mitchell was crushed. And totally confused as to why the doctors could not fix his friend. Mitchell desperately wanted an answer. He tried in his simple capacity to find one. He asked questions with multiple choice options, none of which made much sense.

"Did he have a heart attack or was it cancer? Did he go to the hospital or to a clinic or to an emergency room or was he in an ambulance or at home or on the street where he fell down and someone had to call 9-1-1?"

He needed a simple and clear explanation. And no one could give him one. Once again, Mitchell was alone. Hyman could not believe it. How could his kid have such unbelievably bad luck? Cradling his head in his hands, he told Barry "Some people say that in life you are dealt a hand of cards. Mitchell was dealt a very bad hand."

BARRY AND HIS dad shared some poignant conversations. Hyman felt strongly that his children had been cheated out of so much. Life would have been different if Ruth hadn't died. They would have had a good life, a normal life as a family. Ruth would have been proud of Barry. She would have been a wonderful mother. She would have known how to deal with Mitchell. They would have had money to do some of the things they had dreamed about doing with their kids. Ruth would have been much more patient and tolerant with Mitchell. Things would have been completely different.

Hyman missed Ruth so much.

Growing up without a mother, and with a brother like Mitchell, Barry learned early on that his life was different from everyone else's. His friends and cousins had two parents, a home with several bedrooms, an actual bed for their parents, freshly baked cake on the counter, pets in the yard, plants in the living room, paintings on the walls and newspapers delivered to their house. Some even had two cars, a cleaning lady and family vacations. Siblings who were not disabled.

This was his life. His reality. His difference. He was determined to be happy and successful, despite the obstacles or challenges. Choices, we all have choices.

HYMAN DID NOT have any extra money to give Barry an allowance. Barry collected empty bottles and cashed them in for the two cent deposit. And at eleven years old, Barry got a job doing a paper route every morning. He delivered newspapers before school each day and on the weekends. No matter what the weather was like, he was out working before the sun even came up. And once a week in the evening, he would go door-to-door to collect money from his customers. He didn't mind, because it gave him the opportunity to get out of the apartment.

He used whatever earned money he absolutely needed, and offered the rest to his dad. Hyman refused to take any of it and insisted that Barry deposit it into his own bank account. Barry loved looking through that bankbook at the ongoing list of deposits.

Hyman often told Barry that compared to Hyman's own childhood, Barry and Mitchell were much better off. Hyman had to share a room with all of his brothers. And they were so poor they could not afford warm winter mittens. In the winter, Hyman's mother used to give each of her children two baked potatoes, to keep one in each of their thin mittens until they got to school. That would keep their hands warm, and then they could eat the baked potatoes for breakfast. Barry was happy that he had warm winter clothes and didn't have to eat baked potatoes for breakfast. He preferred Frosted Flakes and milk in a bowl.

From a young age, Barry worried about his father. He was proud of his dad, and knew he was a wonderful, dedicated father. But he also knew that

his father was unhappy with his life. Lonely and preoccupied with worrying about Mitchell. No one knew better than Barry how difficult it was for his father to be a single parent, especially in his particular circumstances. Hyman wanted the best for his boys, and he didn't have any clue as to how he could help make Mitchell's life even slightly better.

Barry spent endless hours away from the apartment, hanging out with the neighbourhood kids shooting hoops at the nearby community centre, and playing hockey and baseball on the long driveway between the buildings. The diversity amongst the kids from all over the world, in the crowded, condensed urban area enriched their friendships. Despite their cultural differences and lack of money, loyalty was a common value. And they all intuitively understood teamwork and sportsmanship. They were in and out of each other's apartments, and parents of all the kids were welcoming and generous with food and drinks.

Barry tried his hardest to include Mitchell with the neighbourhood kids, and the kids did, albeit reluctantly, involve him whenever possible. But everything they did together involved some sort of sport, and Mitchell could not keep up. Not even with the youngest kids. So he stayed in the apartment, watching the small black and white television set, pacing, looking out the window at his brother and his brother's friends, pacing some more, mumbling. Frustrated. Nervous. Jealous.

HYMAN AND THE boys went grocery shopping once a week with Hyman's oldest brother and sister-in-law, Uncle Aaron and Auntie Reba. Barry always asked his father to put the same items in their basket as his aunt was buying for their house. But buying cookies, chocolate and chips was not in the budget, so Uncle Aaron always let Barry secretly pick something special that he would buy for them. "May Wests," a round, chocolate dipped cake with yellow custard between two layers of vanilla cake, was Barry's all-time favourite treat.

Mitchell stayed right by his father's side, exactly as he had been told to do. Hyman couldn't risk Mitchell knocking over a display or getting upset with someone in the store who might have looked at him "the wrong way." So he kept him at his side. And Mitchell didn't dare wander from his dad.

Hyman did laundry one evening a week in the basement of the apartment building. When Barry was old enough, he helped his dad carry down the laundry basket full of clothes and the box of laundry soap. Hyman and Barry would wait down in the small room for the two washing machines to finish the cycle, switch everything into the dryers and then go up to the apartment while the two dryers were running. They brought the clothes up, folded them and put everything away in the bedroom closet or in the drawers in the old dilapidated dresser. Same routine every single week.

Hyman didn't like staying home in that depressing apartment, so the three of them spent their weekends visiting relatives. They appreciated the hearty meals, and often left with containers full of home cooked food. With over twenty first cousins, there was never a shortage of hand-me-down clothes for the boys, and cousins of all ages for the boys to play with. Every one of the Fishman cousins tried their best to involve Mitchell, and to make him feel as included as possible. But the years of bullying, coupled with the constant failures in his struggle to do things like the other kids, left Mitchell resistant and suspicious. Even with people who cared and wanted to help, Mitchell kept his distance.

KNOWING THAT IT was a good idea to add some pleasure to their lives, Hyman tried to do some fun things with the boys. In the winter time, he took them skating and tobogganing. In the warmer months, they swam together at the community pool.

His brother Aaron and his divorced friend, Ruby, were Hyman's closest friends. Aaron spent every Sunday morning with his brother and the boys, so they wouldn't be alone. They had an easy relationship, and the boys were crazy about Uncle Aaron. All of Hyman's brothers, the Fishman uncles, had similar dispositions. They were quiet, gentle people. Easy to please. Easy to be around.

Ruby's colourful personality was quite a contrast to his good friend Hyman. That was probably what drew them to each other. They were both single, but Ruby enjoyed the dating scene. His stories and experiences kept Hyman entertained. And at the same time, they further reinforced his decision not to date. These women Ruby talked about sounded time-consuming and demanding. Hyman certainly had no spare time.

Ruby enjoyed spending some evenings at the apartment with Hyman and the boys. Mitchell was quiet and uncomfortable around people, therefore it was hard for Ruby to get to know Mitchell. But he enjoyed talking to Barry. Having been lifetime friends, Hyman was comfortable with Ruby and appreciative of his support and understanding of how tough things were. Not in a sympathetic way. That was not what Hyman wanted. Just knowing and understanding. Unspoken support.

Ruth's brother, Uncle Len, had kept in close contact with Hyman and the boys throughout the years. He was fond of Hyman, proud of the remarkable job Hyman was doing raising the boys on his own.

Len had a successful business in New Jersey, but he always, always found time for his sister's family. Phone calls and visits, mailing thoughtful birthday presents, it was important to him that he stay connected. Hyman and the boys were crazy about Uncle Len and his family. They particularly loved their road trips to New Jersey and the adventures they had with their New Jersey family. It was such a treat for them to go to Atlantic City, the boardwalk, eat cotton candy, go to restaurants and movies.

And so, the years crept by.

As Barry turned seventeen, he was doing well in his last year of high school. He had applied to various colleges, called CEGEPs, for the upcoming September, and was determined to get accepted at his first choice. He was quiet, focused, and well liked. He had a good group of friends, none of whom were involved with drugs or cigarettes, and he played on the school basketball team. He had a part-time job at a local hardware store, and was one of the only part-time employees in the store who could assemble and repair bicycles. There was always a pile of broken and unassembled bicycles waiting for him at work. While he discovered girls, he didn't have a whole lot of time for them. School, basketball and his job kept his weeks pretty full.

Mitchell had finished with school, and the accompanying ongoing struggles and frustration, for several years. A number of employers were kind enough to give him a chance at a job, but the longest he lasted at any one place was a few weeks. He was either fired or he quit. He was either ready to kill them, or they were ready to kill him. Simple jobs on an assembly line or doing janitorial work, and he couldn't do it. Hyman was beside himself.

I<small>T WAS THE</small> end of April, 1974 and finally, after a long, cold winter, the weather was beautiful. Hyman and the boys decided to wash the car. It was a big 1971 Chevrolet Biscayne, chocolate brown with bench seats. Barry had just finished driving school and had passed the driving test on his first attempt. Hyman let him drive whenever they went out. Barry felt very grown up sharing the car with his father, and he was looking forward to driving it as often as possible in the nice weather.

There was a water hose by the side of the apartment building, long enough to use for washing cars. Hyman and the boys brought down their own bucket, dish soap, towels and sponges. When they were satisfied that the car was clean, they dried it with old towels and went upstairs for a cold drink. Hyman wasn't feeling well and went to lie down. Unusual for him, since he rarely took a nap during the day. Before he could make it to the couch, which he converted to his bed every night, Hyman fell to the floor of the living room. Barry screamed in the hallway of their apartment for help. By the time a neighbour arrived, Hyman had stopped breathing. Massive heart attack. No warning. Fifty-five years old. Beloved father, brother, brother-in-law, uncle, cousin.

Mitchell watched. Stunned. Immobilized. Terrified. He had watched his mother drop dead when he was four years old. Now, at twenty-one, he watched his father drop dead. Both times, there was nothing he could do. Alive and then dead. Black and white.

Mitchell and Barry. Orphaned.

CHAPTER 3

A PPARENTLY IT WASN'T that unusual for aunts and uncles to unofficially form a committee that would meet on a regular basis to discuss what is best for the remaining family members. Especially when the family members were children.

The "Let's decide what is best for Mitchell and Barry" committee gathered to discuss the plan for the boys. Decisions had to be made quickly. The situation was complicated. What should they do about Mitchell? In actuality, he was twenty-one years old, but in reality, he was still a young child. And Barry was only seventeen. He still needed guidance and direction. And they both needed a place to live. Hyman's youngest sister Rose, and her husband Herman, agreed that the most logical place for the boys to live was with them and their four kids. The Silver family had a big house with a large bedroom in the basement for the boys to sleep. Rose didn't work, and since she was already cooking for six, why not cook for eight? So right after the funeral, the boys officially moved in with the Silvers.

Officially moving in meant bringing their clothes and personal belongings. There was no point moving the worn out twin beds, the dresser, couch, or kitchen table and chairs. There were no paintings on the walls, nothing valuable or worth keeping in the kitchen, no plants, no decorative items. Everything they owned fit into a couple of old suitcases.

THE FOUR COUSINS were thrilled to have Mitchell and Barry move in. They were welcoming and proud to be the family that took in the orphans.

Barry could not believe that his entire life had changed. He felt guilty about having to intrude on his aunt and uncle, especially with his brother. He was worried about his and Mitchell's financial situation. He had a little bit of money in his bank account, but not nearly enough to support himself and his brother, and pay for college. He had every intention of following through with his plans for college, and then university for that matter. He felt overwhelmed with the responsibility of Mitchell and, at the same time, completely uncertain about how to deal with him. And in the meantime, he had to worry about his final high school exams.

Barry did get accepted into the college of his choice. He worked the entire summer, earning and saving as much money as he could. He had discovered that his father had a small life insurance policy, very small, that would at least help the boys manage for the next few years. Manage as long as they worked and spent money extremely carefully.

Hyman's brother Perry was the accountant in the family. He was also the administrator of Hyman's Will, which consisted only of this life insurance policy. Insightful and conservative, Uncle Perry offered to handle the boy's financial affairs to be sure that the money stretched as far as it could go. He wasn't about to hand it over to a seventeen-year-old boy and his unstable brother.

Barry found excuses to spend time with his Uncle Perry at his office. Uncle Perry was a calm, logical and capable man who Barry respected and admired tremendously. His practical, solution-oriented approach to the whole situation, and to life in general, provided an immense deal of comfort and hope for Barry.

FRIENDS, NEIGHBOURS, AND business associates connected to someone, anyone, in the Fishman family, were eager to do something to help these orphaned boys. People offered hand-me-down clothes, winter jackets, and plenty of "If there's anything I can do to help, please let me know."

Barry started college in September. His Uncle Herman found him a part-time job at his friend's big retail store where they sold carpets, tiles, and linoleum. Herman was grateful to his friend Shloime, for hiring Barry to work at his store. And Barry was happy to have a job working for a nice man, near their house, with perfect part-time hours, and doing physical labour. It felt good to sweat, moving those heavy rolls of carpets and boxes of tiles, instead of worrying about his brother.

Barry was determined to keep his father's car. It was expensive to pay for gas and insurance, but his aunt and uncle's house was far from where he was going to college, and it would have taken him way too long to commute every day. He knew that somehow he would manage to keep the car. He had applied for and received school loans and grants, and was cautious about how he spent money. It would all work out. It had to.

BARRY WAS THRILLED to have met a friend at college named Leslie. Leslie's parents were friends with Rose and Herman, so the two families knew each other. Leslie had heard all about Barry and Mitchell. Remarkably, the guys had the same school schedule. Having all their classes and lunch breaks together, it didn't take long for Barry and Leslie to become friends. With small town values of hard work and family, Leslie was down-to-earth and easy to talk to. It was almost as if they had been friends forever. Some people even thought they looked and acted so alike, they could be brothers.

Leslie was immediately invited to join everyone for dinner at the Silver's house, especially since he had known the Silver family longer than he had even known Barry. And of course, Barry spent plenty of time at Leslie's house. Leslie's parents lived modestly above their successful retail store in a rural community an hour from Montreal. Country folks. They were delighted that Leslie and Barry were friends. It was obvious to them that they were good kids, serious about school. Mature, responsible, and compatible buddies.

Leslie and his younger brother were very grounded and helped out in the store whenever they had some time. Ironically, these simple, friendly, generous people bought Leslie a flashy, white Trans Am so he could commute to college. Leslie had no idea how cool that car was.

Leslie's parents also knew Shloime, the owner of the floor covering store where Barry was working part-time. Leslie's mother, and Shloime's late wife Rita were first cousins. In fact, Leslie told Barry that he was also good friends with his distant cousin, Lynda, Shloime's daughter. What a small world.

Leslie wanted his friend Barry to meet his cousin and good friend. He thought they would get along famously, and he loved the idea of his two good friends getting together. Neither Barry nor Lynda was interested. College had just started and they were both busy settling into their new routines.

In early October, both Barry and Lynda were scheduled to work at her father's store on a Friday evening and then the next day. There was a big shipment that had to be loaded on a truck, so they spent most of Friday evening getting the order ready. Lynda didn't normally lug rolls of carpets, but on that particular weekend, she was in the mood. Having just met

Barry and thinking that he really was cute may have had something to do with her sudden willingness to endure physical labour. They chatted, they schlepped, they flirted. As soon as Lynda got home on that Friday, she called Leslie to say that she had met Barry and would be happy to go out. Leslie laughed and told her that he had already heard from Barry. They would all be going out the next evening in Leslie's new Trans Am. He asked Lynda to find him a date, and the four of them would go to a movie and out for coffee. He was seizing the opportunity. He didn't want to take a chance that one of them would change their minds.

Barry and Lynda worked the whole day Saturday together and, typical of seventeen-year-olds, neither one of them said a word to each other about going out together that evening.

PART FOUR:

Patience

CHAPTER 1

Dear Diary,
I just came home from my first date with Barry. He is such a HUNK. Tall, dark
and handsome, just like the prince in Cinderella. As corny as it sounds, I think
we fell in love immediately. No glass slipper, but the sparks were flying. I hope he
calls me tomorrow.

He did call. And the next day, and the next.

I WORKED IN the store as often as possible, and certainly when Barry was
working. I treasured the drives to and from work with my father. He always
let me drive, so I could practice my driving skills. And it gave us a chance to
chat. We didn't talk about anything specific, and certainly not about Sonia.
But it was our time together, alone. Just me and my dad. Almost like it
used to be in the rowboat.

My father was thrilled about me and Barry. He told me that he liked
Barry, he knew that the Fishman's were a good family, and could see that I
was happy.

Barry and I saw each other all the time. We studied together in the
library, sat and talked in coffee shops for hours and hours, went for long
walks, and got to know each other better each day.

We had a great deal in common, especially since we had both been
through so much in our seventeen years. The one thing we both agreed on
from day one, was that neither one of us wanted anyone to feel sorry for us.
Sympathy, no. Empathy, yes. There is a huge difference between the two.

BARRY TOLD ME that while his father's death had been awful, his father had
been very unhappy, frustrated with Mitchell, and lonely. It was hard for
Barry to see him that way. He missed him, but he was sure his father was
much happier, and more at peace, now. Finally.

I gasped when he told me that he was seven months old when his
mother died. SEVEN. In 1957. And then seventeen when his father died.

When Barry and I weren't alone, we spent time with Leslie. The three
of us had a blast together, no matter what we did, constantly cementing

the bond we had formed as a threesome. We introduced Leslie to my dear friend Donna, and they hit it off for a short while, but that didn't last. Leslie had no trouble finding girlfriends, and we welcomed each new girl into our tight little threesome.

The Silvers were overjoyed that Barry and I were together. I had known all of them my entire life, because my parents had been good friends with Herman and Rose.

I have always loved coincidences or flukes, because I think they have way more significance and meaning than we realize. I was particularly excited when Barry's cousin came across a picture of Barry's dad, Hyman, that was taken at the Silver's house just a few weeks before Hyman died. And standing right behind him in the picture, was my father. Just the two dads. Freaky. Everyone certainly thought that the irony was pretty amazing. I knew it was a definite sign that Barry and I were meant to be together.

I was so comfortable spending time at the Silver's house. Actually, I was comfortable spending time anywhere and everywhere, except at my own house. I dreaded spending any waking moment there.

Auntie Rose and Uncle Herman's house was noisy, busy and hectic. I loved it. Aside from their four kids, and Mitchell and Barry, they had three dogs and two cats. Their kitchen table easily sat twelve people and Auntie Rose always served enough food for twenty. In fact, their house was always full of people and ridiculous amounts of food.

She was known for her monster rib steaks, delicious chicken soup, and melt-in-your-mouth chocolate brownies. Similar to her mother, Barry's grandmother Annie, Auntie Rose spent endless hours cooking and baking for her family and any strays who wanted to stay for dinner. I was happy to be a stray in that house.

Barry often told me how grateful he was to his aunt and uncle for helping them out by opening their home to them. He also said that eating homemade food every night was such an improvement to the food they ate for so many years. He certainly didn't miss those Salisbury Steak TV dinners with the vegetables and dessert all divided on the same container. He had hated when the gravy from the meat dripped onto his dessert section.

Dear Diary,
I finally understand what people mean when they talk about good chemistry. Good vibes. Good energy. I think Barry and I are actually soul mates.

CHAPTER 2

I̲T̲ ̲W̲A̲S̲ ̲I̲N̲E̲V̲I̲T̲A̲B̲L̲E̲ that I bring Barry to my house to meet Sonia. Things were already strained enough between me and Sonia. I knew that the longer I waited to introduce them to each other, the more awkward it would be. Barry knew quite a bit about what had been going on, but I had certainly not told him all of the miserable details. He had just lost his father, he had no parents, he was living in the basement of his aunt and uncle's house, sharing a room with Mitchell and worried about him, worried about money, determined to do well in school, and now madly in love with me. He had more than enough on his plate.

I felt protected and safe when I was with Barry. He may have been quiet, but he was strong. Inside and outside. Physically and emotionally. He had the most amazing ability to be both sensitive and sensible. He had been through so much in his life, and yet he was actually grounded. Stable and smart. He knew what he wanted, he was calm, focused and honest. I trusted him completely.

I also learned early in our relationship that Barry hates being told what to do. He could be flexible and easy going, as long as he knew that he was holding the reins. And he learned early on with me, that while I may have come across to many people as a strong person, I was actually quite the opposite. People just assumed that since I had survived so much, and still did well in school, had lots of friends, was outgoing and friendly, and had a good sense of humour, that I must be pretty solid. Ha.

Barry was always open to learning and growing. He would never put himself at the centre of attention. He was definitely more interested in sitting back and observing others. "Still waters run deep." I also knew him well enough to know that he formed his opinions about people and situations pretty quickly, and quite accurately. I was amazed by his incredible intuition and ability to size people up. And it certainly didn't take him long to see Sonia's true personality.

I had to stop and take several deep breaths before bracing myself to answer the door and let Barry into the house for the grand meeting. From the minute that he walked in, I could feel the tension. They smiled at each other and we all sat down in the formal European living room with authentic oriental rugs, hardly a room conducive to any sort of comfort and relaxation.

Barry answered all of her questions, which he later referred to as "the interrogation" about his academic plans and his brother, in a polite and pleasant manner, but to me, he was obviously uncomfortable. We were seventeen years old. He had absolutely nothing in common with this woman, and could sense that he was being judged. Carrying on a conversation with her was anything but easy.

After about fifteen minutes, he gave me the "let's go" look and we excused ourselves and left the house. Barry said that from the moment they met, he couldn't stand her. He saw right through her designer clothes and fancy furniture. He found her to be totally shallow, self-centred, superficial and insincere.

The feeling was obviously mutual, since her feedback to me the second I returned home, totally unsolicited of course, was that he was quiet and shy which, she confidently informed me, obviously meant that he was meek and insecure. She also told me that since he came from a poor family, he would never amount to anything, and that he was a package deal with his brother. She emphasized the fact that if we stayed together, I would be "stuck" having to look after his brother as well.

This was coming from someone who never went out of her way for anyone, never did a day of volunteer work, and had no compassion or empathy for anyone unless they registered highly on her Sonia bank account meter. Her opinion about Barry meant absolutely nothing to me.

CHAPTER 3

IT DROVE ME crazy that my father was not on speaking terms with his brother and sister-in-law, my Uncle Dave and my Auntie Riva. After a lifetime spent together, I knew that my father had to feel terribly about the way things were between them, especially because it was apparently related to money. Money had never been that important to my dad, until he met his lovely new bride.

He had been close with both my aunt and uncle. So close with their kids. I tried talking to each of them about working things out, resolving this feud, but I was always told the same thing. I didn't know all of the facts and there were too many issues to resolve. Discussions that started out calmly inevitably became emotional. My aunt and uncle on my father's side were making decisions with their heart, defying their own philosophy about the need to lead with your head. Interesting.

As a young adult, I started to see and appreciate a whole other side to my aunt and uncle. Or maybe they had mellowed with the difficulties they had faced in the last few years. Whatever the explanation, I became much more comfortable in their presence. Oh, my uncle still checked to make sure I had hung up my coat properly, facing the right direction and evenly placed on the hanger. But now I could tease him about it. I could intentionally hang it backwards just to bother him. And I was no longer afraid of being scolded.

The dynamics of our relationship had changed, and I felt connected to them. We could have adult discussions that were meaningful. They liked Barry, they enjoyed our visits, and they were proud of our academic decisions. The only dark clouds were the seemingly irreconcilable differences between them and my father.

EXTENDED FAMILY WAS so important to Barry and he was exceedingly fond of his father's sister, Sarah. She was widowed and lived alone in a cozy little apartment. Auntie Sarah just loved having company, and we often dropped by without an invitation. She always had a moist and delicious pistachio cake on the counter. One evening we were on our way to visit Auntie Sarah, and just a block away from her building, a woman unexpectedly walked out onto the dark street right in front of the car. Barry swerved and thankfully avoided hitting her. We were so shook up by this near disaster, that we changed our minds about the visit.

Auntie Sarah died suddenly that evening. Her son had come over right around the same time that we would have been there, to check on her, and found her dead on the floor of her living room. As upset as we were about her sudden passing, we were grateful that we hadn't been the ones to find her. I was quite certain that one of our angels had made sure that Barry was spared that all too familiar experience.

BUBBY AND ZAIDA were crazy about Barry. We went there every Friday night for dinner, and popped in unexpectedly during the week. My father's store was opened on Friday nights so he couldn't be home for dinner. And I certainly didn't feel badly about Sonia being home alone, or out shopping, or rallying teammates, or doing whatever she was doing.

These Friday night dinners were precious for me and Barry. A treat for us and for my grandparents. Aside from the fact that we knew how much pleasure my grandparents got from our time together, and how much my grandmother loved spending the day cooking dinner for us, we enjoyed our time with them. We sat for hours around their small kitchen table covered in a cheap vinyl tablecloth, long after eating our meal, listening to their stories and experiences, full of advice and saychology lessons. Bubby did most of the talking, but every so often my grandfather would throw in a sentence.

When I tried talking to her about my dad, she would fall back on her consistent philosophy that he is trying his best, he suffered so much he couldn't help himself, and most of all he was a man. Men just aren't the same as women. Fathers just aren't the same as mothers.

As soon as she mentioned mothers I would ask her to explain why Sonia, a woman and a mother, was so awful to me. I thought maybe I could induce her to join me in a bitching session. But no, she rationally but sincerely, with her head and her heart, explained that Sonia was raised differently, with different values and experiences and, since she's not my real mother, our differences clash. She doesn't mean to hurt me; she just doesn't know any better.

Sometimes she would admit that Sonia was a fool, because only fools condemn, criticize and complain, but she would then qualify it by saying that Sonia was obviously never taught about character, integrity and understanding. It was not her fault, it was her parents and their parents before them who were to blame. That usually led to an advanced saychology lecture about how Sonia was teaching me some valuable life lessons about what is and what isn't important, and how to treat others. Instead of getting upset and hurt, learn from her mistakes.

Most importantly, Bubby would remind me that while I may have only had my mother "in this world" for thirteen years, she taught me well, she would always be my mother, my only mother, and would always be proud of me.

Dropping by their house was comforting for all of us. Through their own struggles and pain, they still found many ways to help us see the positive side of life, so we could continue to pick up the pieces and reassemble our lives.

Bubby and Zaida continuously told us about how proud they were of both me and Barry. They were not educated themselves, and were so pleased that we were serious about our studies. They told us how important it was for us to work hard in school, to become successful, to be sure to make a difference in the world. They said that we were both strong, and that we could stand out above the rest. That we should live a meaningful life that feels good for us, while at the same time enriches the lives of others.

I was always fascinated. They may not have been formally educated, but they intuitively understood life. And I found it comforting to hear my grandmother echoing what my mother had always preached, and shown us, through her own actions. It wasn't just talk. I knew it could all be done.

Throughout these visits, we would graduate to the living room where we sat on the white and gold French provincial, plastic-covered couch, and Bubby would talk and knit without even looking at what she was knitting. The wool was constantly wrapped around her finger, coming out of what seemed to be an endless roll of wool in a bag on the floor, by her worn and tired feet. Calloused feet, with bunions, and unpolished toes.

When she had something really important to say, she would stop knitting for a minute or so and look at us with those tender eyes, her passion for her words coming through loud and clear.

She could get pretty intense with her saychology lectures and advice about people and life in general. For years, I had heard how there are always two sides to every story, and that it doesn't matter who is right or wrong, just look for the "right" in every situation. Look for the good, never the bad. The beauty, not the flaws. Be careful what you wish for. Don't wish harm on others, no matter how much you think they have hurt or offended you. Don't hate anyone. Instead, try to understand them.

Saychology 101. Good advice, repeated over and over again.

It was amazing to me that I had met someone who valued extended family as much as I did. Barry was close with his relatives, and I was welcomed by each and every one of them. It was easy to get to know the Fishman's as well as his mother's family in New Jersey. Everyone made me feel comfortable. The Fishman cousins had a cousin's club that met once a month. Many of the cousins were married with children, and each month someone else hosted the club at their house. It seemed as if every week there was something going on at one of his relative's homes. This was a huge family that managed to find many opportunities to spend time together.

We spent so much of our free time visiting relatives. Thank God for that big brown reliable 1971 Chevrolet Biscayne.

When Barry and I had a few extra days off of school, we took that big Chevrolet Biscayne to visit our family in New York and New Jersey. Whether we stayed in New York with my eccentric Aunt Naomi, or in New Jersey with Uncle Len, we got to spend time with everyone. Uncle Len continued to prove that he was just so special, kind and generous. He never had a negative thing to say to or about anyone. Barry could not tell me enough, just how lucky he felt to have Len as his uncle. So full of charisma, with a magnetic personality. Way more than an uncle. He was a mentor. A pillar of strength and optimism.

I thought back to our family trips to New York. My family had always loved New York. We were especially impressed with Naomi's apartment building. There was a uniformed doorman in the lobby twenty four hours a day, a garbage chute, and elevators that we could ride up and down as much as we wanted, obnoxiously pushing every single floor on the panel.

Naomi had five locks and chains on their door, the walls were painted bright yellow, and there was one cupboard in the kitchen that was fully loaded with cookies, chocolate and candy.

During our girls' trips we would shop on the lower east side, eat hot dogs cooked on street stands, drive around staring in awe at the hookers, and walk by the endless number of homeless people. We didn't have any homeless people in Cote St. Luc. We were fascinated.

I don't know how we did it, but we all managed to find a spot for our sleeping bags and sleep in that small apartment. Well, "sleep" is a relative word. My mother, her friends and my aunt Naomi would keep us up for hours talking and howling. Half the time we had no idea why they were laughing so much, but they certainly found it all hilarious.

Naomi was still single, and since she didn't have kids of her own, she loved to mother me and Barry. In an unusual way, mind you, like taking us out late at night to bars, or to the leather district in New York where we could see how the "S&M" crowd lived. Her apartment had round ashtrays overflowing with ashes and butts on almost every flat surface, and gave off a distinct smell of cigarette smoke combined with perfume and air freshener spray. When we packed everyone from the Alpert family into her apartment for dinner, she did her best to let them know that she called me every day, and was practically my mother. As different as she was from my mother, I must confess that I loved the special treatment. It also helped that Barry and Naomi got along well. Some days, even better than I did with her. Barry's family, my family, it didn't matter. They all made such an effort to include each other.

I loved to daydream about how my mother would have loved everyone, but most of all, Barry.

CHAPTER 4

I DIDN'T KNOW that my father had a Will. In fact, I didn't really know what a Will was, and I thought that only old, rich people had Wills. But one day I needed my birth certificate for something and, when I looked through the drawer where we kept all of the important papers, there it was. His Will. I wasn't looking for it, but since I had it in my hands, I read it.

Looking back, I wish I had never seen it, because reading that document was one of the most hurtful experiences I ever had. I sat slumped on the edge of his bed and read, with disbelief, the stinging words clearly written in black type. My father's Will said that when he died, he was leaving the house, which was already in Sonia's name, and all of its contents, to Sonia, and his money and any investments were to be divided between Sonia, her two kids, and me. Sonia was to get half, and the three of us were to split the remaining half.

I had no idea what to do. I was beside myself. Furious, disgusted, and hurt. Sonia's kids had inherited plenty of money from their own father. Loads of it. They weren't even my father's kids. From what I saw, they barely had any relationship with my dad. They were polite and respectful, but that was it. What right did they have to my father's money after he dies?

And why the hell did she need any of it? Some of that money had to have been savings from my mother, who worked, unlike Sonia. My mother had been a productive member of society, not a spoiled, miserable person who judged everyone, only liked people if they were "loaded", and spent her days shopping or pampering herself.

And there was his Air Canada settlement money there too, which may have been what my relatives considered to be a "paltry sum" but it was still his money. She certainly didn't need to dip into that too. In fact, what right did she have to any of our money?

So I called Barry, babbling on hysterically about how disgusting and stupid my father was, and how I wished he had died with my mother and sisters. Then I wouldn't be dealing with a father who was still alive and had no idea how to be a father. He was weak and brainless, and all he cared about was that superficial, self-centred bitch he married, who had plenty of her own money but didn't touch a dime of it. A total taker, who had no idea how to give.

I was crying and screaming, breathing quickly, sobbing, stamping my feet like a toddler having a temper tantrum. I was completely out of control.

I knew that I was saying things that one should never say about a parent. I meant every single word I said about Sonia, but I didn't really wish that my father had also died. I was just so hurt, angry, betrayed and shocked.

After Barry had listened and eventually got a few words in to calm me down, we both agreed that there was not much I could do.

"Your father was not thinking in a rational way. His Will is consistent with his behaviour since he married Sonia. Don't let it bother you. We'll do whatever it takes to make it on our own. Besides, you can't tell him you read his Will."

Barry was right.

I knew that I couldn't confront my father. He was way too fragile, which on that day I obviously didn't really care about, but how could I confess to reading something that I should not have read. And what explanation could he possibly give me that would make it alright? Absolutely none.

What got to me was the realization that this further proved my theory about how much my dad had to do in order to pacify his second wife. Including her kids in his Will must have scored him some serious points with her. I had to let it go. Or should I say, try to let it go.

We have choices. We always have choices. Much easier said than done.

CHAPTER 5

WE WERE ALMOST finished our two years of college, and were in the process of applying to McGill University. I was applying to the Faculty of Social Work where I could receive formal training and a degree in helping others. I still believed, very strongly, that my life was spared so that I could help people. Not in a saint kind of way. Just the regular kind of help that could make a difference for someone in need. I couldn't imagine doing anything else.

Barry was applying to the business program. He was good with numbers and loved going to the library and book stores where he could look through the books and magazines about big businesses. Being practical and sensible, he chose accounting as a solid place to start his career.

We talked about moving into apartments. Separately of course. He didn't want to continue imposing on his relatives, and thought it would be better to find a small apartment for him and Mitchell. He could continue working part time and, as long as Mitchell kept a job, they could manage the rent and other basic living expenses.

There were many who did their best to find a job for Mitchell. While he tried to stay at one of these jobs for more than a few weeks, his temper and mistrust of people got in the way. So did the alcohol that he had discovered. It had been about a year since his father died and, for the first time in his life, he was starting to feel like he had some freedom from the strict rules that he had always lived by. Getting drunk felt great for Mitchell. And as he proudly announced to everyone who would listen, he was old enough to buy liquor for himself, so that's what he did. And he was coming home to his aunt and uncle's house pissed drunk.

The year since Hyman's death had given all of the aunts and uncles a true, albeit slight, taste of what Hyman had dealt with all those years. None of them really knew what to do or how to deal with Mitchell. They didn't consult Barry either, which was probably better. They just assumed that an eighteen-year-old would not have the experience or maturity to make proper decisions about Mitchell. The truth was that Barry didn't know what would work. He had watched his father struggle with Mitchell and, no matter what he'd tried, nothing seemed to work. Barry was open and, at the same time, relieved to let his aunts and uncles try to resolve this issue.

The consensus was to send him to live on a kibbutz, a cooperative, self-contained community in Israel. A decision that all of the aunts and uncles agreed was the best idea. He was definitely strong enough to work hard, and he might feel good about being part of a community where everyone was equal. And something drastic had to be done. Things could not continue as they were.

So off Mitchell went to Israel. Well, he lasted there for a few months. He moved into a couple of different Kibbutzim, and then they finally sent him back to Montreal, and back to Barry, because of uncontrollable fighting and drinking.

As for me, I knew that as difficult as it would be, in so many ways, I had to move into my own apartment. I could not stay in the house with Sonia. I wasn't happy living there, they were not happy having me there, and I was old enough to be on my own. After all, I was already eighteen. Practically middle aged. I could live closer to McGill, easily find jobs waiting tables, and get out of that toxic environment.

As soon as I had an opportunity to be alone with my dad, I told him about my plans. I also told him that I needed some of the Air Canada settlement money, so that I could live on my own and finish university, while working part time. As usual he didn't have much to say, and I assumed that he was okay with my decision. He even told me he would help as much as he could.

I thought that he seemed somewhat relieved. He may not have shown much emotion or insight, but he knew enough to know that our living situation couldn't continue.

A couple of days later, I was studying in my room when my father and Sonia walked in together and presented me with some legal-sized documents. My father explained that these official-looking papers had to do with the money from Air Canada that had been held in trust for me, and the way in which the money had been invested. He went on to say that since I am over eighteen, I had to sign the papers. With the two of them still standing in my room, I tried to read what was written, but it was all legal jargon; I couldn't understand any of it. But when I asked my father to explain it all to me, Sonia actually began screaming at me to sign the papers, and not ask so many questions. "Don't you trust your father? Just sign the papers." So I did.

Something was just not right about those papers, the urgent need for my signature, the whole scene in my room, the screaming. It was nagging at me all night. Something was going on that had me worried. The next morning, I called my Uncle Manny, my mother's younger brother. He was a smart and successful businessman and I knew he would be able to explain to me about what I had signed.

Uncle Manny said that he did not like the sound of what I had described and would have to see the paperwork. He suggested that in the meantime, I should go and speak to his personal bank manager about transferring the settlement money into my own bank account, and he would help me to manage it.

After school that day, I took the bus to the bank to meet with this bank manager. My uncle let him know I was coming, and this soft spoken, polite man brought me into his office. After filling out some papers, he said he would have to call my father to get the details from him about where the money was invested. He would help with the transfer, and the money would be invested in what he called GICs: guaranteed investment certificates.

I sat and watched as he called my father at the floor covering store, introduced himself, and explained the reason for the call. He listened silently to whatever brief message my father gave him. His face had dropped. He ended the call. And then he just stared at me. He told me that there was no money to invest. It was all gone. Every last penny. The big store, my father's dream, would be closing. Bankrupt.

I was completely stunned. Frozen. Silent.

The bank manager called my uncle and, after shocking him with the news, he handed me the phone. I had been as composed as possible until I heard my uncle's voice. Then I was instantly reduced to tears. Hysterics actually. My uncle sounded upset. Angry. He reassured me that he would help me do whatever I had to do to get my money back. Even if it meant taking legal action against my father.

This could not be happening.

I called Barry and, in a completely frenzied state, tried my best to explain. He picked me up, took me home, and came in with me while I frantically packed up some of my belongings. I would move in with my Aunt Nicky and Uncle Issie. I couldn't stay in that house another minute.

My father came home as I was putting some of my things into Barry's car. I had stuffed my clothes and shoes into garbage bags. The clothes and shoes that I liked. Not the expensive Sonia stuff. I left all of that in the closet. I took my pillow, my school books and supplies, my diary and scrapbook, my parents wedding album, the box of pictures, mementos, and newspaper clippings, my mother's beaded purse, and the needlepoint picture of a deer with some trees and grass that Carla had been working on. She hadn't quite finished it, and it was still rolled up and held together with the needle.

I looked at Barry's car and realized that everything I owned was in that car.

My father just stood and watched. He didn't try to stop me. He didn't help load the car. He just stood there. I hated him for taking all of my money and investing it in his stupid store. And at the same time, I felt intense pity for how pathetic he was. So desperate to keep her happy. So totally dependent on her. So castrated. It made me sick. She made me sick, and I told her so.

The crying and screaming was suddenly out of control. I told them both that I knew about the Will, and that I thought it was disgusting that Esther, Harry and I were considered to be equal by my father. I told Sonia that I thought she was an evil person who had turned my father against his brother and sisters, his friends, and now his only remaining daughter. I reminded them again about what a good kid I was, that I had never done anything wrong, that I knew other teens my age who were so messed up, and that they would be sorry for ruining my life.

There were so many hurtful things flying between us, but the one thing that remains forever imbedded in my memory was when Sonia told me, in a voice that practically pierced my eardrums, that they did not have a revolving door. Once I left, there was no coming back. She also assured me that the locks would be changed immediately.

BARRY STAYED WITH me at my aunt and uncle's house and tried, along with my aunt and uncle, to calm me down. My little cousins were completely puzzled by what must have appeared to them as an emotional disaster. They had no idea what had happened and they just watched innocently, as we all talked and cried, and I just cried and cried.

My aunt and uncle called my dad and asked if they could come over to talk to him. They were not gone for long, although it felt like hours to me. When they got back, looking drained and defeated, they told me they could not believe some of the things that were said, and that they would not allow me to go back there, even if I wanted to. They said I could live with them for as long as I wanted to. Thank God for family.

CHAPTER 6

Sitting in the plush conference room of my Uncle Manny's offices, I was surrounded by my uncle's lawyer, his accountant, and both of my uncles, my mother's two brothers. We were having a business meeting about what I was going to do to get the settlement money that was supposed to have been in trust for me until I became an adult. According to all of the professionals, it wasn't very much. Nevertheless, everyone agreed that it was my money and I was entitled to it.

How could I be having a legal meeting about my own father? How would I ever be able to get the money back from him? The bank manager had told me that the money was gone. All of it. Finished.

My head was reeling with logical, practical thoughts about the money, but my heart was saying something else. Do I lead with my head, or do I lead with my heart? Everyone was talking about how to take legal action against my father. Could it be that my mother's relatives were leading with their heads?

Apparently my father had invested the money in his floor-covering store, pouring money into a dying business. Good money into bad. He had gone bankrupt. And there went all of the money. Not only mine. His settlement money too. And God knows what other money he had lost.

One thing I knew for sure. Sonia hadn't given him any money. She certainly didn't invest in his business. And the house was in her name. The furniture was hers. My father had absolutely nothing.

As furious as I was with him, I was also overcome with enormous pity for this man who had lost everything he ever had. How could someone have such horrible luck? He had lost his wife and two kids, his home, his identity, his relationship with his brother and sisters, his business, and most of all, he had lost his spirit. His giggle. And now, he had lost me. How could I ever speak to him again? How could he have done this?

We were going to do what we had to do to get my money back. The house was worth a decent amount, and Sonia had a hefty bank account. The decision was made. I was going to sue my father.

And despite Sonia's best efforts, she was not going to ruin my life. It may have been too late for my father, and for that I felt terrible, but I was determined to be happy. And there was nothing she could do to stop me.

WITHIN A FEW days, I was back talking to the therapist who had known our family and always made me feel much better. The one who Sonia hated. She was shocked when I told her what was going on. And hearing about my current situation, she agreed to see me as often as I needed her, for a significantly reduced fee. Another angel on earth.

Those sessions were invaluable. As much as I knew that I could talk to Barry and my relatives about the newest developments in my saga with my dad and his poor excuse for a wife, I needed the objective support and reassurance from this therapist to proceed with this lawsuit. And she certainly provided that. Without any hesitation.

As much as I wanted to blame Sonia for absolutely everything that had gone wrong, I felt that my father had let me down tremendously. Abandoned me. The profound anger, hurt and disappointment about my father permeated through my entire body, replaying in my mind like a broken record. It had taken control. It surfaced at school. While I was working at the restaurant, particularly if I was serving a family. A happy family. At the dinner table with my relatives. My cousins looked bewildered when I fell apart in the middle of a bite of chicken, sobbing. In the shower. Uncontrollable, unexpected, intense emotion.

There was no break from it while I was asleep. The nightmares were getting worse, and they were so vivid. This time when the man with no face delivered the big plywood box, he just dropped it right in front of the house. Where everyone could see it. People were driving by just to look at it. The police had to come and direct the traffic. Keep the cars moving. I tried to drag it inside but it was so heavy. I could only move it a few inches at a time and then I had to take a break. I was wearing my big dirty construction boots, jeans and a t-shirt. Sonia kept telling me to change my clothes. She thought I looked sloppy. I didn't care. I had to move the box. I couldn't leave it outside.

I decided to empty it so it would be lighter and I could move it. When I opened the lid, the strong odour of the smelling salts almost knocked me over. There was a body inside. A huge body. It reached out for me. It had no face but it had long arms. I turned away to run but everyone was standing there, wearing dark sunglasses, blocking my way. No one was talking. They were just watching and waiting. Leaning on each other. The arms continued to reach towards me. I didn't know what to do. No one was telling me what to do. I asked them but no one was answering me.

I woke up shuddering and dripping with sweat. I started to sleep with a night light. Eighteen years old and now I was terrified of the dark.

I WORKED SO hard to pull myself together. I had to finish college with good marks, or I would not get into university. I had the most amazing support from Barry, all of our aunts and uncles, cousins, friends, and my wonderful therapist. I refused to give up like my father had and live a life of sadness and misery. I chose to live a happy life and I was determined to stay true to that goal. Everyone was looking after me. Deep down, I knew I would be okay.

Just be patient. Patience is the secret. Remembering that always made me feel so much better.

CHAPTER 7

B<small>Y THE SPRING</small> of that year, and right before my nineteenth birthday, I found a tiny apartment that I just loved. Since I had no credit, no regular income, and I was a full-time student, my Uncle Manny had to sign my lease for me. He did so without hesitation.

It was only one room, with a closet and a bathroom. No separate bedroom, no separate kitchen. But I loved it. Between all of my relatives, I had no trouble furnishing my new home with whatever I could find lying around their basements. A twin bed, an old dresser, a small table and chairs, and a weathered but totally comfy small couch. Dishes, cutlery, pots and pans, towels and bed linen. Whatever else I needed I found while trolling through the Goodwill store. I had a mixture of items from so many places, that absolutely nothing matched. But knowing that I was surrounded predominantly by things from all of the different people who cared about me, filled me with a strong sense of love and support. The vast mixture of items was proof of that.

As soon as I was settled in, I got myself an adorable little kitten, and named him Tiko. From the moment I brought Tiko home to our apartment, we were madly in love with each other.

I was proud of my apartment, and obsessed with keeping it clean, neat and organized. I needed order in my life. Predictability. Everything had to stay in exactly the same spot. Things couldn't change or be moved. And I definitely could not throw anything away. I had already parted with so many things, that I now needed to collect items. What may have been junk to others was precious to me. As long as I could fill my closet, my cupboards, my life.

I planned everything. I had a routine, agendas and lists. I felt like I had some control.

B<small>ARRY AND</small> M<small>ITCHELL</small> moved into a similar apartment to mine, only a few blocks away from where I was living. Two people living in that tiny room seemed impossible, but that was what they could afford. Barry wasn't planning on spending too much time in the apartment, so he wasn't concerned about the lack of space. He thought the location was good, especially for Mitchell to access public transportation, and he was relieved to be moving out of his aunt and uncle's house. They had been generous to him and Mitchell, but the brothers had been there long enough. It was time.

Barry bought two twin hide-a-bed couches. That way they could double as couches during the day, and beds at night. That sort of sleeping arrangement had been good enough for their father, it would be fine for them. Unfortunately, the mattresses that came with these hide-a-beds were thin, and only when they actually slept on them did they realize that the springs were poking through. For the time being, they were sufficient.

Mitchell was involved with a community vocational centre that helped people with disabilities find meaningful employment. He was working at a sheltered workshop, on an assembly line where he was receiving ongoing support and coaching from an experienced job coach. Finally, someone had taken an interest in him and was able to help him develop some work skills, as well as ways to deal appropriately with his frustration and anger.

Barry and I were both accepted to McGill University. We knew that we would have to work part-time while going to school, but we wanted to save as much money as we could. We worked our butts off that summer. My feet were so sore after those twelve hour shifts, I could hardly move. But sitting on the floor of my apartment rolling the coins I had earned as tips made it all worthwhile.

Barry was working at two different jobs. He certainly didn't spend much time at his apartment. In fact, he barely slept at all. He worked the graveyard shift at General Motors, which was amazing. Well, "amazing" is a relative word. He was earning almost three times the minimum wage, working on the assembly line. As a welder, he had burn marks on his chest from the sparks that ricocheted off the cars and hit him. But he could overlook the terrible hours, and the burns, when he cashed that hefty pay cheque every week.

His day job was pumping gas at a downtown gas station. People who filled up their cars downtown were happy to generously tip the attendant. Especially if he also cleaned their windows and checked their oil. Barry had plenty of his own coins to roll.

Once we were back in school, Barry seemed to cope easily with the stress of his brother, a full course load, and part-time jobs. He admitted that immersing himself in an extremely busy schedule worked well for him. There was less time to think about his problems, which he always claimed were nothing compared to those of his brother. He missed his dad, but found comfort in knowing that his dad no longer had to live an unhappy life, spending so much time worrying about Mitchell.

I WAS TOTALLY in my element at McGill. I found the subjects and formal training interesting and meaningful. And the best part was the size of the campus. It was huge. I loved getting lost in the crowds, rushing to class, grabbing a slice of pizza, lining up at the library, meeting people. It was all so exhilarating.

The social work program was a combination of classes and on-the-job training in a field placement. My first training location was The Douglas Psychiatric Hospital where I was assigned to a social worker, my supervisor, and given a small caseload to manage. Despite the amount of work that was dumped on me, and there was a lot, I always found time once every week, without fail, to go and see my "cousin" Howard in the locked unit that was specifically for people with Schizophrenia. I talked nonstop to Howard about all of the fun times our families had shared. I guess I was hoping that something would trigger a reaction. A memory. A smile. Anything that might bring him back. But Howard just stared at me. Vacant staring. Empty. Alive and dead, both at the same time.

I found it difficult to understand or relate to the whole psychiatric environment. Why did these patients with Schizophrenia plummet to such depths of despair and immobility? There had to be a way for them to pull themselves together. Fix their problems.

That school field placement definitely confirmed that I did not want to be a psychiatric social worker. No way.

Howard's life made me think about and evaluate the meaning of life, death, tragedy, luck, destiny. Was it better to be alive in his state, or would it have been better for him to have died? What's worse, a tragic death or a tragic life? Sixteen seconds or sixteen years?

Would I want to be visiting my mother and sisters in a locked unit of a psychiatric hospital? Was Howard actually alive, just because his heart was beating?

Was my father any better off? He couldn't seem to find a way to recover from our tragedy. To appreciate that he still had me. To realize that I still needed him. He seemed to have succumbed to a permanent robotic state. Denial about the accident. Perhaps he had even managed to erase the fifteen years of his life with my mother, as if they had never existed. A little denial. A dash of erasing. Turn in your personality, spirit and ability to laugh. Blend it all together for a life and future of profound sadness and misery.

It gave me a lot to think about. I may not have come up with a lot of answers, but it sure made for some interesting conversations for me and Barry. We loved having these philosophical discussions. We would talk for hours and hours about this sort of stuff, about our values and feelings, and of course, about our dreams. Our plans for the future. Our future together.

CHAPTER 8

THE STORE WAS closed, gone, finished, and my father was working as a salesman at a chain carpet store. For the first time in his entire life, he was an employee, punching a clock and accountable to a supervisor.

It was blatantly clear that he did not have any money at all to pay me back for investing and subsequently losing my settlement money. There was no point pursuing the lawsuit. As my uncles continued to say, "You can't milk a rock." Besides, this whole suing-my-father thing did not feel right to me. He didn't lose the money on purpose. He was obviously hoping that the self-serving investment would have ended up differently than it did. And most importantly, I felt such pity for him to be that insecure in his relationship with his wife, that he had to resort to drastic measures to keep her happy. To keep his marriage going. To prevent yet one more loss in his life. That would have done him in for sure. Instead, he lost his business, his livelihood, his confidence, his pride. No longer a king wearing a crown covered in big red stones, he was now a beaten, defenseless and terribly sad man.

Pity. Anger. Pity. Anger. I went back and forth.

I WAS NOT able to go very long without talking to him. I wanted to be sure he was okay. I missed him. And I needed him way more than I had ever admitted. When we talked on the phone, our conversations were full of tension, anger and resentment, inevitably ended abruptly, or else in a fight. I could always tell that Sonia was in the background, coaching him, telling him what to say. Or just standing there, saying nothing. Passive-aggressive listening. He spoke to me with Sonia as his audience. With each of us vying for his attention, he was not able to be the daddy I knew, because that would have caused problems for him with her. So he was cool. Aloof. Matter of fact.

I always told him that I knew she was standing there and I did not want to continue this upsetting conversation, this performance he was putting on for Sonia. It was full of negative undertones. We could meet somewhere. A coffee shop. Any place. Without her around.

My theory was definitely accurate, because whenever I saw him in person, things were relatively fine. He would never be the same as he was before the accident. That man was buried with my mother and sisters. Even though he was in some other zone, at least he was much warmer; loving and caring in his own way. Alone, he had no need to put on a show. Not the way things were in our rowboat, that's for sure, but more comfortable than we ever were on the phone. I took what I could get.

One day when Sonia was out of town, my father let me come over to get a few of my mother's crystal bowls. Apparently a couple of the bowls I had taken had actually belonged to Sonia. Obviously, that was a mistake. Totally unintentional. I definitely did not want her bowls, or anything of hers for that matter. Before I even had a chance to get them back to my father, she sent me a lawyer's letter demanding their immediate return. A lawyer's letter. By registered mail. And just to make matters even worse, my father called me, with her in the background of course, and told me that if I didn't return her bowls, he would burn all of the reels of our family movies that he had apparently kept. I had no idea that he even had them, and he obviously knew that the threat to burn them would be far more powerful than threatening me with anything else.

Perfect. I told him that when he brings me the reels of family movies, I will give him the bowls. The exchange took place within the hour. All of that disgusting, hurtful drama over her Jed Clampett bowls that I had no interest whatsoever in keeping.

I WAS DETERMINED to live the life my mother would have wanted me to live, and I so badly wanted to be similar to her. The best compliment anyone could ever have given me, was to tell me that I was just like my mother. By doing some of the things that she had done, and repeating her behaviour, I was able to feel more connected to her.

After talking to Donna, Barbara and Shelley, and confirming their definite interest, I approached a group of other school friends about starting our own chapter of the M.A.M.R., the Montreal Association for the Mentally Retarded.

I hosted the first meeting and was ecstatic over a turn-out of over twenty young women packed into that tiny apartment. There were two women there, named Lana and Ruth, who introduced themselves and explained that they were there because Lana had recently given birth to a little girl with what we would now refer to as Down Syndrome and, when she heard about this new chapter, she was eager to join.

I had coffee, tea and a variety of sweets all set up, which people munched and sipped throughout the evening. The plans and discussions went so well, no one left until well past eleven o'clock. Ruth and Lana, the only ones already married with children, joked about how their usual bedtime was nine-thirty.

We decided on several fundraising activities and set up the next meeting at someone else's house.

Dear Diary,
Actually, this one is for you Mom. I just finished tidying up from the MAMR meeting that I hosted and I am so excited. Everyone seems really pumped about belonging to this group and organizing some great events. Lana and Ruth are older than the rest of us, but they are really nice and funny. I think it will be so good for Lana to do this, since she has a very good reason to help this cause.

I know that you were at this meeting tonight and I hope you are very proud of me. I love you so much.
Love,
Lynda

CHAPTER 9

M ITCHELL WAS DOING well in his job, and had also found himself a girl-friend. Elaine worked with Mitchell at the sheltered workshop, was a year younger than him, and apparently they were madly in love. He talked about Elaine as if she were the greatest person alive. He described her as beautiful, popular and smart. He showed us pictures of the two of them crammed together into those little photo booths at the shopping centre. They constantly called each other on the phone, and went to McDonalds for lunch on Saturdays. Mitchell was so excited to have a girlfriend, and he told us over and over again that he couldn't wait for us to meet her.

Meeting Elaine and her family was one of those experiences that you just never forget. Nor will I ever forget Barry's face when we walked into Elaine's family's apartment.

The building was in a poor neighbourhood, and their apartment was up three flights of stairs. The filthy dark stairway was littered with beer and pop cans, broken glass, apple cores, wads of gum, and all kinds of garbage. There was a stench of fried food and cigarettes, and racket of talking stifled by loud music.

The garbage and noise continued through the hallway that led to their apartment. A bent nail held "3C" on the door, and the button for the buzzer was dangling by its wires.

We were greeted at the door by Mitchell and Elaine, and were quickly introduced to the most unusual group of people either of us had ever seen. Everyone there was obviously delayed: Elaine, her parents, her sister, her brother, her sister-in-law and a six-month-old little boy.

The apartment was packed with a mixture of furniture, none of which was placed logically in the room. We had to step over a random foot stool to get to the tattered beige couch that was covered in holes with the stuffing coming out.

There were wrappers from several fast food restaurants, empty cups with lids and straws, and an old sheet hanging over part of the window, held up by nails hammered into the wall.

It was an excessively hot day, and they had a window air conditioner blasting cold air into the room, yet all of the windows were wide open. Barry diplomatically explained that the air conditioner would probably work more effectively if they closed the windows. Elaine's father admitted that he never knew that and eagerly jumped up to close the windows.

We chatted with them about the weather, their obvious love of fast food restaurants, and the baby. The way in which they related to one another, their views and opinions about anything we discussed, the state of their home...the whole scene was just surreal. Bizarre. I watched Elaine's sister-in-law pour Coke into a sippy cup and feed it to the baby. They all laughed at the expression on his face when he tasted it. It was all so strange and inappropriate. Here I was, this idealistic social work student ready to rescue the world, watching my boyfriend's brother interact with a totally dysfunctional family. Barry and I couldn't get out of there fast enough.

Having connections in the world of social services came in handy. It didn't take long for me to get the scoop on Elaine and her wacky family. I learned that they were famous in the local social service world. Actually known to every social service agency in Montreal. There had been multiple social workers closely monitoring and intervening with this family for years and years, and one worker was currently working the system to remove the little boy and get him into child protection. The advice I was given was to get Mitchell as far away from that family as possible.

That was just great news. Mitchell finally found a girlfriend and was so proud of this "normal" accomplishment, and we were about to burst his bubble.

As predicted, Mitchell was furious with us. From his perspective, Elaine was perfect, so was her family, and he was not about to end this love affair. In fact, he told us he was going to marry Elaine.

We told him how we felt, and a bit about what we knew about the family, and then we backed off. We certainly could not forbid Mitchell from seeing her. We had no control over him. In fact, he was so angry at us for what we did say to him, that Barry was worried about staying at the apartment with him. He had been pretty good about controlling his temper, for quite some time, but we had no idea how he would deal with these latest developments. We packed up all of Barry's personal belongings, left everything else in the apartment for Mitchell, and Barry moved in with me. Twin bed, tiny couch, table for two, crowded closet, not an inch of space to move. So cozy and so full. My cup runneth over.

Opinions and advice were flying. In the seventies, nineteen-year-olds did not live together. It was just unheard of. We didn't care. We couldn't.

It was a practical and emotional decision. A combination of leading with both our heads and our hearts.

My grandparents were totally supportive, and their opinion meant a lot to us. They knew that we were planning to get married as soon as we graduated university. They knew that we were organized, disciplined, methodical. We had plans, we made lists. We were in control.

Amazingly, they had no problem with us living together. Obviously modern thinkers for that generation, they encouraged us to do what we had to do to move forward with our lives. They did have a tendency to repeat themselves, probably to be sure we were hearing them. *Don't worry about what others think. You know what is right and what is wrong. Work hard in school. Become successful. Make a difference in the world.*

It didn't take long for Mitchell and Elaine's love affair to end. They were both strikingly similar and drove each other crazy. Mitchell obsessed about it for a while, but he managed to move on. He was feeling much better about his work performance, and he knew that if he continued to progress well in the sheltered workshop, he would be placed in a real job. He liked having that goal.

Mitchell was living on his own in the apartment and managing, relatively speaking. Living a primitive sort of lifestyle. We came over as often as we could to help him clean his apartment, and show him how to do things on his own. He would make himself sandwiches, TV dinners, and other easy-to-prepare foods.

Despite the numerous attempts to coach him with the laundry machines in the basement of his building, his clothes and towels still always smelled stale and felt damp. His table had a huge burn mark in the centre, most of his dishes and glasses were chipped or cracked, and the knobs dangled from the drawers. We replaced things. He broke them. We coached. He got frustrated. We gave advice. He got angry.

When we weren't in that tiny apartment of ours, Barry and I had full agendas and long to do lists. Between school, field placements, studying, writing papers, helping Mitchell, working part-time, organizing and working on MAMR fundraising events, visiting relatives, connecting with friends, shopping for food, doing laundry, cleaning the apartment, and occasionally sleeping, there wasn't much time left for anything.

My father and I saw each other once in a while. They had sold the house and were renting an upper duplex, which I had heard through the grapevine was beautiful. I had never been invited over. Guess that house didn't have a revolving door either. Occasionally my dad would agree to come over and have dinner with me and Barry at our little apartment. But most of the time, he told me that he couldn't leave Sonia alone and, if I invited her too, they would both come. No thanks.

He was absolutely adamant that he was the one who was reluctant to leave his wife at home, alone, so that he could spend time with me. He claimed that Sonia was encouraging him to go. She wasn't stopping him at all.

"Go visit your daughter. Go spend time with your kid who respects you and me so much. Don't worry about leaving me at home alone. I'll find something to do, alone. Go. Enjoy yourself."

That would have been the Sonia way of encouraging him. There's no way my father had the backbone to have left her without feeling totally worried and guilty. My father tried to convince me that Sonia was keen on working things out with me, confident that we could learn to get along, maybe even become friends. If only I would get to know her better, I would see that she was a terrific person. My response to him was always the same. Actions speak louder than words.

Her daughter Esther and Esther's husband Jacob had relocated and were living in Ottawa. My father often went with Sonia to spend time with "their kids'" in Ottawa. But many times, Sonia went alone. She had no problem leaving him at home, alone. No problem at all.

My grandmother added a new saychology theory to explain the situation between me and my father. She told me, in Yiddish of course which made it sound even better, that a woman leads with her heart, and that a man leads with his penis. Since Barry didn't understand Yiddish, she kindly translated by telling him that it meant that my father was thinking with the wrong head. Now there was an interesting addition to the debate about how to make decisions. Head, heart, penis.

CHAPTER 10

Sharon and I had met when we were both sixteen, and instantly became friends. She was unlike any other person I knew. She came from a wealthy family, but their financial situation had not affected her at all.

She was a beautiful girl: popular, smart, and fun. She had a perpetual smile on her face. Most of all, she was honest and down to earth. She didn't live in my neighbourhood, and I had to take two buses to get to her house, but the distance didn't bother me. Sharon introduced me to all of her friends, who welcomed me into their world without any conditions or hesitation. I loved hanging out with her, with or without her friends. We spent hours together in her huge bedroom, flipping through teen magazines and calling people on her pink Princess phone. With our heads close together, we held the receiver so we could both talk and listen at the same time. I couldn't help but laugh nonstop when I was with that happy-go-lucky, funny Sharon.

There was never a problem setting an extra plate at the dinner table for me. Sharon had three younger sisters, and sitting at that table with everyone brought back fond memories of pre-crash life in my house. The chatting, laughing, passing of serving bowls, clearing the table, cleaning up, washing, drying. It was comfortable, relaxing and fun. And when I told Sharon's mother how well I could scrub the sink, she was happy to hand me the Ajax.

On the beautiful summer day of her nineteenth birthday, Sharon was killed in a terrible car accident. Her death hit me like a ton of bricks. Getting that early morning phone call wrenched me right back to that awful morning almost six years earlier. Like a powerful suction. I was so distraught I could hardly move. Getting out of bed in the morning, I felt heavy and achy, like my limbs were made of brick, and stuck together with thick mortar. The days passed in a lethargic blur, a constant throbbing in my head and twinge in my stomach. I didn't care about my social work patients on my placements and simply went through the motions, saying the things I was supposed to say. They needed me but I couldn't deal with them. I just couldn't give anymore. Sharon had been young and vibrant. Her house was busy and noisy. Her family was so normal. And happy.

And she was gone. Slaughtered in a brutal, gory accident. How could this have happened?

No matter how much time had passed since the plane crash, and how hard I tried to convince myself that I was getting on with my life, coping well, in control, this death of a friend kicked me hard, right in the face.

That funeral was treacherous. Like walking through a field of land mines. I grieved for Sharon, her parents, her sisters, her grandparents, my grandparents, my dad, her relatives, my relatives. I stared at that coffin and wondered if Sharon was still smiling in that darkness. I couldn't even picture her without a smile on her face. There was just nothing dark about her.

I leaned heavily on Barry and watched as they lowered that solid oak box into the ground. Gasping and crying, I felt like I could hardly breathe.

I STRUGGLED TO understand why I was having such a terrible time dealing with Sharon's death. Deep down, I recognized that most of this profound grief was really related to my mother and sisters, grief that I didn't allow myself to feel when they died. A delayed reaction. As if the anaesthetic had worn off and exposed cuts that I had temporarily and superficially covered, because they were just too deep and too painful to deal with at that time. My father had shut down. I had escaped into daydreams. But now...

Now, six years later, the scabs were ripped off and the wounds were bleeding again. Fresh, new blood spurting out all over the place.

Poor Barry. He had no idea what to do with me. He would find me out on the balcony, sobbing. Screaming into the sky. Shaking like a drug addict.

"I can't help myself. You just don't understand. I don't know how to stop myself from crying."

"You have me. And I'm not going anywhere. We have each other."

"That's not helping me. I'm sorry. I'm so sorry...."

These uncontrollable crying spells lasted for weeks. It wasn't passing. Here I had been this relatively together girl, moving forward with her life, and this death of a friend set me back in ways that Barry didn't feel equipped to handle. To solve. That was tough for him. He focused on solutions. Answers. He never let himself surrender to a state of weakness. His attitude about dealing with difficulties was simply to adapt and move forward. When things weren't working properly, they had to be repaired. Don't dwell on the problem, resolve it. If your rainbow is shattered, repair it.

At school or work, I found some relief in the routine: in not feeling, just doing. But when I had time to think, my tortured psyche took over. The nightmares started again, I was falling apart, bursting into tears at the most unexpected times, and reacting to everyone and everything with uncontrollable emotions. One night, after finding me shivering on a plastic lawn chair on the balcony at 3:00 a.m., Barry gently covered me with a soft blanket and, just as gently, suggested I go back to the therapist. A solution.

Now she had plenty of material to work with. All those documented stages of grief, combined with some post traumatic stress disorder, just like they described it in the textbooks. It's not often that a therapist gets to work with a young patient who is determined, open, and insightful. A professional's dream come true.

I SAT FROZEN on the couch with tears running down my cheeks. I had just finished telling the therapist about Sharon.

"You're strong. You've done so well."

I felt anything but strong. I let out a deep breath.

"I know. I have…in the past. But now…Now, I am so upset about Sharon's accident that I can hardly function."

"You've had a huge shock."

"It's been weeks."

"It takes time."

"My friends don't understand why I am still such a wreck. Barry doesn't understand."

"I think he does."

"Well, he just deals with it differently. He wants to fix me."

"Because he loves you."

She was right.

"I know. And I'm driving him crazy with my crying and mood swings."

"Look, you have a boyfriend who is responsible and caring. He really has his act together. You have wonderful grandparents and extended family. And good friends. Let them support you."

But it had always been enough to do it myself: to keep busy, to daydream. The grief passed. And now I couldn't stop crying.

"Ugh, why has this affected me like this? I'm not myself at all."

"But you are yourself. This is how you feel."

"I feel like I've gone back in time six years.

"It's okay to regress. To backtrack. You had a lot to deal with at such a young age, a major trauma, and you are still working it through in your own way."

"But it was *six years* ago."

"And you were very young. You were living in a household stricken by multiple tragic deaths. You buried a lot of the grief that you felt, and it's surfacing now."

I felt tears welling up again. When would it stop? When would this ever stop?

"You've kept yourself so busy that you actually postponed some of the grieving, which is fine. It worked for you. But it's coming out now."

"What do I do? I'm just so frustrated. I can't go to work without crying. I can't study without crying. I can't sleep but I want to sleep. My friends and family don't get it. I don't get it. I'm exhausted. I don't know how to get though each day without crying."

My voice cracked and my head pounded. The room blurred.

"Somehow, you learned how to live with your terrible losses six years ago. You will learn again."

"I just want to feel normal. To not always feel like this awful misery can just seep into my life at any time."

I was sobbing uncontrollably now. Tears and drool and all the messy ugliness of not being in control. Of being completely devastated.

She handed me the box of tissue and waited until I calmed down. Until a rhythmic breathing had settled into my chest.

"I'm sorry. I'm not like this...."

"Let me explain something to you. You will never fully recover from losing your mother and sisters, and essentially losing your dad as well. But throughout your life you will do your best to heal. The scars will never go away. This death of your friend has disturbed your scars and you hurt again, no different than if you had picked a scab off your arm. Now you have to let the scab form again. And you will."

"I will?"

"Of course you will. It can be a painful and exhausting process. As time goes on, the pain lessens. You will find your spark again. Your hope and enjoyment."

"I can't see how. I'm just so drained. So tired."

I leaned back in the couch, defeated.

"There's no right or wrong amount of time to mourn. It's a long process and for the rest of your life it's normal to have good days and bad days. As long as you have more good ones than bad ones."

Two weeks later and therapy was slow going. But I had to admit, those therapy sessions were brief moments of honesty and wellbeing in what had become my rather unhealthy existence of profound sadness.

"I really appreciate coming here."

She smiled.

"Sometimes I feel like I'm on a roller coaster."

I looked at my hands in my lap. They were dry and rough. Old-looking. No wonder. I wasn't eating or drinking properly. Or sleeping. I especially wasn't doing anything for myself like applying hand cream.

"I'm always so agitated, crying all the time. I feel weak. I feel this terrible sadness. An emptiness. All I want to do is cry."

Today I had tried to dress nicer for my appointment. Lately all I had worn were ratty jeans and Barry's old shirts. My hair was in a ponytail and the bags under my eyes were dark. But today, I had at least attempted to conceal them with some makeup. I even put on a little lip gloss. I had read somewhere that if you did little things to make yourself feel normal, you will actually start to feel normal. I didn't know if it made sense and couldn't tell if it was working.

"There are times when I feel like it didn't really happen. Like I'm sleepwalking."

"Denial can be a powerful emotional anaesthetic."

"I keep thinking about what might have happened to her body during the accident. She was so beautiful and I have these horrible images of her being hurt. It's making me sick."

I had thrown up at least a few times in the past several weeks. Out of nowhere: just ran to the bathroom and heaved my guts out. It was like the pain had to get out and was doing so any way it could.

"I remember hearing the adults talking about my mother and sisters bodies being pulverized. I was too young at the time to know what that meant. Now I know and those gruesome thoughts scare the hell out of me."

"How is Barry handling all of this?"

Ah, my Barry. My lifeline.

"He is amazing. Strong. He listens to me babble on about how miserable I am, and he just hugs me. I know I'm lucky to have him."

I hadn't completely lost it.

"Have you tried talking to your dad about any of this?"

The question should have been, have I talked to my dad about anything of importance in the last six years?

"No."

Silence.

"My father shut me out of his life when he married Sonia."

"What do you mean?"

"It's like he threw his life before the crash into the garbage, and now he has a new life with a new wife and a new family."

"How do you feel about that?"

"Well, I know my dad and he isn't happy. He is so different than he was before the accident. Now he's always sad."

"But how do *you* feel?"

"I don't want to be like him. He is stuck in this terrible place of grief."

I paused.

"Kind of ironic, huh? Like father, like daughter."

"No, I don't think you're like him. Deep down. You've already proven that."

"It would just be nice if he could act like a father. To help me get through this."

"You can't make your father behave like a father."

"I know. Trust me, I know. I'm just saying…"

She shook her head.

"It's impossible to change your father. He in stuck in chronic mourning. He lost so much that he just can't find a way out of that constant state of misery. But you can. You're not your father."

"I sure feel like him right now. Seriously, this must be what he feels like all the time. It's awful."

"That's an important insight. So, what can you do to move forward?"

"I don't know, I just don't know. It's like I'm stuck. I'm afraid to move. I'm afraid it's just going to get worse again. Like I'm going to start feeling better and then something else will make it all bad again. Like what's the use...."

"The use is, you either move forward or you become your father."

She was right.

"You have a supportive and wonderful boyfriend who cares deeply about you. Let him help you."

Barry had gone out and bought me a book on controlling stress and tension. He wrapped it up so carefully with gorgeous paper and a huge bow.

"He's very tuned into you. Very sensitive."

"He is. He got me a card with a love poem, and then he wrote the most amazing message about how much he loves me."

I smiled, remembering. It was the first time I smiled in as long as I could remember. I touched my hand to my lips as if to check if it was real.

"See? Embrace that and try to see what you have through all the sorrow. Respond to it. Next time you're out on that balcony, wailing at the world and he offers to take you for a walk, make a decision, and go."

"Okay, I'll try."

When I left, I was starting to actually feel better. A little unstuck from that dark place of grief.

Choices. We always have choices.

CHAPTER 11

B Y THE TIME we were twenty-one, we were living together in a comfortable one- bedroom apartment, engaged to be married and busy planning our wedding which was to be held a month after graduating from McGill. What I wanted more than anything was to have a beautiful traditional wedding, a happy celebration with dancing and good food. Just like I had imagined. A Maid of Honour. A Best Man. Several Groomsmen. No Bridesmaids. No Flower Girl. Since my sisters were not alive, I could not imagine anyone else filling those wedding roles.

And no sadness. No tears. No crying. This was going to be a party, not another funeral.

Many of our friends were planning their weddings at the same time as we were, and every one of them had their mothers' complete involvement in every bit of it. I was achingly jealous. I had no mother and no future mother-in-law.

I was determined that our wedding was going to be equally wonderful, even though neither of us had a mother to help us decide, plan and organize, and our budget was considerably lower. We booked the local synagogue, and when the Rabbi heard that Barry and I were planning and paying for our own wedding, he significantly reduced the rental rates. The caterer had never worked with a twenty-one year old couple on their own, so he threw in the appetizers and wedding cake. We signed a contract with the band for half of their usual fee. While the photographer gave us a huge discount, I let him know how important it was for us to have a beautiful wedding album with pictures of every person there. I sat in shock as the florist committed to providing centrepieces that were far more lush, bright and beautiful than we would be paying for.

Auntie Nicky took me to a wholesale place to buy my wedding dress. I chose a white traditional dress with a long train, just like the one my mother had worn. Barry and I made sure that Mitchell knew how important it was that he was our Best Man, and Barry brought him to rent tuxedos for the two of them. I asked my dear friend Donna to be our Maid of Honour, and she immediately went out and bought a lovely rose-coloured dress. And to be sure that we could do a traditional first dance as Mr. and Mrs. Barry Fishman, without tripping on each other's feet, we took four dance lessons.

In the midst of final exams and papers, working part-time, shopping, cleaning, laundry, and all the rest, Barry and I worked hard to plan our wedding. We did our best to control all of the things we could control, since we knew that we had little control over the emotions of our relatives on the day of the wedding. I was so worried about how I would react if anything went wrong, or if people were visibly upset. So everyone on all sides, was instructed, begged, warned, to remember that this was a wedding. A celebration. A party. There was to be no crying. We told everyone how important that was to me and Barry.

I kept my father well informed about the wedding plans. I was sensitive to the fact that he didn't have any of his own money to contribute towards the wedding, but I didn't want him to feel excluded. And the one thing I made sure to tell him, was that Barry and I had met because of him. Because of his store. In the end, investing my settlement money in his store was the best thing he could have done for me.

Hearing that from me had to have meant a lot to him. It was hard to know for sure, because he didn't react or comment. As usual, and ever since the plane crash, talking to my father was like talking to an empty shell. Hollow and vacant. But I needed him to know that, indirectly, he had given me the best gift in the world. He brought me and Barry together, and he could and should feel good knowing that his daughter would be taken care of by this quiet, driven and wonderful person.

WHILE I WAS planning, Barry was busy interviewing for jobs. Full-time jobs. His career. Businesses and organizations came to the McGill School of Business to recruit graduating students. They did on-the-spot interviews and made offers to the students they were eager to hire. It was a stressful and exciting process.

We talked about the various career opportunities in other places, away from Montreal. Maybe even as far away as California. Since Barry was born in Florida, moving to the United States was an option. Uncle Len offered to take Barry into his business with him, but we had already seen what had happened to my father and his brother, and knew of other family members who were in business together and ended up destroying their relationships. We were not prepared to do anything at all that would potentially jeopardise our relationship with Uncle Len.

We both agreed that we had to get away from Montreal. There wasn't much keeping us there. In fact, there were many reasons to leave. I had a hard time driving by the street where I grew up. I missed my house and all of the items inside of it. I was sorry that my father hadn't thought to save some of the things that he and my mother had bought. They must have chosen many things together. They obviously liked, or maybe even loved what they had bought. Furniture. Vases. Pictures. Our piano. That big kitchen table. I would have treasured every single item.

There were so many places, landmarks, that had significance and held years of memories for me. It was like being surrounded by constant reminders of what I had lost.

I wasn't part of my father's life. He had a new life with Sonia, Sonia's kids, Sonia's grandchildren, Sonia's imported furniture, the clothes that Sonia bought for him, his toupee, and my mother's Rosenthal dishes.

And then there was Mitchell. It seemed as if staying or leaving would not make much difference when it came to Mitchell. He wasn't happy when we were around and involved in his life. And he wasn't happy when we kept our distance, giving him space and independence. We felt as if it was a no win situation.

We needed a fresh new life, together, just the two of us. My only big concern was how I could leave my grandparents. I loved spending time with them, and I knew that they cherished our time together. We struggled with how we could move away without further destroying them.

After many, and I mean *many* discussions with them, lots of tears and hugs, my grandparents encouraged us to follow our dreams, and to do so with their blessings. In fact, they insisted that we try living some place away from Montreal. They said it would be a great experience for us, and something we could only do now, before having kids, before we were too established to pick up and relocate. As difficult as they knew it would be for them, they thought about us. About our happiness, career opportunities, life in a different city. A brand new start. So supportive. So selfless. Through their own struggles and intense pain, when life as we all knew it was extinguished in an instant and all of our lives had essentially fallen apart, they still managed to find ways of helping me to pick up the pieces.

We promised them that if we did move away, we would come back to Montreal every year. And they promised to visit us annually, wherever we were.

We looked further into some of the opportunities in California, specifically with *Deloitte Haskins and Sells*, one of the largest and most prestigious accounting firms in Costa Mesa, California. Their hiring standards were incredibly high. They flew us to Orange County, paid for us to stay at the Disneyland Hotel in Anaheim, wined and dined us in restaurants we would never have otherwise walked into, and offered Barry a job. He was thrilled. We discussed and discussed and decided we would do it. We would move to California. Barry was ecstatic to be starting his professional career with a team of talented, motivated and driven individuals from top business schools across the U.S. They were even prepared to move us there, cover all of the moving costs, help us find a place to live, and pay Barry a whopping twelve thousand dollars a year. How could we pass up such an opportunity?

CHAPTER 12

WE COULDN'T UNDERSTAND how Mitchell managed to crease the tuxedo so badly before the wedding even started. We had arranged for Barry's cousin to bring him to the synagogue early, so that he would be there for pictures. When he walked in, sheepishly, and kissed me on the cheek, he reeked of vomit. He mumbled something about being proud of his little brother, but pissed off that Barry was getting married before him. He was the older brother, he should have been first.

We spent the afternoon with everyone from the wedding party, with the exception of my dad who was late, posing for pictures and watching as the organized catering staff scurried around setting the tables. As soon as the vibrant flower arrangements were placed on the tables, the room came alive.

In the chapel, where the wedding ceremony would take place, the florist was draping greenery around the altar, known as the Chupah. This canopy represented the bride and groom's home together. The couple and their immediate family stood under the Chupah, while the Rabbi recited the blessings of the marriage ceremony.

I was proud of my grandparents for keeping themselves so together during a day that I knew was tremendously bittersweet for them.

My father finally arrived at the end of our scheduled time for pre-wedding pictures. In fact, he got there with his wife just in time for the ceremony. Just like all of the invited guests. This was his daughter's wedding day. His only daughter. I had asked him to be there by three o'clock. If only he could have put Sonia on the back burner, just for this one day. To be there for me. I ran over to him, grabbed him by the arm, and pulled him to where the photographer could snap a few pictures of us.

And then I calmed down. Nothing was going to ruin this day.

Julie was one of the first guests to arrive—and she came to take a peek at me before scurrying to her seat. She had gotten married. Her daughter was tall for a six year old, and she looked as proud as could be wearing Wendy's pink flower-girl dress. I couldn't have thought of anyone more appropriate to wear that dress than Deedee's little daughter.

ONCE EVERYONE WAS seated in the chapel, the whole wedding party proceeded to the area just outside the double doors that led to the aisle.

As soon as we were ready to start, I heard the soft background music that we had selected. It was my mother's favourite song, *Sunrise Sunset*.

Is this the little girl I carried?
Is this the little boy at play?
I don't remember growing older
When did they?
When did she get to be a beauty?
When did he get to be so tall?
Wasn't it yesterday
When they were small?
Sunrise, sunset
Sunrise, sunset
Swiftly flow the days
Seedlings turn overnight to sun-
flowers
Blossoming even as we gaze
Sunrise, sunset
Sunrise, sunset
Swiftly fly the years
One season following another
Laden with happiness and tears

Mitchell paced and mumbled while waiting for his turn to march. Everyone was so sweet to him all afternoon, and throughout the pictures he was calm and cooperative. A smile can go a long way, especially for Mitchell, and I realized that everyone was smiling warmly at him as he approached the doors to walk down the aisle.

My beautiful maid of honour, Donna, was next. She walked to the Chupah and then stood facing the seated guests.

Then Barry's tiny grandmother looped her arm in his, and together they were next.

My grandmother wore a long turquoise dress trimmed with tiny sequins. Her hair was done in a lovely updo, and one of my aunts put her eye makeup on so well it looked professional. My grandfather looked handsome and proud in his black tuxedo. Guests sniffled and softly cried during their turn.

My dad went next, by himself.

And quite magically, as soon as the doors opened for me to walk, I heard nothing. I felt as if I were floating down the aisle with absolutely no one else there except for Barry. I glided towards him as he faced me from the alter, with his genuine smile and that posture of strength and confidence.

My dad was waiting, as instructed, halfway down the aisle for me. I put my arm through his, and together we walked to Barry.

The room was completely silent. I heard afterwards that there wasn't a dry eye to be found, but I was spared the drama that apparently took place in every seat.

The Rabbi delivered a speech about how he had met us and spent time with us. It became clear to him that we were all about moving forward, finding the good, focusing on what we had in each other. He said he was truly inspired by us: a young couple who had been through so much and, together, had persevered in a positive way.

The wedding was truly everything I dreamed of, and so much more. Traditional. Fun. Beautiful. Surrounded by friends and family who had always been supportive and loving to both of us. Other than the obvious regret that so many significant people were not there, it felt perfect. And, even though they may not have physically been there, I knew, beyond a doubt, that they were present. As the Rabbi had said, "This is truly a match made in heaven." I felt their presence every second of that day and evening. They wouldn't have missed our wedding. They didn't miss it.

WE DID IT. We planned, organized and paid for the wedding ourselves. It wasn't the discounted cost of everything that made it fantastic, that just made it affordable. The band outdid themselves. Other than the short amount of time it took for people to eat their meal, the dance floor was never empty. The band made sure that everyone was up and dancing the whole time, having fun and celebrating. And they did.

The only thing we had ordered for dessert was wedding cake and fruit, so I panicked when I saw the catering staff rolling out carts of squares, stunning cakes and colourful dessert platters. It's difficult to run in a full-length wedding dress, but I sprinted into that kitchen. The caterer actually smirked when he told me that he wasn't charging us anything extra for the surprise sweet table. He told me that it was his absolute pleasure. His gift to us.

I had been so careful all evening to hold back my tears, to heed to the warnings I had given to everyone about crying, but that caterer pushed me over the edge. I stood in that kitchen bawling my eyes out. Tears of gratitude and appreciation. For him, for the Rabbi, the band, the florist, the photographer, our wonderful relatives and friends, and mostly for my life. I had just married the most wonderful person in the world, and was surrounded by precious relatives and friends. I felt lucky and blessed.

To this day, I have yet to see a sweet table that doesn't bring tears to my eyes. Sweet tears of appreciation for all the wonderful people out there, who have no idea how a small gesture can mean the world to someone.

PART FIVE:

Resilience

CHAPTER 1

WE WERE STARTING a whole new chapter of living meaningful lives, feeling good, productive and satisfied. It was the continuation of "our movie" and we were both equally determined to stay focused on our goals. We had career goals, but most importantly, we were focused on that happy ending, if it ever really ends.

Immediately after our wedding, we devoted our time and energy to moving to California. We had send-off brunches, dinners, small groups, big groups.... Our friends and relatives were supportive, making sure that we knew how happy they all were to see that we were starting our newly married life in an exciting place like California.

Not only did the accounting firm arrange and pay all of our moving costs, but they flew us to Orange County, California, a month before our official move, so we could find a place to live. All expenses paid. Air fare, hotel, meals, a rental car. We were ecstatic. We looked at a number of apartments and townhouses for rent, and when we walked into the small, brand new, sunny two bedroom townhouse, I knew it was perfect for us. Not only because Barry and I liked the unique Spanish style, the little garden in front and the deck off the kitchen, but because of the lizard in the bathroom. As soon as the rental agent told me that lizards are good luck, I wanted this house. It was a sign.

ONCE THE MOVERS had unloaded the last box off the truck, we began unpacking all of our things. Shockingly, we actually had enough to fill a small moving van. What a nice change from garbage bags stuffed into the 1971 Chevrolet Biscayne. We had packed up every single item that was in our apartment in Montreal. No matter what it was, I kept it. Everything had some meaning and was treasured. And now we had wedding gifts to add to our collection, things to fill our closets and cupboards.

Barry and I stayed up the entire night unpacking and organizing our new home. My obsession with being neat, clean and orderly provided that crucial feeling of control. Predictability. No changes. No surprises. Please, no shocks.

Tiko, our pampered cat, was a bit wobbly from the tranquilizers we had given him for the flight to California, but he quickly recovered and settled into our new home. As long as he could sleep in our bed, he was happy.

We were definitely the most decisive shoppers ever to hit the stores. Within a few days, we found the best deals on two small off-white couches that could convert to beds, a wicker coffee table, big floor plants in baskets, a desk and chair, and a floor lamp. For our stereo and television, we used clay bricks and brown laminate shelves. We made a big book shelf in the second bedroom with the same pattern of bricks piled on each side and shelves in the middle. Everything fit perfectly in that cute little townhouse.

I bought a few bird houses and bird feeders for both our front garden and back deck. By attracting the birds, I would have constant reminders to be brave through the scary parts.

BARRY STARTED HIS job as an accountant and came home motivated and excited about the office, the work and the people. He surprised me with his work ethic and discipline. I already knew that he was willing to work long hours and function with little sleep, but that had always been for either money or marks. Now, he wasn't making any extra money for working long hours, yet he was determined to do a good job, to learn as much as he could. I loved that he was so serious and responsible. So motivated. By working in an accounting firm, he had the opportunity to learn a little bit about a lot of different businesses. He realized early on that public accounting was not something he would do forever, but it was a surefire way to learn and to help him decide what direction to take his career.

In addition to working long days, Barry began studying for the Certified Public Accountant, or CPA exams. That took up a considerable amount of time, which left little time for us to enjoy life in sunny California. But we managed to sneak in trips to the beaches, the biking trails, the modern shopping malls, and the gorgeous drives through magnificent neighbourhoods.

It was a little bit like playing house. We got up early and ate breakfast together. Then he would kiss me goodbye and leave for work, all dressed up in a suit, a white buttoned down dress shirt, a tie, and carrying a black briefcase. When he got home, dinner was ready and the table was set. He told me about his day as we ate, we would clean up together, and then we would go for a walk. I was so happy. I was proud of Barry. I loved our house. I loved living in California. I loved our life. And I was terrified that it would end. It was all too good to be true.

WITHIN A FEW weeks, and after interviewing for a variety of social work positions, I found a job at St. Joseph's, a large, reputable hospital close to our house. The hospital had a big social service department with eight social workers. There had been one position available on a medical floor, predominantly filled with elderly patients. Perfect for me.

I went through a full two-week training period along with various other hospital employees. By the time I was ready to officially join the department and take on a caseload of my own, I was convinced that I had made a huge mistake. I wasn't a student any more. I was a real social worker, wearing a lab coat, carrying a beeper, with access to patients, their families, doctors, nurses, dieticians, therapists, and medical charts. The nurses on my floor asked me questions. Doctors referred patients to me. Families looked to me for help and support. I was expected to do a job for which I would be paid. Well paid, actually. More money than Barry was making at the accounting firm.

My grandmother laughed when I called and told her how scared I was. It didn't take her long to restore my confidence. To remind me that I had extensive training at a wonderful university. She also encouraged me to ask for help. Turn to the other social workers. They all knew I was fresh out of school. They were social workers. If they couldn't be supportive and helpful, then who could?

As a hospital social worker, I was part of the social work department, and assigned to a specific floor of the hospital. Not only were the social workers in our department competent, but they genuinely cared about the patients, the hospital staff, and their fellow social workers. This was a group of professional women who understood the true meaning of compassion and sincerity. I could not have asked for a better job, a better hospital to work in, and a better team to be a part of.

It didn't take long at all to feel a strong sense of belonging. I loved that. Along with belonging came confidence, trust, appreciation, and motivation. I was helping others. I was making a difference. And I was meeting some incredible people.

I realized quickly that the nurses on my floor worked unbelievably hard. They had to deal with various body fluids (and solids), overpowering odours, vicious tempers, condescending attitudes, patronizing instructions, changing sheets, serving meals, answering call bells, chronic complaining, death, emergencies, non-emergencies, phone calls, lineups at the desk and countless other minutiae.

They had to document in the charts, report at the end of their shift, competently multi-task, ensure accuracy and consistently remain patient, kind and sweet. They were stressed to the maximum.

Move over Mother Teresa. Lynda to the rescue. Between the patients, their family members, the nurses on my floor and the doctors, I was as busy as could be. I started a support group for overworked nurses, a support group for families of stroke victims, and a support group for families placing loved ones in a nursing home. I felt needed, appreciated and useful. I was willing to work long hours, and managed to get on the weekend emergency call list. That way I could carry a beeper, which made me feel important. I could intervene in crises and emergencies, and I could get paid for overtime.

I was doing whatever I could do to make a difference. Giving way more than was expected. Trying to stand out above the rest. Using my training as a social worker, combined with my grandmother's rich advice about how to relate to people, find a way to live a meaningful life and, at the same time, enrich the lives of others.

My grandmother loved hearing my stories. Our phone calls lasted much longer than Barry and I could afford, but that didn't matter. I needed to talk to her and I knew she treasured the calls as much as I did. I would work a few extra weekends if I had to. I wasn't cutting back on my phone time.

It was hard to be away from our relatives and friends, but we were busy building our careers and our new life together. Whenever I felt myself slipping into that dark tunnel of fear, worry or guilt, I spent time with my latest therapist.

Bernie was recommended to me by one of the social workers in my department, and I found our sessions invaluable. The main concern for me was that everything was going so well, too well to last. I was happy. I had a great job, I loved our home and our new friends, and I was terrified that it was just a matter of time and it would all end. Life can change in an instant. Life as you know it can just stop. No one knew this better than me and Barry.

Along with the fear and worry, came guilt. I felt guilty about being happy. I felt guilty about the almost non-existent relationship I had with my father. I felt guilty for leaving my grandparents. I felt guilty about Mitchell's life. I felt guilty about being alive when my mother and sisters were dead.

My sessions with Bernie had less to do with the past and more to do with the present and future. He wasn't big on me digging up all of the feelings and emotions I had felt since the plane crash. He didn't believe that you have to talk about your past in order to move forward with your life. He wasn't keen on me spending any time talking about what was. We can't change what was, but we can learn from it, grow, and focus on the present and the future. Focus on what you have now and what you want, moving forward in a positive way. Bernie was always preaching positivity.

I heard this over and over from Barry as well. Barry never felt sorry for himself, never complained, instead saying that he just did what he had to do. You can't change the past and you shouldn't worry about the future. Live the present to the best of your ability. Plain and simple.

Barry and I loved talking about our life together, and planning our future. I was always amazed by how well Barry understood people and situations. He had a way of looking at everything with a perfect balance of his head and his heart. He was practical and logical, yet sensitive and thoughtful. He knew how to access his emotions without being emotional. No wonder he was so well-liked by both my mother's and my father's families.

He was also supportive of my rapidly growing bird house collection and some of my outlandish beliefs and feelings about life after death. I told him that his parents, my mother and sisters' spirits had all followed us to California. It wasn't the sort of thing I talked to anyone else about, but I brought the subject up every now and then, and Barry listened. He knew it was something that gave me significant comfort.

IT WAS JUST a few days before Passover, the first Passover we would be away from extended family. I focused on all of the positives: stimulating jobs, a fabulous house, a loving marriage and who could knock the California weather.

Nevertheless, I was worried about being drawn into that dark place. How could I get through another special day without my mother and sisters? Was my father going to be leading the Seder sitting at the head of Sonia's dining room table surrounded by Sonia's family? Could I have done anything differently to be part of that family?

I stopped on the way home from work at a store that sold Judaica, Jewish cultural and religious items. It was not on my usual route, and I had never been in there before. One of the doctors on my floor mentioned it, so I went. I bought a Passover cookbook and a traditional Seder plate and, for some reason, I asked at the cash to have them both gift wrapped. I always loved getting wrapped presents as a child, and liked the idea of bringing them home wrapped in pretty paper, but I had never done anything like this before. It just felt like the appropriate thing to do.

The whole drive home I was thinking about my mother and Barry's mother. I tried to envision what Passover would have been like if they were both still alive. I pictured a big table set for lots of people: Barry's parents, his brother, my parents, my sisters, my grandparents. I knew that I couldn't have that in real life but it sure felt good thinking about what it would have been like if everyone had been alive. Our two families together as one. I just wanted to keep the image in my mind for a bit longer. Savour the few moments in my head. Imagining. Dreaming.

I left the beautifully wrapped boxes on the wicker coffee table and when Barry got home, I told him they were gifts from both our mothers. I ignored the look he gave me, and went on to tell him that they knew each other on the other side. They were friends. And they were both proud of us.

We sat on the couch and opened the gifts. Barry was so good about the whole thing, going along with my claim and apparent need to believe that they were from our mothers. Whether it was an intuitive spiritual feeling, or something that I had thought up to make me feel better, either way it was the first time that we had done anything tangible related to our two mothers. We never talked about our mothers knowing each other, we didn't visit the cemeteries together, yet this few minutes of opening gifts "from them" felt so real. I told Barry that they were in the room with us. That part I knew for sure.

CHAPTER 2

I HAD BEEN working at St. Joseph's Hospital for over a year, feeling comfortable in the department, in my role, happy on my floor, learning a lot. I was valued, appreciated, busy and committed. Our offices were amongst many others in the hospital basement, close to the cafeteria and the doctor's lounge. One morning as I raced through the basement hall carrying a stack of files I stopped dead in my tracks smack in front of Harry, Sonia's son. I hadn't seen Harry in a few years, and he looked different in his white lab coat, smart glasses, and stylish hair cut. Much more packaged-looking than he ever looked when he was under Sonia's wing. Or maybe he had never let her control him. Maybe she hadn't tried as hard as she did with me to control his packaging, manage his time, judge his friends.

Now Harry was a doctor and was doing a surgical residency in my hospital. My father hadn't even told me that Harry and his wife had moved to California.

I quickly dismissed my first thought of "oh shit" and decided that this could all be a good thing for me and my father. I would look at the potential positives in this situation. *We have choices. We always have choices.* If Harry and his wife Gloria lived in California, then my father would surely be visiting them, so I would get to see him. And being three thousand miles away from Sonia meant that Harry and I might even be able to develop a nice sibling relationship that we could never do when Mrs. Critical Judgmental was around, budding in with her nasty comments artfully disguised as concern and sincerity.

Harry must have been choosing to look at this in a positive way as well, because he invited me to join him that day for lunch in the doctor's lounge. After chatting for a couple of minutes, we agreed on a time to meet.

I walked into the main social work office area where I was sure to find our department's administrative staff and at least one social worker. I closed the door behind me, put the stack of files on a chair, and announced my latest news. I found the whole thing so ironic, and so typical of my father. With all of the hospitals in the states, and particularly in California, how did Harry and I end up in the same one? And how hard would it have been for my father to pick up the phone and tell me that Harry and Gloria were moving to Orange County and Harry was doing his residency at an Orange County hospital. I babbled on to my department friends and then I called Barry. We both agreed that this might be a great chance for the four of us to get to know each other and, at the very least, I would get to see my dad. I even imagined that Harry would tell my father and Sonia how well-liked and respected I was and they would finally realize that, despite their stupid allegations, I was valued and appreciated as a good person.

We did get together with Harry and Gloria a few times, but unfortunately our one common denominator, Sonia, was enough of an issue that we each kept up our guard, our walls, the resistance to us ever becoming close friends. Too bad, because we liked them. But I understood, probably better than anyone, how Gloria would have had major mother-in-law issues if she ever got too friendly with me. Even from three thousand miles away, Sonia would have made her life a living hell.

While Barry and I were living in California, my dad and his brother, my Uncle Dave, were trying to repair their damaged relationship, bury the hatchet, let bygones be bygones. I was so happy for my dad. Having his brother and sister-in-law back in his life, in whatever little way, gave me comfort. My Auntie Riva was so different from Sonia, and I knew from my lengthy phone conversations with my aunt, that they tolerated Sonia for the sake of my father. And Sonia didn't dare say a negative thing to them about me or Barry. Sonia was well aware of the relationship I had with my aunt and uncle, which was based on trust, honesty and appreciation.

As for Mitchell, he still worked for minimum wage at the sheltered workshop where he continued to receive ongoing coaching. Companies paid the workshop to do menial jobs, primarily the packaging of products in an assembly line fashion. The goal was to eventually place the participants in permanent jobs once they could demonstrate the ability to manage on their own. From the descriptions we got from Mitchell, he was definitely one of the highest functioning participants in the program.

Uncle Perry helped Mitchell as much as he possibly could. Mitchell had no idea how to manage money, so his paycheque was going directly into his bank account. Every few weeks, Mitchell would go to Uncle Perry's office to get some cash. Uncle Perry helped him budget his money by letting him know exactly how much he should spend every day.

Since his phone was disconnected because he didn't pay the bills, Uncle Perry took over paying his phone bills. He also gave Mitchell post-dated cheques for his rent. He told Mitchell to give the envelope to the landlord.

Mitchell had moved around quite a bit, usually getting evicted after a few months. Things were fine at the beginning and then he would quickly feel out of place. He didn't have to look too far to see couples, families, people going about their daily lives with way more going for them than he had.

The building managers would lose their patience with him when he couldn't or wouldn't follow the rules of the building, and he damaged the furniture in furnished apartments.

He always managed to find another one-room hole that was noisy, poorly heated in the winter and stifling hot in the summer, and reeked of fried food combined with smoke and mould.

Mitchell loved to read about politics and actually knew more about the subject than anyone else we knew. He became obsessed with anything related to the military. He started shopping in Army Surplus stores and wearing military clothing. We knew because he had just come back from spending a weekend with Uncle Len, who told us that Mitchell had an amazing time loading up on all kinds of military attire.

We sent him packages. Black, green and brown camouflage clothing, vitamins, books. We called him at least once a week, having the same conversations with him each time. He would update us on the most recent political situation in the news, he told us about what he was doing at his job, and complained that all of his co-workers at the sheltered workshop were driving him crazy. He said they were all retarded or stupid. He told us over and over again that he might be a lot of things, but he wasn't stupid.

CHAPTER 3

As usual, I used my two weeks of vacation to go to Montreal. Barry only recently started his new job, so he couldn't come with me. But Donna and Lorne were getting married that summer, and I did not want to miss their wedding in Montreal.

I arrived on Friday evening and stayed at my cousin's house. The wedding was on Sunday. I spent the entire day Saturday with my grandparents. We visited family, went out for lunch, talked, laughed, hugged a lot. I took pictures all day long. It felt good to be with them. So easy. So comfortable. So important.

The next morning I got the phone call. Oh how I hate morning phone calls. Bubby had passed away during the night. Suddenly. Unexpectedly. My poor, sweet Zaida had found her dead. He called for an ambulance, but it was too late.

As shocked and devastated as I was, I was also thankful that she waited for me to visit and have a special day with her. So typical of my Bubby to be thoughtful and considerate. I was grateful for that day, and the pictures I took would be treasured forever.

We had funeral arrangements to make. We would be sitting Shiva. I missed Donna and Lorne's wedding.

I fought with Air Canada about the charges for delaying my flight back. I tried talking to a supervisor and, even after explaining about the plane crash, there was nothing they would do. It continued to amaze me that Air Canada had truly walked away from the victims' families, paying the paltry sum of money and then closing the file. Families had been devastated because of Air Canada, left to carry on with the lifetime sentence of pain and loss. And they couldn't even waive some surcharges? Air Canada's view regarding how victims should be treated was diametrically opposed to my own. Clearly, there would be no red carpet service for me.

Zaida was crushed to have lost his wife of over fifty years. I was worried about how he was going to cope with her death, and about how he would manage living on his own. He had always done the food shopping, but he had no idea how to cook or do laundry.

I stayed in Montreal with my devastated grandfather for the remainder of the Shiva and long enough to feel confident that my uncles and aunts, as well as Julie, would help him out as much as possible. While he was still independent, and had been working at a lottery booth, I worried about him.

Julie, who I still referred to as Deedee, reassured me that she would continue coming to his house at least once every week to clean up for him and do his laundry, just as she had done for the past few years while my grandmother was still alive. Her relationship with my grandparents had always remained solid, as if she were family. Julie knew that they would never have spent the money to hire someone to help clean the house, and my grandmother couldn't do it by herself, so a couple of times a month, Julie just showed up. She told them that she was in the neighbourhood with nothing to do, and she wanted to see if they needed any help. With young kids of her own, it was highly unlikely that she ever had free time, but she fit my grandparents into her life without giving it a second thought.

With reluctance, I headed home.

LIVING IN CALIFORNIA definitely had its advantages. The weather was amazing, we had rewarding jobs and met some wonderful people. We always had visitors, and knew that we could stay and make a life there. But something about being so far away from Montreal nagged at us. We visited Montreal whenever we had vacation time and were always on the phone with relatives or friends. Still, I was having a hard time dealing with my grandmother's death and the fact that my grandfather was alone.

Barry and I both agreed that Montreal was not where we wanted to live. Too much had happened there. We could visit, but not settle there. After several discussions, we decided that Toronto made the most sense. It was close enough to Montreal to drive back and forth. Our good friends Donna and Lorne had moved there and loved it. Barry was interested in the pharmaceutical business and I was keen on going back to school to get my Masters in Social Work. Toronto it was. Barry began sending out resumes and I applied to the University of Toronto.

OUR TOWNHOUSE DEVELOPMENT was unique, and looked more like a group of individual little houses all clustered together. There was a long driveway that we shared with eight other houses, and at the end of the driveway were individual mail boxes made out of old barn wood. Behind the mail area orange and yellow flowers grew on vines, wrapping themselves around the wooden support posts. I loved going to get the mail and flipping through it right there at the end of the driveway. I once told a neighbour that the only thing missing was a park bench, and I would be happy sitting for hours in that pretty spot reading my mail and feeding the birds.

Surrounded by the manicured mailbox garden with the sun shining brightly was where I opened that big envelope from University of Toronto. I had been accepted. I ran into the house to call Barry and tell him the news. Getting into the graduate program in Social Work was highly competitive and notoriously difficult.

And I was chosen.

CHAPTER 4

GOING BACK TO university after being in the working world for four years was a challenge. Far removed from the student routine, it felt weird being married and older than most of the other students, sitting in lectures and juggling assignments as well as a field placement. In addition to pressuring myself to get all As, I had to adjust to a brand new city, make friends, learn my way around, manage our home, and try to find a few minutes here and there for Barry.

Having started his career in public accounting, Barry felt that he had been given a solid introduction to the business world. He worked with a team of motivated, competitive high achievers. He had an inside glimpse of various businesses, small to large, in diverse industries such as a sports team (California Angels) and Fortune 500 companies.

Once he passed the CPA exams, he had to decide what to do with his career: stay in public accounting and get promoted or get into a business in the health care industry. He wanted a career where he could make a small contribution to improving health. Barry did not need to be converted by me or anyone else to a life of doing things for the sake of others. Having grown up in a home with unusual circumstances and the ongoing need for flexibility, sacrifices and compassion, he naturally understood that it is important and it feels good to help. To make a difference. To live a meaningful life.

His new job as a Financial Analyst at Eli Lilly, a major global pharmaceutical company, was incredibly demanding. He left the house at seven-thirty every morning, and often worked twelve-hour days.

Because I already had a bachelor's degree in Social Work, I was accepted into the one year Master's program at University of Toronto. I was turning twenty-seven upon graduating in June, and we decided we were ready to start a family.

FROM THE DAY I found out I was pregnant, my anxiety level peaked. I panicked that all of the good things in my life would abruptly end. I was scared stiff. I called Barry at work ten times a day to make sure he was okay. I was nervous driving. I worried about going on the subway. I fretted about money. I was anxious about the health of my baby, the delivery, the risk of post-partum depression. I was afraid that I wouldn't know how to look after the baby and didn't want to keep bothering my aunts.

I missed my mother, my sisters and my grandmother more than ever.

I sensed the onset of that all-too-familiar cycle of grieving. Slipping into that deep, dark tunnel of self-pity, fear, panic, worry, negativity. I felt like I was drowning. I needed help.

We could not afford to pay a private therapist, so my doctor recommended a psychiatrist, which would be covered by the Canadian medical system. Between school, my field placement, keeping my home clean, spending time with my husband, going to my prenatal check-ups, and lugging around my huge bag of worries, I now had to fit in my therapy sessions.

I knew myself well enough to know that all I really needed to hear from that psychiatrist was that everything was fine, life was good, and there was no reason to worry. Look ahead, not back. You can't change the past. Lightning doesn't strike twice.

I would have believed her. I always believed Bernie, my trusty therapist in California. And life was good in California. Great actually. But no, this female Dr. Freud, had to dig deep into my past, to all of those painful times where I was dealing with tragedy, with horrendous loss and legitimate worry. She wanted me to talk about the nightmares so she could analyse them.

She obviously thought it would be valuable to bring it all up again and go through as much agony as possible right there in her office. As if when I originally went through everything, I hadn't felt lousy enough. Why not relive it and resolve it once and for all? That was her theory.

I always walked out of there feeling worse than when I walked in. After torturing myself for two months, I stopped going. Somehow I was going to have to stop freaking out about everything that could go wrong, and learn to trust life again. To focus on the positives. Things were good. Barry was loving and supportive, we were happy together, and now we were having a baby. Worrying and reliving the past would not do any good. It was debilitating. I had to stop. And I knew that Barry would help me: my wonderful husband and very best friend in the whole world. Supportive, logical, loving—and here for me.

Dear Diary,
We had our last prenatal class tonight and both of us really like the people we met. We all went out for coffee, decaf of course, after class. It's been fun talking to other couples who are equally excited and nervous about becoming parents, sharing ideas and plans.

Our new pregnant friends all have parents who are buying them most of what they need, getting them set up and shopping with them. Highly involved in their pregnancy. Many brought their mothers with them to their prenatal appointments. They seem to have storybook lives.

We will make our own storybook life.

I don't mind going alone, and whenever Barry can leave work for a few hours, he surprises me and meets me there. He knows that I really appreciate having him at the appointments. Listening to the heart beating. Excitedly anticipating the birth of our baby. The start of our family.

My father still hasn't offered to buy anything for us. I speak to him on the phone about once a week, but all he does is ask how I am feeling. Our conversations are always short, superficial and strained. He never has anything to tell me, and I don't really know what to tell him. Our lives are so separate. So detached. I am desperately grasping onto a relationship that has diminished to almost nothing. It is so sad.

BARRY AND I had spent many weekends shopping and getting organized for our new baby. I loved the way the baby's room had turned out. We had a honey-coloured oak crib, with a matching change table, rocking chair and dresser. Barry hung pastel-coloured wallpaper on all the walls. The change table was stocked with tiny diapers, wipes, receiving blankets, little yellow and white sleepers, and miniature yellow socks. We had a plastic baby bath tub in the bathroom and a bucket car seat that was sitting at the front door.

Dear Diary,
I am writing this from my labour and delivery bed at Mount Sinai Hospital. It is about 3:00 am on October 25th, and Dr. Engle says that our baby will be born soon. I already had an epidural. Barry is asleep on the chair next to me. I am way too excited to sleep.

The two of us were standing in the kitchen cleaning up from dinner when my water broke. I was shocked. I am not due for two more weeks. We called the hospital and they told us to come right in. I was so scared, but at the same time really excited, and grateful that my hospital bag was packed, and that the nursery was totally organized.

IT'S A GIRL!

The minute we were in a room with access to a phone, Barry and I called my dad, my grandfather, every single one of our aunts and uncles, many of our cousins and our friends, to tell them that our beautiful, healthy baby daughter, Rebecca Wendy Fran, was born.

Dear Diary,
The first time I stared into the eyes of my precious little newborn daughter, I was fully absorbed in the moment of intense maternal love. I knew instantly, deep down, that the love I feel as a mother is more powerful than anything I've ever felt before. I just hope and pray that we will all stay together, happy and healthy, for much longer than my family did.

I WAS DETERMINED to breastfeed. I knew that there were many health benefits but my main reason for breastfeeding was its accompanying closeness with the baby and the fact that I was the only one who could feed her. I did not want to share this baby with anyone other than Barry, and I knew that he would rock her, hold her, bathe and change her. I wanted to feed her.

The nurses were very patient with us as I tried to breastfeed in the hospital, but I could not seem to figure it out. I didn't know how to hold her, and she wasn't latching on properly. The nurses hooked me up to a breast pump and we fed her with a bottle.

I had only been a mother for a few hours and already I felt like a failure. I was starving my baby, and I was hungry for the kind of support and help that only a mother can provide.

Thank goodness for the La Leche League. Seeing that I was adamant about breastfeeding, my solution-oriented husband must have sounded totally desperate when he called the La Leche League for help because, within a couple of hours of being home, the doorbell rang. I was in the nursery holding my precious baby all wrapped up in a pink receiving blanket, fast asleep in my arms, when this sweet woman walked into the room. I burst into tears. She was so calm and loving, spending well over two hours with us, and successfully coaching us on breastfeeding.

While I was ready to adopt this woman right then and there as my new mother, the one person I desperately wanted and needed was my own mother. I was absolutely aching for her.

THERE WAS SO much I had to learn. I loved the idea of being a mother, and I was madly in love with my baby, but more than ever, I struggled with being motherless, frightened to face the day-to-day routine of motherhood without my own mother by my side. No matter how many times I had convinced myself that I was finished mourning my mother and sisters, the pain and longing for them resurfaced, and continued on and on. I constantly saw the support and guidance that my friends received from their own mothers and mothers-in-law; everything from babysitting, shopping for or with them, that extra pair of hands, advice, reassurance, and someone to turn to with a shoulder to cry on when it all felt so overwhelming.

I often questioned my competence, wanting to be perfect, worrying about absolutely everything. *How long should I nurse? Why is she crying? Why isn't she crying? What is this rash? Should I take her temperature? How do I take her temperature?* Of course, the combination of sleep deprivation and the reality of having a baby with no mother of my own made it tough to stay positive. I had to remind myself that I had chosen life. I had chosen to be happy. I had chosen to look at the good, not the bad. To look at what I have instead of what I had lost.

It took work on my part, hard work, and the commitment to stopping myself from indulging in self-pity and, instead, focusing on the good.

For at least the first two years, we never went anywhere without Rebecca. I just could not leave her. There was no one I trusted enough to babysit and, thank God, Barry never pressured me.

For the most part, I did it. We did it. Barry and I.

CHAPTER 5

Dear Diary,
There is a beautiful bird who has come back for the second year to her nest on the
window sill of Rebecca's room. I can't open the window in there because I don't
want to disturb the nest. We are loving the opportunity to see the tiny eggs and are
awaiting the hatching of the baby birds. I especially love the reminder this is giving
me about the movie The Birds, and all of the lessons I learned from that movie.

I HAD ANOTHER great pregnancy with our second child, Jonathan Terry, who
was due mid-July, 1987 when Rebecca would be just over two and a half. I
was energetic, active and busy right up until his birth.

During most of my pregnancy, my dad, Sonia and I were having one of
our short but nevertheless positive runs. He called more often, was sweeter
and more natural on the phone, interested, caring. He was being somewhat
fatherly and it felt good.

During their visits to Toronto, I was hospitable, cautious about not
letting Sonia's passive aggression, criticism and potentially offensive comments upset me, and very aware of how my father just loved the harmony.
Sonia's niece lived in Toronto so, deep down, I knew that the real reason
they came to Toronto was to visit her niece, but I chose to look at the
bright side. They were spending some time getting to know Rebecca, and
my father appreciated the time with us. Sonia had even promised that if we
had a boy, she would bring her famous traditional dish made with chick
peas to the Bris, a ceremony where a Jewish boy is circumcised.

Maybe I was gullible, overly optimistic, or I just wanted to believe that
things had finally turned around, and we would all manage to stay on this
positive path. But it didn't last.

I went into labour two weeks early and on June 29th, 1987 ironically
on Sonia's birthday, I gave birth to a beautiful little boy. The timing was
actually perfect. I was worried about giving birth on either June 28th or
July 5th. The Bris is always one week after the delivery, and I did not know
how I could handle a Bris and a house full of people on that monumental
date of July 5th, the anniversary of the plane crash. And I certainly did not
want my baby's birthday to be on that date.

Knowing that I gave birth on Sonia's birthday gave me a certain sense
of satisfaction. Maybe I was digging deep for some message or meaning,

but it did provide me with further proof that she did not succeed in robbing me of my pursuit of happiness. And just to prove that to her, I experienced ultimate happiness and joy on her birthday.

Dear Diary,
We had the Bris for Jonathan this morning. We were overwhelmed by the number of relatives and friends who were here, from Montreal, New Jersey and New York. The procedure went as well as could be expected and my sweet little baby boy seems to be fine.

My dad came alone. The bitch never even showed up and we have no idea what she's upset about this time. She also must have forgotten that she had promised to make her chick pea dish. She makes me sick.

IN JULY OF 1987, when Jonathan was barely two weeks old, we had a bizarre experience. Barry had literally just walked into the house, through the entrance from the garage which opened right into the laundry room. Within seconds of his closing the door and walking into the kitchen, we heard a huge bang. He ran back and opened the door he had just walked through, and his car was pushed up against the door, the shelves adjacent to the door flattened against the wall. His first thought was that he had mistakenly left his car in gear, but he quickly realized that the garage door was damaged and there was another car pushed up against his car. With the smashed garage door between the two.

Within no time, we all stood in the laundry room trying to process the whole insane situation. Apparently, our next door neighbour, Rose, was backing into her own garage when she lost control of her vehicle and did a u-turn across our lawn, up our driveway and right through our garage door.

The event quickly drew a ridiculously large number of neighbours to the front of our house where they were discussing and debating how the whole thing had occurred. Someone called the fire department, assuming they were needed, so it didn't take long for the bizarre situation to further evolve into quite the dramatic scene. Rose was enormously embarrassed and felt terrible about the damage. The garage door was demolished, the car was damaged both in front and in the rear, there were tire marks across the lawn, and the garage shelves and all its contents were crushed.

Our neighbours thought the whole thing was hysterically funny; they wanted to install a "No U-turn" sign on our front lawn. I personally chose to join them and declare the entire incident totally hysterical. Considering that I was hormonal and sleep deprived, I could have chosen other ways of responding. Negative ways. But, no one was hurt, which was the most important thing and actually quite miraculous, considering that Barry had walked through that door just seconds before. In fact, the fire fighters were laughing and relieved, and it did make a great story.

Poor Rose found absolutely no humour in the situation, especially because it cost her several thousand dollars to replace the garage door and repair the car. She didn't believe me when I told her over and over that I wasn't upset with her. She felt guilty and was convinced that I was lying. I ended up having to console and reassure Rose that everything was fine, no one was hurt, and she didn't have to sell her house and move to Siberia.

The truth is that I thanked my angels endlessly for doing whatever it was they did to prevent such a near tragedy. It had been a close call. A matter of seconds. Maybe even sixteen seconds.

LIFE WITH TWO children was busy, and I did my best to stay positive, and grateful. I had two sweet kids, an adoring husband, and lots of friends. But there wasn't a day that went by when I didn't miss my mother and sisters terribly, particularly when the kids were sick or needed minor surgery. As Barry and I sat in waiting rooms, once again we were the only couple there without grandparents. Having no mother or mother-in-law meant I had no one to turn to who was both my mother and my children's grandmother. Someone who could not only understand *my* fears and worries but who would also support me unconditionally as only a mother would. Aunts and cousins are great, and I appreciated everyone, but when they are not your own mother or sisters, well, it's just not the same. It can't be.

I watched with pure envy as my friends and their kids had those special relationships that you can only have with a grandmother and grandfather. I knew that we were definitely cheated by those huge voids in our lives: special occasions, birthdays, anniversaries, grandparents day at school, holidays, even important decisions and the day-to-day events in our lives.… My friends knew better than to ever complain about their parents or in-laws in our company.

My father visited occasionally but, within a short time, he was itching to leave and get back to his wife. I couldn't force him to spend more time with us, and while I didn't understand him, I had given up trying.

Learning how to mother was an ongoing process for me. I read every parenting book I could get my hands on, desperate for information and confirmation about the growth and development of our kids, the parenting decisions we were making: health, education, everything and anything. In the back of my mind was that ever-present worry that we were doing something wrong, or that the next setback lurked around the corner like an evil villain.

For me, that expression "history repeats itself" was a horrifying statement. I already knew only too well that life could be extinguished in a second. As a young mother, I was petrified about losing another family member, and particularly terrified about anything bad ever happening to my precious children.

I drove my paediatrician and his office staff crazy with my phone calls and appointments, my questions and concerns, and my inability to stop myself from suggesting that everything was potentially sinister. I was a regular at their office, freaked out when the kids had a common cold, the flu, a headache, a rash, a sore leg. I worried about their internal organs and their limbs. I panicked about the possibility of brain tumours, cancer, heart disease, Meningitis, food poisoning, choking, concussions...

Sitting in the waiting room with other young mothers, I felt as if I was the only one there without my own mother.

Having already lived through the profound sudden loss of people who I had loved so much, I braced myself for the certain catastrophe that would shatter my world.

I had to peel myself away, fighting back tears, when I was required to separate from each of my kids at their first drop-off program. I mimicked what the other mothers told their kids, reassuring them that "mommy always comes back" but, in my heart, I knew otherwise. Mommy doesn't always come back. Loving relationships could end instantly, at any time.

Leaving them was beyond horrifying for me, a huge obstacle for a young mother to overcome. Once again, I drew from my previous strategies of focusing on the good, and applying one of my newest tactics: a mental picture of sending those morbid thoughts off into space in a rocket ship. Count to sixteen. As I did, I could almost see the trail of smoke as the rocket ship blasted into space. Thank God there was so much room up there.

CHAPTER 6

B Y THE TIME Jonathan turned two, I was eager to go back to work but determined not to leave the kids for long. Most of the time it is the kids who suffer from separation anxiety, but in my case it was me, the mother. That ruled out the various clinical social work positions that were available, since all of them were full-time jobs.

I had always loved camp, I enjoyed being around children, and I was super organized and energetic, so I decided to look for a job at a day camp.

Timing is everything. I landed the perfect job as a Camp Director at a day camp just ten minutes from our house. It was a small camp, but had the potential to grow with hard work and strong leadership. Neither of those requirements worried me.

I never needed that much sleep, so once the kids were in bed I got to work. I was hired to run the camp, but it didn't take long for me to discover that my employers had handed me a blank slate. The camp had just moved to this new location, having lost their previous director, their customers, and all the paperwork necessary to operate safely.

Faced with the challenge and difficulty of essentially building a day camp from scratch, I buckled down to creating a brochure, registration forms, policies and procedures. I recruited and interviewed staff, wrote staff manuals, planned programs and activities. I did my best to attract customers through my large network of friends and through word of mouth.

Being aware of the limited resources out there for children with special needs, I wanted to integrate these kids. Since I had the professional training, and knew how valuable camp was for all children, I saw every reason to operate a camp where those with Autism, Down Syndrome and developmental delays, were welcome.

I made a point of hiring teens who were bullied or shunned. By giving them a leadership role along with some meaningful training and ongoing coaching, they could go from being timid, victimized and insecure, to sought out by their peers and in some cases, even popular.

Using creativity, basic marketing, and strong customer service, I managed to attract enough customers for that first summer.

I had found a job where I could have my kids by my side, my husband involved, and an opportunity to make a difference. Bubby would have been proud to know that I was living a meaningful and enjoyable life, while at the same time enriching the lives of others.

After the highly successful completion of our second camp season, the word was out. I was also pregnant with our third child. But, by the fourth month, things weren't going well with my pregnancy and my doctor sent me for tests.

I soon found out that I had a Molar pregnancy which was extremely rare and did not involve a live fetus. I required surgery to terminate this abnormal pregnancy, along with a variety of follow-up blood tests. In some cases, chemotherapy was necessary. Fortunately, very fortunately, the only follow-up I needed was daily blood work to ensure that my body was going back to normal.

We were upset but relieved that I didn't require aggressive follow-up. In fact, we didn't realize just how serious a Molar pregnancy could be, which was probably a good thing. What value was there in knowing the worst scenario? Just much more to worry about.

VERY SOON AFTER, an opportunity came up for all of us to go to Florida. Barry had a conference, the hotel was paid for, and the flights were cheap.

Rebecca, now six years old, and Jonathan, now four, were so excited about going on a real vacation, and on an airplane. Oh God, I had to pretend to be excited too, but even though we were all flying together, I was still petrified.

I triple checked that my bottle of Valium was in my purse, we locked up the house and left for the airport. Barry kept asking me if I was okay and while I continued to respond with a perky "of course" he knew that inside I was a wreck. I popped a Valium in the car, before we even got to the airport. I had to stop the panic that was quickly mounting.

By the time we boarded the plane, I was calmer and trying hard to relax. I told the kids that we would be so high up in the air, we might even be able to see the top of a rainbow. Maybe rainbows are always high up in the sky just waiting for a rainy day, so they could come out and show off their beautiful colours and perfect shape. Red, orange, yellow, green, blue and purple. That never changes. Despite the lightning and thunder of the most vicious storms, the rainbows that come out afterwards are always perfect and beautiful.

Rebecca's astute and profound theory was that "God probably fixes the rainbow after the storm so we never have to see it when it's broken."

As the flight took off, the four of us were in the middle of quietly singing every rainbow song we could think of. I never realized that between us, we knew so many of them.

I HAD TO wait almost a year before getting pregnant again, and once I did my doctor carefully monitored my pregnancy.

I should have known during my amniocentesis that my little sister Wendy was back, growing inside of me. Hyper, funny Wendy. They had to stop the test and send me into the waiting room to rest for a while because the fetus would not stop dancing around in there.

From the moment that Kimberly was born, she looked exactly like Wendy as a baby. When Deedee came to visit and saw Kimmy, she actually burst into tears.

Since I knew Deedee well enough to know that her St. Lucian accent only surfaced when she was really tired or emotional, I too fell apart when she started talking in that different English of hers. She picked up that baby, mumbling, crying and hugging her so tightly, I teased her that she would hurt her.

Rebecca and Jonathan took care of our new baby with tenderness and immense amounts of love. That kid was never left alone. They carried her around, brought her into bed with them, held her, rocked her, kissed her and hugged her. Barry and I could not get over how they mothered her. For two adults who had lost their own mothers, we were delighted to witness all that mothering in our home.

From the moment she could talk, Kimmy made us laugh. The memories of Wendy and her entertaining personality came flooding back. There were times where I slipped and called Kimmy, Wendy. I had her back in my life, my precious little Wendy. It was actually uncanny.

Whether it is God, or the Universe, or whatever, rainbows surely can be repaired if you are patient, determined and positive. That's my quick summary of Saychology 101.

CHAPTER 7

B ARRY CLIMBED THE corporate ladder rapidly at Eli Lilly, spending time in finance, human resources, operations, business development and marketing. He was pleased that his career allowed him the opportunity to learn about all aspects of business, in a respected, well-run organization. He was amazed to have been actively involved in bringing Prozac to market, which meant he truly had a small hand in transforming the treatment of depression. His job required that he travel quite a bit on business, for either meetings or conferences. Occasionally spouses were invited to join in on the trips. No way would I go. I wouldn't and I couldn't. First of all, we had no one to leave the kids with, but for me, the biggest issue was my absolute refusal to get on a plane without my kids. There was not enough therapy or tranquilizers to get me to agree to do that. Unfortunately Barry had to go on some of these trips alone, even though everyone else brought a significant other. I felt terrible about it, but I just couldn't do it.

IN AN IDEAL world none of us would ever need to fly. But, unfortunately for me, planes just couldn't be avoided. We had to get to New York quickly. I had no choice. I had to get back on that horse yet again. Auntie Naomi had stayed single for many years, but eventually married a man named Artie. Together, they smoked, drank and ate ridiculous amounts. Despite their eccentricities, they were family and I knew that my aunt really did love and care about me and my family.

They visited us about once or twice every year, throughout their ten years of marriage. And then Artie was diagnosed with lung cancer. Shocking, considering that he only smoked four packages of cigarettes each day. We always joked that his excessive daily consumption of one hundred proof vodka would preserve his body forever. The truth was that their self-destructive behaviour went against everything we believed in, but after all of our saychology lectures from Bubby, we were not about to judge them. They did what they did, and unfortunately it cost them both their health.

Artie died first. Barry and I knew that we had to go to Artie's funeral, but our same old dilemma was back. I refused to fly without the kids and, even if we drove, we wouldn't make it for the funeral and we had no one to watch the kids. So, the five of us flew to New York for the funeral on a ridiculously expensive early morning flight. It was a costly, rushed trip but we did it for Auntie Naomi and she certainly appreciated that we all came.

As we waited to check in at the Air Canada ticket counter, I overheard the ticket agent telling a man that because he travelled so much and was away from his family, his special status at Air Canada would hopefully make him more comfortable, by offering him better seats, admission to the Air Canada lounge and other advantages.

When the ticket agent was done, I asked her if there was any room in First Class. Yes, there was, the flight was not full. I asked if our family could be upgraded. When she said no, because we did not have the proper status with Air Canada that entitled us to upgrades, I felt my blood start to boil. This man qualified because he was away from his family, travelling on business or whatever. Poor guy. I lost my family in an Air Canada plane crash. An Air Canada pilot error. My kids lost their grandmother, essentially their grandfather, their aunts, potential cousins, and everything else that goes along with those losses. And we don't qualify? *Oh yes, I forgot. The file was closed.*

But for me, *the file* was never closed. For me and my father, it had remained open and active.

I couldn't help myself. I burst into tears, telling her, politely but emotionally, that I had lost my whole family in the 1970 Air Canada plane crash, and I could not believe that we didn't "qualify." She looked at me as if I had just told her that it was raining outside, and said that she was sorry but that is just the way it is. When I further mentioned that I would love to write a letter to Air Canada to tell them that even when there is room in First Class, their representative refused to move us, she said that I should go ahead and write whatever letter I wanted to write, and then she offered to give me the mailing address.

I walked onto that plane sobbing. Obviously the Valium had not yet fully kicked in.

Zaida was turning ninety, and my uncles and aunts planned a party for this milestone. Unfortunately, he had been in a nursing home for the last few years. Julie had taken care of him for as long as she could at his home, but when his health deteriorated to the point where he had to have one of his legs amputated, a nursing home was the only option.

We went to Montreal as often as possible and visited him. Poor man. He was completely lucid, bored and lonely. He had lost his leg, his independence, his freedom and definitely his will to live. Fresh bagels every day were only a memory for him now.

I wondered why such a good man, hardworking, honest, never greedy, always generous, had so much tragedy in his life. He had buried his daughter and two of his grandchildren, and then his precious wife. What did it all mean? Where was the good in the last part of his life? The lessons? The half-filled glass?

He must have been overwhelmed and maybe a bit disoriented at the party, with all the relatives, many of whom he hadn't seen for years, gathered in his honour, because he stroked Rebecca's face calling her Rita, my mother's name. That just broke my heart. But Rebecca didn't correct him. She just hugged him in a gentle hold that lasted way longer than sixteen seconds. Rebecca had definitely learned saychology from the previous generations. I was so proud of her.

Zaida died a couple of years later, finally able to leave a life overloaded with sadness and loss.

CHAPTER 8

M Y DAD SAW the kids a few times a year, mostly when he was accompanying Sonia to visit her niece and nephew and their kids. We benefited by those *Sonia* trips with five minute drop-in visits by my doting father. He threw bits of his time at us, in much the same way as you would toss bits of bread at the pigeons in the park.

I explained to our kids his minimal involvement in our lives was because he had special needs and, while he loved all of us, he just couldn't help it. He really wasn't normal. That explanation seemed like a reasonable way of making it clear to the kids that this pathetic relationship they had with their grandfather had nothing to do with them, and everything to do with him.

Our kids were exposed to more than enough grandparents who were completely involved in the lives of their grandchildren. They knew what they were missing. They may not have ached for it as much as I did, but it drove me crazy knowing that he put so little into the lives of his own grandchildren. Considering everything that he had lost, here were three adorable little kids who wanted more of their grandfather, and he wasn't there for them. It was just bewildering.

One day we were all in the car and the kids were mentioning something about grandparents, that highly sensitive subject for me. Instead of getting emotional, I tried to stay as calm as possible as I told the kids that if Barry's parents and my mother were still alive, they would have been so proud of what great kids they were.

Kimmy was about four years old when she innocently asked whether I reminded my dad that I have kids, because if I did, she was sure that he would visit more often and would also be proud. She went on to suggest that I call him and remind him again about his grandchildren, because she was sure that he didn't remember about them.

Dead silence in the car. Priceless innocence.

There were the rare visits when he arrived by train on a Saturday afternoon and went back on Sunday. We made a big exciting deal about him coming to visit, and the kids and I looked forward to seeing him. Barry's attitude wasn't all that positive about my father. He was polite, and went along with whatever we were doing, but had zero relationship with his father-in-law. While Barry could carry on a conversation with ease with just about anyone, he had given up trying to talk to my father. Aside from the fact that my father was usually zoned out, Barry was sick of every conversation with my father inevitably evolving into something about Sonia.

We always planned a Sunday breakfast which, according to my childhood memories, had been a special time in our house. And the kids were anxious to bring him along to their activities, proudly showing off their talents to their grandfather.

I always hoped that he would enjoy these visits and want to visit more often. See what he was missing. Instead, we usually ended these short reunions with a fight, admittedly initiated by me and always related to either Sonia or his lack of involvement in our lives.

During one of those sad and infuriating arguments, my dad made a surprising comment that stung, hard. He complained that every time he came to visit, we were running around the city, going to watch the kids at an activity. He said that if he was coming to spend time with us, he didn't see why the kids have to go to gymnastics, ballet, or hockey.

The tears began, as usual, and I fired back emotionally, telling him I was stupid enough to have thought he would enjoy watching his grandchildren at their activities. That he would be interested enough that he wanted to watch them. Or did he prefer to sit at my kitchen table, stare into space and drink tea?

Catching the tears with my tongue as they were falling down my cheeks, I further enlightened him about the fact that every time there was an event at one of their schools where parents and grandparents were invited, my kids were the only ones there without any grandparents.

These frustrating melodramatic arguments continued as they had played out so many times. I cried and yelled at him and he looked at me with that same blank look, as if he were fully deaf and unable to read my lips. I told him that he was a fool for failing to see how we all need him to step up and be a grandfather.

"If being a father to me is so impossible, at least be there for my kids."

What I didn't elaborate on as much as I could have, because actually saying the words would have been far too truthful and painful for me, was that no matter where I went with my kids, there were grandparents everywhere. Birthday parties, the waiting room at our paediatrician's office, dropping off and picking up at preschool, grandparents day at school, class performances, restaurants, stores, gymnastics and dance programs, activities, hockey arenas, local swimming pools, kiddie haircut shops.

Beaming, bragging, hugging. Buying ice cream, buying toys, having grandma time at the manicurist. Speaking in loud, proud voices so that everyone would know they were the lucky grandparents.

I saw grandparents everywhere, in the same way that childless couples see pregnant women and young children. With pure envy. An aching desire for my kids to be getting the same unconditional love and attention from grandparents that it seemed as if every other child in our neighbourhood was lucky enough to have. The kind of special relationship that I had with my grandparents.

THE REALITY WAS obvious that the most my father was able to do was to continue with his rare visits, in that trance-like state where he just sat and stared. Inevitably, he would tell me that he felt guilty about leaving Sonia at home. He claimed that she was fine with it, but he didn't feel right. And then I would hear about how she never did anything to hurt me. Why can't I include her in my life?

Even on Father's Day one year, after begging him to come and spend time with us, he arrived late on Saturday and then woke up on Sunday morning only to announce that he was taking an earlier train home to be with Sonia. How could she be alone on Father's Day?

I reminded him that he was my father and that for my sake, the kids, and even Barry, couldn't he please stay the day and go back in the evening. He completely refused. It was like he had strength only when it had something to do with Sonia. Otherwise he was as weak and pathetic as a wet noodle.

There it was, that pull and tug of conflicting emotions. I wanted to feel sorry for him because he was so totally dependent on her. I didn't want him to be alone, but I was angry at him for emotionally abandoning me, for his lack of interest or ability, or backbone, to spend some time as a father and grandfather.

It was clear to me that all these years, he had wanted me to accept her unconditionally, to look the other way despite her manipulative, malicious and passive aggressive behaviour. Maybe on some level, he realized that she would not have been the one to change, and I guess he was counting on me. But I had tried and I just hadn't been able to do it. As a young teenager, I didn't have the maturity or confidence to go head-to-head with Sonia in vying for my dad's attention. Having lost many attempts, and suffering the consequences, I quickly learned that this was not a competition I was able to safely enter.

Politely put, we were like oil and water, and no matter how badly I wanted to improve things between me and my father, I could not find a way to have a relationship with Sonia.

I KNEW THAT Sonia was constantly going to visit her kids and grandchildren, with and without my father. I even told him that he should look at what she does with her family and do a quarter of it with me and my kids. Like walking into a store and picking up a little toy or game for the kids. Something that would show them that he thinks about them once in a while.

Every time we had it out, I realized that I may as well have been speaking a foreign language. He didn't get it. He couldn't or he wouldn't.

I SOMETIMES SLIPPED into that fantasy world of mine where my kids did have grandparents with them for the regular stuff and all the special occasions. And then one day, I had an epiphany. I needed to stop begging, screaming, hoping and praying that my dad would wake up one day and become the father and grandfather I wanted him to be. He obviously could not do it, and I needed to relinquish the hope that he would ever change. I decided that instead, I would go out and find grandparents for my children. Surrogate grandparents. There had to be older couples out there who wanted grandchildren as much as I wanted my kids to have grandparents. I enjoyed my fantasy of time with this make-believe couple who were just waiting to answer our ad. People who would come to our house for dinners or brunch. They would get a kick out of the kids, and would appreciate what great parents Barry and I were. They could join us for holidays, birthdays, anniversaries. I would bring them to grandparent's day at school, ballet performances, hockey games. I so enjoyed my fantasy time with this couple that I could hardly wait for them to join our family.

I told Barry about my idea to advertise for surrogate grandparents in the Canadian Jewish News. He knew me well enough to know that once I had made up my mind about an idea, there was no turning back for me. What did we have to lose? I assured him that I would screen the applicants on the phone, and we would only meet the ones who sounded good. Then we would "interview" them together.

The more we talked about it, the more encouraged we both were to see if this turned out to be a good solution.

In theory, the whole thing could have been great. There are undoubtedly many older couples who would have been ideal surrogate grandparents, but instead, the people who responded to our ad were lonely, needy individuals, looking to meet their own personal needs, with little to give to three kids.

Rather than the fantasy grandparents I had imagined, most of the applicants were estranged from their own children, defending themselves as the victims of their ungrateful, selfish, money hungry offspring. Bitter, angry, miserable. One woman reassured me, after a long winded and terrible rampage about her own kids, that she would be a perfect grandmother to our kids. However, her disturbing tone of voice and definite fury had me picturing her with a hatchet in one hand, which reinforced my decision to end that conversation quickly. If I wanted my kids to have an evil witch as their grandmother, I didn't have to advertise. I would have just pursued Sonia.

Some were curious enough to call, but apparently suspicious about our motives. One woman said she had seen the ad and was offering us the opportunity to come and pick up several boxes of old toys *in great condition* that she had in her garage.

We invited one couple to our home, Doris and Morty. Doris sounded so "normal" on the phone.

Doris walked in first, Morty schlepping along behind her. She removed her shoes and bent over to line them up with the grout lines on the tiles.

"Morty, take off your shoes." She scowled and then looked at me, rolling her eyes. "Such an idiot."

Every time Morty said something, Doris would cut him off. He could barely finish a sentence. "He doesn't know what he's talking about."

Doris sat on the living room couch with her purse right by her side. She even brought her purse to the washroom.

JONATHAN WAS TAPPING a dinky toy on the side of the couch. Rebecca grabbed the toy car away from him. He grabbed it back.

"Why are your kids fighting?"

I was dying to respond with "because they are so bored. And probably scared of you. And surprised by your behaviour."

But instead, I just said that I had no idea. Barry and I exchanged looks and we silently agreed that this lovely visit had to come to an end, quickly.

WE MET WITH one man who was very persistent and seemed so sweet on the phone, I thought he was worth meeting. His wife had been ill for a few years and had recently been placed in a chronic care hospital. Their two sons lived out of town, rarely visiting Toronto.

We arranged to go out for brunch, so we could meet him and see how he was with the kids. That was the number one priority for us. But from the minute we picked him up, all he did was talk about himself and his life, barely even looking at the kids. He stuffed his pockets with all of the pink packets of Sweet'n'Low on the table and, as we walked away from the table, he lingered long enough to pick up one of the five dollar bills that we'd left as a tip. That was one long brunch.

We dropped him off and the minute he closed the car door, the five of us laughed hysterically at how ridiculous the whole outing had been. In fact, the kids pointed out that every time they tried to talk to him, he cut them off with yet one more story about himself. The consensus was that his own kids probably moved to get away from him because he bored them to death with his stories. We certainly weren't going to see him again.

The kids let me know how they felt.

"Please Mommy, this surrogate grandparents plan is probably not one of your better ideas."

They were absolutely right. Instead of feeling sorry for all of us, I needed to listen to my kids and realize that we may not have had the grandparents I had growing up, but we had each other and that was more than a lot of people have.

CHAPTER 9

D ESPITE MY TRAINING as a social worker, and the many saychology courses I had taken both in my grandmother's house and at university, I wasn't at all prepared to turn forty. The memories of the big birthday bash for my dad's fortieth came to life in painful detail. He had never again celebrated another milestone birthday that way, and he had certainly never been the same dad.

Since my mother had died just months before turning forty, my fortieth birthday meant surpassing the age she was at the time of her death. How could I feel good about moving beyond forty when my mother was robbed of her life before reaching this milestone? All I could think about was that she never even made it to forty.

I was plagued with guilt, anguish and heartache. And since my birthday was right around the same time as Mother's Day, I felt even worse. It was hard to feel good about life, to feel gratitude and appreciation for everything when guilt assaults you with an arsenal of negativity.

That's when you have to hope that something—or someone—smacks you in the face as if to remind you to look at the good, the half full glass, the beauty not the flaws, the scrapbook pictures and not the lumps of glue.

Barry took me to a movie I was eager to see in the late afternoon. When we returned home, we walked into a house packed with friends and relatives. There were balloons everywhere, mostly purple ones since those were my favourite. Well, actually purple was my mother's favourite colour, which was why she loved purple lilacs, so I made purple my favourite colour too.

I was shocked and speechless.

And then I got busy hugging and crying and laughing. Shelley and Jon and their spouses had come in from Montreal, as had Barbara and her husband. Our friendships had remained strong through the years, and we all did our best to stay connected. Of course Donna and Lorne were there.

The kids just beamed the entire evening. They had completely planned and organized the party, from the lavish catering to the birthday cake with a giant candle in the middle. They said that they couldn't possibly fit so many candles onto the cake, so the giant one represented all forty plus the one for good luck. They claimed little help from Barry, except for use of his credit card.

Rebecca was right around the same age as I was when my own mother died. Her party planning skills were highly developed for a kid and, throughout the party, she made sure that everyone was in high spirits. It was remarkable seeing her in her element, so grown up and happy.

Thinking back to my teenage years and remembering how desperately I wanted to be normal and do all of the things that my friends were doing, I was always acutely aware that I wasn't a normal teenager. I had the responsibilities, worries, fears, issues, and will to survive that normal teenage girls just don't have to deal with.

In order to dull the pain and distress I felt at my house, I left whenever possible. When I lost my mother, I was still young enough that I had not yet entered that challenging teenage stage of rebelling. Our relationship hadn't yet turned into a typical mother and teenage daughter relationship, loaded with roller coaster emotions and conflict, while remaining sheltered by that unconditional love that only a mother can provide. When my mother died, I lost this perfect woman to whom I was still tightly bound. I had still enjoyed spending time with her, telling her everything and looking up to her. She was truly my best friend, my confidant, my mentor.

That's how things had been with me and Rebecca, until recently. Suddenly, I was no longer her perfect mother. And mothering a teenager destabilized my world. I did not know how to deal with a daughter struggling to become independent, to separate from me, especially one who questioned my abilities, my competence, and her need for me in her life. I still yearned for my mother, yet wanted to be a perfect mother to my teenager who was rejecting me. I was totally unable to cope with this stormy time.

Fortunately, there was an abundance of information at the library and book store, where I soaked up everything I could on the rocky stage of mother and teenage daughter rebellion. And as soon as I felt satisfied that Rebecca was doing all of the normal things that every teenager does as they move through the normal stages of growing up, I calmed down.

But that night, I saw that beneath the teenage sullenness and struggle to grow up was a young woman who truly loved me, just as I loved her.

As for my other kids, there was always a kindness and sweetness about Jonathan that was obvious to everyone who met him. I watched as he talked to the adults with his perpetual smile and effortless ability to carry on a conversation. Of course Kimmy was being Kimmy, the entertainer, the actress, the comedian, working the room with ease and enthusiasm.

When Barry wasn't schmoozing, he was by my side, telling me how happy he was that we had so many people celebrating with us. I was surrounded by friends and relatives, and aware of the indisputable fact that I had the most amazing husband and incredible kids. How could I even think about letting the guilt and sorrow intrude on what was such a wonderful evening? Such a wonderful life.

We have choices. We always have choices. I chose to feel gratitude, happiness and pride.

CHAPTER 10

Uncle Len never dropped the ball in his continuous devotion to his sister's two kids, Mitchell and Barry. He spoke to our family as well as Mitchell on a regular basis, and there was never a long stretch of time where we didn't see one another. In our eyes, and quite certainly in Mitchell's, Uncle Len was the most incredible man: thoughtful, considerate and sincere.

The kids were excited to be going to New York and New Jersey for an Alpert family get together. Uncle Len had arranged for Mitchell to fly to New York, landing at approximately the same time as our flight from Toronto. Since Barry knew the La Guardia airport well, he gave Mitchell simple instructions about what to do and where to go when he got off the plane.

Our flight was delayed, arriving about an hour after Mitchell's flight, and when we couldn't find him in the designated spot, we searched the airport. It took a while and we were becoming frustrated and annoyed that he wasn't where we had asked him to be, but when we located him we could not stay upset. He was elated to see us, and the kids were so happy to have finally found him.

Dressed in his army clothing and carrying an army green bag stuffed with his clothes and God knows what else, Mitchell was pissed drunk. He said that he was waiting for us in a bar and, while waiting, he had a few beers.

Within no time, Mitchell had us all roaring with laughter. He was so drunk and happy about being drunk that he lay down on the floor in the middle of La Guardia airport, laughing and rolling around. Our kids were beyond hysterical. I was laughing so hard, mostly at their reaction and at the fact that this was all happening in a busy airport, that the tears were streaming down my face. And when I looked at Barry and saw that he was no longer amused and, in fact, looked rather disgusted, I elbowed him and told him to lighten up. The kids were enjoying themselves and Mitchell was getting some desperately needed attention.

In order to get our rental car, the six of us had to pile into an elevator that was already half full. Mitchell was the last to walk in and, fascinated by the sensor that would prevent the door from closing, he continually put his hand in front of it every time the door started to close. Of course, this got the kids laughing again, so Mitchell continued to do it. With an elevator full of strangers, and the kids howling with laughter, the game went on way longer than Barry's patience. He finally pulled Mitchell closer to him and firmly told him to let the doors close. He was not amused. The kids and I quickly stopped laughing, the elevator closed, and we all stood silently, choking back our giggles.

Mitchell was on a roll that weekend. Having discovered that his silliness was highly entertaining, he tested his audience throughout the weekend. Some of it was funny, and some was overdone and just obnoxious. The winning performance was on Sunday morning. Mitchell's hotel room was down the hall from ours, and we had arranged for all of us to meet in the hotel coffee shop for breakfast. The hotel, which was all on one level, had a long hallway with the coffee shop and lobby area at one end, and at the other, all of the rooms. We were already in the coffee shop when Mitchell came running out of his room in his boxers, laughing and announcing that his toilet was overflowing. The kids instantly doubled over. We ran to his room to find the carpets completely soaked and the toilet overflowing.

By the end of that weekend, my stomach was actually sore from all the laughing. And knowing that Uncle Mitchell had enjoyed himself for an entire weekend was amazing.

KIMMY COULDN'T WAIT to spend time with her uncle again and insisted that he come to Toronto for her upcoming birthday party. From her perspective, Uncle Mitchell was just perfect. He was funny, he played with her, and he was willing to do anything Kimmy wanted. A big grown up kid who she truly adored.

The grand finale and highlight of her birthday party was painting her Uncle Mitchell. Having stripped him down to his boxers, he was completely covered in paint, laughing and enjoying the experience as much as all of the kids. The kids at the party all agreed that Kimmy's uncle was just fantastic.

But no matter how many weekends we spent with Mitchell, he was still the same guy who resented Barry, yearned for a normal life, and went home to an empty room which was generously called an apartment. He didn't want to live in the shadow of our life, and yet nothing in his own life was very positive. A heart of gold, and a desperate need for attention and recognition, Mitchell has always had the saddest life of anyone we know.

CHAPTER 11

O F COURSE IT had to happen on my parent's anniversary, in the year 1997, and on Highway 7, since the number seven seemed to have continued to be a significant number in my life. Not always bad, just significant.

My father may have forgotten about his November 13th anniversary, or maybe he hadn't, but every year I acknowledged it in some way. In 1997, I acknowledged it by having a life-threatening car accident on what would have been their forty-second wedding anniversary.

I was driving my Toyota Previa van, enjoying the unusually beautiful Fall day when a red car driving in the opposite direction turned left without even looking. I barrelled into the passenger side of his car, and then spun around barely missing a hydro pole.

Having never taken any illegal drugs, I can only imagine that the high I felt during the seconds that followed were as euphoric as any drug-induced high. My van was totalled, I had whiplash and broken ribs, and yet I was completely enveloped by an inexplicable feeling of peace and happiness. Totally bizarre and surreal yet that was my experience. I have no idea how long it lasted, maybe three minutes, maybe sixteen seconds, but it was only when I heard the sirens that I snapped out of it.

I had never lost consciousness, but as I later told Barry, my kids, and anyone else with whom I was close, my mother was in that car with me. Without any doubt. I felt her presence so strongly and, based on the irreparable damage to my van and the fact that the fire department and paramedics all claimed that it was an absolute miracle that I wasn't killed, I knew she really had been there.

THAT WAS IT. Enough of this. Life is short and unpredictable. I didn't want to, nor could I possibly find enough worrying time in each day, to drum up every possible disaster that could potentially strike us. I made four major decisions.

First of all, I decided that it was time to stop worrying about flying without the kids. It bothered me that Barry was going on these deluxe business trips alone, when everyone else was there with a spouse. If I could be in a serious car accident practically around the corner from my house, on a clear, sunny day, totally out of the blue, then it must have happened for a reason. There had to be a lesson in all of this. A message.

Before the pain from my broken ribs had fully subsided, I announced my decision. From now on, as long as we could find someone trustworthy to watch the kids, I would join him on his trips.

I was taking the plunge, but not all the way. I had one condition. I knew I would always be terrified of flying, but I had my Valium so if I made the decision to fly, I would find a way to manage. My stipulation was that I would not fly on the same airplane as Barry. We would have to fly separately. That was the only way I could actually follow through on this.

Barry was so happy. We would now have a whole new experience of travelling together. Exploring. Enjoying.

THE SECOND MAJOR decision was that I was now "the second wife." I had heard over and over, from the emergency crew at the site of my accident, to the insurance adjusters who saw the state of my van, that it was nothing short of a miracle that I hadn't been killed. When Barry went to the compound, where they had towed the ruined van, to get all of my personal items, he came back really shook up. He couldn't believe that I was relatively fine considering the extent of the damages.

Having been well taught by Sonia, I knew only too well that the second wife has a spending attitude and privileges that first wives just don't possess.

I notified Barry, half joking and half serious, that since I had apparently come so close to being killed and then subsequently replaced with a "second wife" I would take full advantage of the second wife privileges. Within reason, of course. But if I really wanted something I would buy it. No different than my mother, I had spent cautiously and often regretted walking away from something that I really wanted. We were both doing well, so why not enjoy it?

I was so excited about my new status as second wife that, as I told many of my friends about my new attitude, I realized that many women out there wanted to be treated like the second wife. It should not take a near death experience for them to gain that improved status.

GETTING RID OF things was always difficult for me and a source of debate in our marriage. Barry is practical, neat and tidy. He likes everything put away, and he doesn't need trinkets. He calls it all "clutter."

He draws from his childhood to decide what is important and necessary, and I draw from mine. I love my extensive bird house collection, the pictures all over our shelves and walls, statues, vases, bowls, wind chimes, plants, flower pots. I call it organized and decorative.

I keep everything. I have every term paper I ever wrote in both undergraduate and graduate school, every book I ever bought, clothing and shoes from twenty years ago. My attitude is that we never know when we may need something again and, as long as we have enough space to store it all, why not keep it?

Undoubtedly, having lost so much as a child, abundance gives me comfort and security. While I may not easily get rid of old clothes or items, I did reach a point where I was prepared to get rid of the negative and miserable people rotting in my life. Those people who blame, criticise, find fault, complain, waste energy and time, essentially sucking the life out of others. They are dark, toxic and remarkably contagious. As the saying goes, misery loves company.

I knew from experience that spending time with the right people is probably one of the most important things you can do to get through difficult times. I would even go so far as to say that by spending time with positive, upbeat, good people, you could actually dodge some of the negative things along the way.

I looked at my hoarding habits, my life and my friendships differently after the car accident, and made my third decision letting go of the relationships that really didn't feel good any more. And I vowed to stay clear of anyone who was miserable, bitter and angry. They didn't deserve the time or attention.

My fourth and final decision was to put an end to the ongoing dread and worry about the number seven. I was finished with allowing myself so much worry about that number. I had wasted so much personal energy anticipating "seven" milestones. I actually lost sleep worrying about the kids turning seven months old, seven years old, grade seven, visiting houses with a seven address.

It was irrelevant that my mother and sisters had been sitting in row seven, since everyone on board, in every row, had died.

But I didn't die. Perhaps that Sunday, the seventh day of the week, in that seventh month of the year, in the year 1970, had saved my life. And now my life had been spared again, miraculously, on Highway 7. In 1997.

CHAPTER 12

D URING THE SUMMER of 1999, my father called to tell me that he had pancreatic cancer. He said it without emotion, in a flat tone of voice, as if he were talking about the weather. He said there were some experimental treatments for him to try, but the doctor was not optimistic.

Feeling defeated once again by something completely out of his control, he seemingly succumbed to the prognosis. He had no will to fight. To continue. I hadn't thought it was possible for him to plummet to any place lower. Apparently I was wrong.

I made a couple of trips to Montreal to see my dad. Whatever tiny bit of life he had left seemed to have been sucked out. His needle was below empty. He was running solely on fumes. He looked terrible, so thin, he could hardly walk, and he said absolutely nothing. That all too familiar vacant look.

During one of my visits, he was weak but still well enough to go out, so we went for lunch at a restaurant of his choice. *Eggspectation.* I thought it was no coincidence that he had chosen this restaurant for our time together. For so many years, we had both let each other down, having held mutual feelings of disappointment and expectations of each other that had never been fulfilled. While the name was a reminder of the endless let-downs, I searched to find some comfort in it. What I found was recognition and acknowledgment of the way things had been between us. I had constantly expected my father to be more than he could be. Even the basic expectations were not met. That was just the way things were with us.

HE WAS DYING. I desperately wanted to say and do the right thing. I brought photo albums of my kids. I hoped that looking back, together, we could connect again, and somehow make amends for the many years of disappointment, hurt and anger. I flipped through the pages and described some of the pictures. He just stared at them. No reaction. No comments. No smiles. No tears. Nothing.

Towards the end, I called him on the phone in his hospital room every day and struggled to find some words that would make us both feel better. I told him that I loved him and that I was so sorry to have let him down. I told him that I knew he loved me too.

My sweet, devoted Auntie Riva rarely left my dad's side. They had not only reconciled their differences, they had actually connected on a whole different level. My aunt took care of him with tenderness and love, soothing him with her words and constant presence. She was as devoted to my dad as she had been to her own husband when he was dying.

Every time I called she was there, assuring me that she would not leave him alone. She said he was like a kid brother to her and she would stay with him right up until the end.

From the time of my father's diagnosis, Auntie Riva had complained to me about her disgust in Sonia's behaviour. For whatever reason, Sonia was not around much. And as sick as my father was, Sonia had apparently insisted that he shower and shave downstairs in the condo pool's shower area, in order to keep her bathroom clean. Nothing had changed. For Sonia, it was always about appearances.

THE LAST TIME I spoke to my dad, Auntie Riva held the phone to his ear and I asked him how he felt. I knew it was a stupid question, but I didn't know what else to say. He was in the hospital, dying, and drugged on pain killers, so I wasn't about to give him an update on Jonathan's hockey or the girl's activities. He said he was fine.

The silence was awkward. I thought back to when silence with my dad was peaceful. When I felt safe and loved. In the rowboat anchored in the middle of the lake. Waiting patiently for a fish to bite.

I told him again that I loved him. I told him I was coming to Montreal the next day and would see him then. He said a few words that I couldn't understand. And when I asked him to repeat what he had said, he told me, as clear as a bell, "I'm doing the best that I can."

Somehow he had found the strength to tell me that he had always done the best that he could. Words that meant more to me than he probably ever realized. And words I will never forget.

Deep down, I always knew that he was doing his best. He was so shattered, so wounded by the trauma and torture he had endured, that he was never able to pick himself up off the ground.

My dad didn't have a mean bone in his body. I knew that in different circumstances, and probably with a compassionate second wife, he would have been the best grandfather to my kids. He had such a sweet disposition, he was never in a rush, he was flexible and easy going. But instead, he was dead inside, manipulated by a totally self-absorbed woman, and my kids never had the grandfather they would have had. We were all robbed.

MY COUSIN MARK picked me up at the airport. When I got into his car and looked at his face, I already knew. I was too late.

He had died that October 15th morning, in my Auntie Riva's arms, a sad, heart-broken man.

Mark and I went to his mother's house. I waited there for Barry and the kids, who were on their way to Montreal by car. We called the funeral home and were told that Sonia had made arrangements for a graveside funeral for Monday afternoon. Shocking news for all of us, since my father had been so good about going to funerals for anyone he had ever known who had passed away. We felt he was being cheated out of the tradition of having a service in his honour and memory at the funeral home, followed by the burial at the cemetery. Mark called Sonia and tried to convince her to do both, but she refused. I watched and listened as Mark spoke to her. I saw that sombre head shaking so I knew that she was not going to budge. She told Mark that all of the arrangements were made and would not be changed.

Barry and the kids arrived and we all had Friday night dinner together at Auntie Riva's house. A quiet, sad dinner. My aunt told us all that she felt satisfied about having been there with my dad, cradling him in her arms as he took his last breath of air. I felt relieved. He was no longer suffering. He had endured more than enough pain in his lifetime and I knew he was now at peace. And I also knew that he was with my mother and sisters. They were waiting for him. I just knew it.

THE OBITUARY WAS in the Sunday morning paper, the information having been submitted by Sonia. My name was misspelled "Linda," and there was no mention of my mother, my sisters, my father's late sister Bella or her late husband Sol. Sonia had listed all of her children and grandchildren by name.

THE GAZETTE, MONTREAL, SUNDAY, OCTOBER 17, 1999

OBITUARIES & MEMORIALS

DEATHS

WEINBERG, Saul. On Friday, October 15, 1999. Beloved husband of Sonia. Loving father and father-in-law of Linda and Barry Fishman. Cherished grandfather of Rebecca, Jonathan and Kimberly. Step-father and father-in-law of Dr. Harry and Gloria Lifschutz, Esther and Jacob Cepelinski. Step-grandfather of Morris, Joe, and Max Lifschutz and Ariella, Marissa and Nathan Cepelinski. Brother and brother-in-law of Rose and the late Lionel Williams, Riva and the late David Weinberg. He will be sadly missed by his many nieces and nephews. Special thanks to Dr. Adrien Langleiben for his care, kindness and devotion. Graveside service on Monday, October 18, 1999 at 1 p.m. Burial at the Eternal Gardens Cemetery, Beth Zion Congregation Section, Beaconsfield. Shiva at 5950 Cavendish, #1208, Cote St. Luc. Donations can be made in his memory to the Royal Victoria Hospital Foundation. Funeral arrangements entrusted to Paperman and Sons.

THE GAZETTE, MONTREAL, MONDAY, OCTOBER 18, 1999

OBITUARIES & MEMORIALS

WEINBERG, Saul. On Friday, October 15, 1999. Beloved husband of Sonia and the late Rita. Loving father and father-in-law of Lynda and Barry Fishman, the late Carla and the late Wendy. Cherished grandfather of Rebecca, Jonathan and Kimberly. Step-father and father-in-law of Dr. Harry and Gloria Lifschutz, Esther and Jacob Cepelinski. Step-grandfather of Morris, Joe, and Max Lifschutz and Ariella, Marissa and Nathan Cepelinski. Brother and brother-in-law of Rose and the late Lionel Williams, Riva and the late David Weinberg, the late Bella and the late Sol Epstein. He will be sadly missed by his many nieces and nephews. Special thanks to Dr. Adrien Langleiben for his care, kindness and devotion. Graveside service on Monday, October 18, 1999 at 1 p.m. Burial at the Eternal Gardens Cemetery, Beth Zion Congregation Section, Beaconsfield. Shiva at 5950 Cavendish, #1208, Cote St. Luc. Donations can be made in his memory to the Royal Victoria Hospital Foundation. Funeral arrangements entrusted to Paperman and Sons.

I was stunned and furious. Barry and I headed directly to the funeral home and met with the director who happened to have known my father well. We asked about upgrading the funeral to include a service at the funeral home, and we let him know that we would pay whatever costs were involved. We also showed him the page in the newspaper with the incomplete obituary notice. We made it clear that if Sonia refused to place another obituary notice with the complete and accurate information about my father, in the next day's paper, we would take out an ad on the front page that would describe my dad in an appropriate and respectful manner. We didn't care how much that would cost.

We sat across from him in his office as he called Sonia. He calmly explained the reason for his call and within seconds we could hear her voice blasting through the phone, as she screamed at him. He actually had to hold the phone away from his ear. She was adamant about a graveside funeral, and would not agree to rerun the obituary with the appropriate corrections. The discussion continued until she heard about our plans to take out a front page ad. Then she finally agreed to the latter request. After all, she was reminded by the funeral director that Shloime, or as she called him, Saul, was the "beloved husband of Sonia AND the late Rita." He was a "loving father and father-in-law of Lynda, spelled with a 'y' and Barry Fishman, and the late Carla and the late Wendy."

The next morning, the obituary was correct.

WE STAYED IN a two-room hotel suite which was perfect for the five of us. Aside from being much easier than adjoining rooms with three kids, it was a sad time of my life and I wanted my husband and kids close by. Early in the morning on the day of the funeral, I awoke abruptly to the television set turning on and then off. I bolted up in bed. Who had turned on the television? The room was dark. No one was awake. And then I felt this unusual whoosh sensation. Like a big breath of air had been forcibly sucked out of my body. An extremely powerful moment, cathartic, like a weight lifted, a cleansing, an unbelievable feeling.

From that moment on, I have not felt one bit of anger, disappointment or hurt about my father. Only a sense of peace and harmony. Freedom from that heavy burden of negative emotions that I lugged around for so many years. As crazy as it sounds, I felt it all leave my body. On the morning of my daddy's funeral.

There is no logical, verifiable explanation, but I have no doubt that it happened, and I have my own spiritual theories. The part that makes me feel good is knowing and believing that my father is where he belongs. Where he is happy again. In a good place, with his wife and two little daughters.

As soon as they woke up, Barry and the kids noticed a change in me. They said I seemed relaxed. So calm. I explained that I was no longer upset with my dad, with their Zaida, and that I felt better knowing he was in a good place.

We went to the cemetery. It was a cold, miserable day, and I was overwhelmed with gratitude by the number of my relatives and friends who came. There was a big pile of dirt with the shovel stuck in the middle like a candle in a cake.

There were some rumblings amongst my relatives about this being a low budget funeral. They were disappointed that the service was graveside, and that the coffin looked cheap. It was a far cry from when he was crowned King at his fortieth birthday, but I was grateful that he was buried in a coffin instead of a plain plywood box. I guess my relatives had forgotten about that.

Barry, the kids and I stood close by the big hole as the Rabbi spoke and prayers were said. I didn't look for Sonia. I didn't look for her children. I felt the tremendous support and love from the people who were there for me. And there for my dad. Despite the horrible weather, many people came to pay their respects to this sweet, kind man whose life had actually been taken from him so many years earlier.

This time I took a turn shovelling some dirt onto the coffin at the bottom of that big, deep hole. I did it because I knew it would have meant something to my dad. He went to so many funerals, he obviously felt some sort of comfort by going. I wanted to find some comfort at his funeral. His official funeral, when his profound sadness could finally be declared over.

And then we left.

As far as I knew, Sonia was sitting Shiva in her own apartment. I planned on sitting Shiva at my own home in Toronto.

Ironically, Sonia and my father had lived in the same apartment building as my Aunt Nicky and Uncle Issie. My aunt and uncle offered to have the first day of Shiva at their apartment. Then Barry, the kids and I would return to Toronto and resume the week of Shiva at our house.

The whole funeral and Shiva situation was unusual, but it was what it was. There were some people who were at the funeral and never said a word to me. There were others who did not speak to Sonia. And there were some who paid their respects to both "teams."

Straight from the cemetery, Sonia's relatives and friends went up the elevator to her apartment, and mine went up to my Aunt and Uncle's apartment. Off we went, each to our own separate Shiva houses, our separate worlds, with no reason to ever have any further connection. No more hurt or discomfort. It was finally over.

THE REMAINING WEEK of Shiva in Toronto was exactly what I wanted it to be. While Barry and I are not religious at all, we did everything we could do to follow the Jewish customs of Shiva. That's the way my dad would have wanted us to do it. Mirrors covered, special candle burning, a low uncomfortable chair for me, daily prayers. Meals were sent in and our house was packed every day with friends and relatives.

I didn't have to lock myself in the bathroom, there was no blood curdling wailing coming from the backyard, and no one did that horrible, sombre head shaking. Everyone knew only too well that this Shiva was different. I lost my dad when I was a child, and had lived a lifetime watching this wounded man drag himself through each day of a profoundly heartbreaking life.

I was grateful to have so many people around for the week, and I did scrub my kitchen sink with Ajax and make sure that the kitchen was spotless before I went to bed every night. Some habits just can't be broken.

CHAPTER 13

I COULDN'T POSSIBLY join Barry on all of his business trips, especially because
he was flying to New York almost every week. He had left Eli Lilly
after seventeen years of invaluable experience, to become the CEO of the
Canadian operations of a small specialty pharmaceutical company. He was
scheduled to fly to New York on September 11th, 2001. He called me from
the airport to tell me his flight was cancelled. I knew. I was watching the
news, horrified, actually unable to function.

July 5, 1970. The day my world changed.

September 11, 2001. The day the world changed.

I wasn't prepared for the panic and anxiety that was stirred up in me as
I watched the continual replay by the media of the plane crashes. Hearing
those all too familiar words—disaster, identifying bodies, devastation—set
off a whole chain of events.

I was a mess for weeks.

I pulled out the box of newspaper clippings and legal documents that
were down in my basement. I couldn't help myself. I had to read through
all of it. I wanted answers. I needed answers. What I got was legalese: "Pilot
error...Gross negligence...Failure to adequately inspect and maintain the
said aircraft...Failure to properly and adequately train its pilots and crews
as to the safe methods of using the ground spoiler mechanism of said
aircraft during a landing approach..."

An airline's mistake. A pilot's mistake. One man's mistake changed my
whole life. My dad's life. My grandparents. My relatives. And most of all,
robbed my mother and sisters of their lives.

I could identify with the families of 9-11 victims and I felt compelled
to join them in their misery. I understood what they were feeling. I was
drawn to them. I watched them on the news as they clung to each other.
I never had a group of strangers, other families to cling to, who had also
lost people in a plane crash. There hadn't been any support groups for the
families of our plane crash. I realized then that my dad and I had suffered
alone, rather than having any opportunity to share our sorrow with others
who understood. Somehow suffering en masse seemed to be something
I now wished could have happened for us. I had always felt so alone as a
victim left to deal with everything on our own.

Dear Diary,

It's been a few days since September 11th, a day of devastating news for the entire world. As traumatizing as the reports have been for me to watch, I just can't seem to peel myself away from the television. Aside from everything that is so horrible, the part that is ripping my heart out is watching the ongoing news reports about the devastated family members of the victims. The interviews. Wondering if they will ever identify the bodies. Their stories. The sobbing. The hysterics. The head shaking.

Every time I think that I am fine, that time has healed the wounds, that I have moved forward and am continuing to look ahead, something happens to suck me back in. I thought it was buried. It never is. Oh, those poor families...

What really gets me is that the media keeps talking about how devastating 9-11 has been for the airline industry. Oh, poor them. Asking for financial aid from the government, that no other industry would even contemplate asking for. I read and listen with disbelief how they use language such as "bail out" "deserve" or "special circumstances" in their plea for assistance.

HELLO, airline industry, Air Canada. Remember me, and my family? Remember the family members of the other 106 victims on flight 621? Where have you been all these years as we have all struggled to pull ourselves out of the dark, terrifying tunnels that swallowed us up on July 5, 1970? Haven't we deserved any special treatment for our "special circumstances"? Some perks. A bail out? Wasn't our status special enough to warrant a little compassion, upgrades, waiving of cancellation fees when my grandmother dies and I want to stay and help my grandfather settle into his life alone? It's unbelievable to me that I have to take my "happy pills" for an artificial feel good when it would have been so easy for the Air Canada employees to help with some genuine warmth and compassion. How hard would it be for them to dole out some authentic feel-good words? I bet that the people who clean the toilets on the planes are entitled to way more "special treatment" than we were ever given.

CHAPTER 14

DURING THE SUMMER of 2004 I was shocked and devastated to read several articles in major Toronto newspapers, stating that the remains of the victims of the 1970 disaster were still visible at the crash site. Apparently there were bones that continued to surface in the field where the plane crash occurred, despite the original clean-up. How incredibly ironic. That was exactly the way the tragedy played itself out in my life. No matter how many years went by and how much therapy I had, the memories, nightmares, fears and worry continued to surface. Startling flashbacks. Lifelong hauntings. Once again, I was drowning in a flood of memories and hysteria. An arm, a leg, a finger…

I hoped Air Canada would take some responsibility for cleaning up the field in a sincere and courteous way. My immediate reaction was to do what I could to determine, through my DNA, whether any of the bones in that field could be identified as either my mother or sisters, and to bury those bones with the respect and dignity they deserved, according to my religious customs.

After two days of complete emotional turmoil and frantic phone calls to the Deputy Chief Coroner for Ontario, Dr. Cairns told me that there were bones found on the site, but ninety nine percent were animal bones. Though there were some human bones, they were smaller than a piece from a jigsaw puzzle and impossible to identify.

On the one hand, I felt better knowing that the papers had exaggerated and sensationalized the story. But it didn't calm me down to know that only one percent were human bones. If there were any human bones buried there, then it was a grave. Period.

In my mind, that field needed to be declared a cemetery with a proper memorial garden and monument in tribute to the 109 people who died, and whose partial remains would forever be buried there.

CHAPTER 15

M Y FRIEND JOANNE'S husband had recently committed suicide. He had been diagnosed with a medical condition that progressed quickly, debilitating him along the way. He ended his life at home, leaving the family car running with the garage door closed, with the family dog by his side.

Joanne and I had consistently tried to find time in each of our busy work schedules to meet for lunch at least once every few months. I was pretty taken aback when I walked into the dimly lit restaurant for our long overdue lunch date. Every table was occupied by well dressed patrons rushing through their lunches, young servers racing through the narrow paths with plates of food, and there was Joanne sitting alone at a small table for two, bawling her eyes out.

She told me she didn't want to cancel, and apologized for being so emotional. She had just come from seeing a medium, a woman who spoke to spirits on the other side. She was so moved by the experience, so amazed at what this woman told her, that she was completely out of control. The part that freaked her out was the fact that there was no way the medium could have known any of the things she told Joanne, unless she had heard it directly from Joanne's late husband.

The medium had taped the entire session, but Joanne remembered most of what was said and reiterated some of the messages.

I was in awe. We both picked at our salads, neither of us too interested in food.

I have always believed in life after death, angels, signs, messages, all of this spirituality. I always felt, or needed to believe, that my family was with me, but I never knew of anyone who had gone to a medium and actually communicated with their relatives or friends on the other side.

Joanne said that the medium Sandy had a long waiting list, probably about a year, and that I could always put my name on the list and then decide if I want to go. *Decide if I want to go?* There was no doubt in my mind. I couldn't wait to get home and tell Barry all about it.

I CASUALLY BROUGHT the subject up after dinner, while we were clearing the dishes and loading them into the dishwasher.

"I met Joanne for lunch today. She had been to a medium and got messages from her late husband."

Barry stopped clearing the table and looked at me.

"Do you think this woman is authentic?"

"She told Joanne some things that no one could ever have known," I said, my back to Barry as I scraped leftovers into a Tupperware container, trying desperately to appear very nonchalant. "Secret names they used to call each other. Personal things about their kids that no one else knew…"

I turned around and caught Barry, his hand frozen mid-air, holding a dirty dinner plate, as he stared into space.

"Barry?"

"Hmm?"

He shook his head slightly as if woken from a trance, handing me the plate.

"I've heard of mediums."

I was shocked.

"You have?" I put the plate in the dishwasher and straightened up, excited. "Well, Joanne insists that this woman really does have extraordinary powers."

"I don't know. I doubt that they are really able to communicate with the dead," he said, walking over to the fridge to put the ketchup away.

"Oh." I put soap into the dishwasher and turned it on.

"But I kind of find the whole idea interesting."

"Really?" I leaned back against the counter. "Interested enough to put our names on her waiting list and go see for ourselves?"

"Sure," he said, walking over and giving me a kiss on the cheek.

I WAS SO surprised that Barry was open to the experience and had agreed to put our names on the list. I hadn't been sure what kind of reaction I would get from him but, as usual, he was positive and supportive.

I called and left my first name and cell number on her answering machine. No other information.

PART SIX:

Presence

CHAPTER 1

W^{HEN} S^{ANDY CALLED} my cell phone to book the appointment, almost a
year after I had put my first name only on her waiting list, I could
hardly contain my emotions. I felt excited, nervous, uncertain, thrilled and
scared, all at the same time. She told me that I was not to tell her anything
about who I was, who was coming with me for the reading, or who we
wanted to connect with on the other side.

The appointment was set for one week away. While Barry and I weren't
sure what to expect, we were skeptical, but wanted to be as open-minded
as possible. If there was a chance of this being authentic, the thought of
any contact with our families was beyond our greatest hopes.

Our family talked a lot about our visit as we waited. I could hardly
sleep the night before and, throughout the morning I didn't know what to
do with myself.

The kids were all at school and, in the quiet house, I studied my
reflection in the bathroom mirror. Pretty good for someone close to fifty. I
hardly had any wrinkles, my green eyes looked bright, and my once light
brown and blond curly hair was dark brown and blow-dried straight. I
chuckled to myself as I thought about whether or not my family would recognize me. And then I became serious and spoke quietly to myself, to my
family, to Barry's family, about this upcoming event. I told them that we
really needed them to communicate with us. I told them that deep down, I
knew that they had stayed close by, and I liked believing that, but I needed
some proof. *Please, somehow, let us know that you have been and are still with
us in some way.*

Barry went to work but was back home by lunch. He didn't know what
to do with himself, knowing that we had to leave soon, and particularly in
light of where we were going. We finally agreed that we should just get in
the car and go. As we drove we were both unusually quiet. Solemn. Deep
in our own thoughts.

Once on the highway, we talked about what we hoped to get out of
this meeting. Barry said that he wanted to know for sure how his mother
had died. Apparently there had been rumblings through the years about
the cause of her death possibly being suicide, and that bothered him. He
had never talked to me about that before. He needed to know for sure.

I wanted to know if his mother was happy that I wore her diamond engagement ring. About a year earlier, Barry and I had agreed that leaving his mother's ring in the safety deposit box was ridiculous. It had obviously meant a lot to her and I wanted to wear it, in her honour, in her memory. I already had my own engagement ring, so I took hers to a jeweler and had it made into a more modern looking ring that I wore on my other ring finger.

I also wanted to know for sure that my dad was with my mother and sisters. Knowing that was very important to me.

What were we doing? This whole thing was crazy. How could someone talk to dead people? I turned to Barry in the car and told him that we had obviously lost our minds. Why didn't we just buy a Ouija board and do this in our living room?

But at some level, I actually felt like this might be for real. Keep an open mind. What did we have to lose?

WE WERE SO early for our appointment that we stopped in a coffee shop just a few blocks from Sandy's home. We barely spoke: waiting, wondering, hoping.

The house was in a suburban area, and looked just like every other house on the street. We were pleasantly greeted by a woman in her early fifties who looked totally normal. Sandy's brown hair was short and she wore pants and a sweater. No scarves, no beads, no candles burning, no incense. Just an average looking woman in a house that could have been next door to ours.

She brought us into her family room that held several comfortable chairs and shelves neatly filled with books and framed family photos. There were a few boxes of tissues on the coffee and end tables.

Barry and I each sat on one of the chairs, facing Sandy's chair. She told us that she would tape the reading, and that we should not offer her any information. She would give us messages from the other side.

"They will prove to you that it's them by the information that they bring to you. Don't give me more than I need. As long as you understand the messages, they mean nothing to me."

She also warned us that she had trouble with certain names that sounded alike, and certain words that may be hard for her to comprehend.

Then, she began.

Today is December 2, 2004
   She looked at Barry.
   I am connecting to Pauline.
   Your dad is also passed.
   Pauline says she's got him with her.
   I know she's not your mom.
   She seems to be the spokesperson for your dad. He seems to be quiet so she's going to help him come through because I feel like he's having a hard time. He wouldn't have been a believer and he was also a very quiet man. She's going to help.

   Your dad went quickly, but it was illness related, not accident related. Like a heart attack. I feel the shooting pain. He never got to say goodbye. You never got to say goodbye to your dad. Well you don't have to, he's here, and Pauline's helping him. She was a talker in life.

   I was absolutely stunned. I actually began hyperventilating. Barry's Aunt Pauline, who had recently died, was married to one of Hyman's brothers, and she was an extremely energetic and talkative woman who "organized" everyone and, without a doubt, stood out in a crowd.

   I can tell because the talkers come through always. She just wants to keep talking.

   Now, your dad is coming through. He had a heart attack, but he says there are two people here with heart attacks. Both of us. That's important for you to know.

   There was Barry's answer. I thought I was going to need oxygen.

   Now, there's an A connection to you. An AN name like Annie that has significance to you. Annie is also there. Annie is also connected to Pauline. She says same side. Same side. Same side. Which means we are connecting to your father's side.

   Annie. Barry's grandmother. The one who helped raise Mitchell and Barry in the first few years following the death of their mother.

   Pauline likes to talk. You remember her, don't you? She had cancer? She says pain, pain, sick, sick, me, me. Pauline says that your dad passed before her because she says he was there to get her.

There's an R connection. She wants to give me the R name. There's a Ruth with them. They are telling me that she is with them.

Pauline wants to be the organizer in this reading.

Pauline was the organizer in the family when she was alive. Amazing.

Your mom is there. Ruth. The ring lady. Your dad says he's got his wife there. I've got the ring lady with me. The first thing he did was show me the wedding ring on his finger.

At the mention of the ring, I gasped for air. Astounded. I touched the ring, with an overwhelming sense of connection to my mother-in-law who I'd never met.

Pauline is helping them come through. They must have been quiet people because Pauline wants to do this for them. So your mom is Ruth. OK. Well they both stepped forward together. There's no divorce here. You have a brother. Your mother wants to say hello to your brother. Your mom is acknowledging the three others. She says it's important that she acknowledge your three kids.

Then she turned to me.

Jack. Male Jack like a dad or grandfather. Jack says he has the three girls with him. He needs to acknowledge that you understand three. Three, three, three.

My Zaida's name was Jack. My mother's father.

You've lost a sister. There were three girls. He's acknowledging the three girls together. These were not babies. One was little. They were both children. Not babies. And there's an older one. I'm connecting to the older one. The one that was oldest.

The one who had the headaches. Major headaches. She had something in her head. There's one who is older, that's who I'm connecting to now. The one who had something wrong with her head.

Your mother. That's who I'm connecting to. She feels young. She's younger than you are. Jack is her dad. She says, he's mine. She's connecting. She's been gone for a while, but she is very emotional. She can't stop crying.

The tears were pouring. I must have gone through an entire box of tissues. I could not speak. I could hardly breathe. I was absolutely flabbergasted.

There's an accident connection. Her head was sore. There was something wrong with your mother's head. Something with her head. Her head wasn't right. They all passed together. She's very emotional.

Of course my mother was emotional. She was overly emotional in life. *Now there's a Miriam. She's going to take over. She's going to calm people down. Miriam says you weren't there when this accident happened. You were away. Miriam helped you in some way. Now your father is also there. She brought him in too. He is also there. Miriam acknowledges the closeness she had with all of you.*

So much for being skeptical. I was so taken aback by what she was telling us. Miriam was one of my mother's best friends, and had passed away a few months earlier. I had remained extremely close with her, Kimmy and I staying at her house in Florida several times. Miriam and Kimmy had developed a wonderful relationship, and Miriam constantly told me that Kimmy was exactly the same as Wendy, in looks and personality. I often told Kimmy how much she would have loved my mother, who, in many ways was a lot like Miriam. Warm, sincere, loving.

Miriam says I'm here and I'm going to help.

Of course she would help. Oh, how much I loved and missed Miriam.

Now there was an eight year old. She wants to acknowledge the eight year old little girl that's with her on the other side. She is safe. The eight year old wants to talk. Miriam says there is something about a trip that needs to be acknowledged. Your sister says yes.

A trip.

There's also an S name with them. One of your family members. Your dad. And there's a T connection. A Tony or Toby. She's letting me know that all the family is there. They've all come together.

My Bubby's name was Toby, my mother's mother.

They are telling me that they had gone somewhere without you. You were the last one left. They all passed together. There's a three-girl connection. They are all here with you today. Now Carla is coming through. She's the older one. Not the eight year old. The older one. But not the oldest. They are all very emotional.

22nd or 2 2. Someone has been married two times. He says he's been around you a lot. He sends you a lot of love.

My dad and Sonia got married on October 22.

He comes to your house to see you. You were the oldest of the three. He says you are number one. Number one.

This was too unbelievable. I had always loved when my dad introduced me as his number one. The last time I remembered hearing him call me number one was when he introduced me to his buddies in the fish market. Years and years ago. In another life.

There is a boat. Your dad says he loved the boat. He is acknowledging the boat. It's not a current boat. It's a memory for you with the boat and the water. A happy memory. Not an ocean liner. A small boat. The two of you were on the boat.

Our rowboat. Fishing. Oh my God.

There's a D connection to your father. Someone he's with. Dave.

His brother. My Uncle Dave. My Auntie Riva and I had many conversations about life after death and she was a huge believer in life going on after leaving this world. Auntie Riva admitted that I was the only one she ever talked to about this, because no one else would believe her when she told them about the messages and signs she got from her late husband.

Miriam is going to come back in. She feels really close to you. She's saying hello to you Barry. She says you would know her too.

Absolutely. Barry and Miriam have always enjoyed a great relationship.

Your dad wants to talk about the little black dog. You have a black dog. Your dad sees the dogs when he comes to the house. There are two dogs, and he tries to give you signs through the dogs, so pay attention, alright. There's an older one. A brown one. And there's a younger dog. The black one. The funny one. The one that makes him laugh. The more excitable one.

The one who makes my dad giggle. I knew that I had heard that unique giggle when Amber, the black dog, had done funny things. It was my dad giggling.

Your dad is very close to you.

Finally.

Toby is your mom's mom. There's a strong connection to your mother. Your dad wasn't with them when they passed because Toby says that dad was at home. He wasn't there. That the two of you were left behind.

They are acknowledging a blackness. They were going away. Not just a day trip. Overnight. Going away for longer than a few days. They were going somewhere. Your dad is talking about a telephone call he got as well as a telephone call that you received. Your mom is very emotional. There was a phone call. A phone call came.

That unforgettable, horrific phone call early in the morning of July 5th, 1970.

Your two sisters are coming through. One was eight and one was eleven. This is so emotional for them too. They say they have been here for a long time. This is not recent. You have a daughter. The eleven year old is acknowledging her. Carla is speaking now. There is an eight-year span. They are eight years apart. You have a grown daughter in her twenties and out of the house. Carla says she follows her. She is very much watching over her. Carla says there is another C or K girl? She's acknowledging that one.

Rebecca and Kimberly are eight years apart.

There's a yellow room. Freshly painted. You just painted it yellow. She's telling you that she knows and that she comes to visit in the room with the yellow. It's her way of saying that she's around you and she knows. So Carla is in your house very much now.

We literally just finished painting our kitchen and all of the hallways in our house, a soft shade of yellow.

The three of them passed together. Every time I get connected to your mother, I really feel like she hit her head. She is sorry. She's saying over and over that she is sorry. I know this isn't a suicide, but she is saying she's sorry and it's about her head. Oh, she hit her head and that's why she couldn't help anyone. She had a head injury. She hit her head. Definitely a head injury—an impact. Related to a movement. A contact. Some kind of impact. The head, the head. It was fast moving. She shows me moving. I feel a movement.

Apparently when the plane landed the first time, it hit the ground with incredible intensity, hard enough to knock off one of the engines. The pilot then unfortunately decided to take off again, circle around and come in for another landing. The plane then crashed into a field seven miles from the airport. People on the plane obviously got hurt during that first impact. My mother must have hurt her head. I felt completely sick learning that.

Your mom says you have two girls. She shows me another child. A boy. She sees the boy. She's acknowledging him. He is Jon.

She turned to Barry again.

Your mom is telling me that your dad has a few brothers with him over here. The brothers are very close. He's with them and they are very close. Pauline is looking after all of them. Pauline's husband is also here. Pauline says my husband is with me. Everyone is together. All together.

Just like they were in life. Close, loving and supportive.

I feel like there are two of your moms here, or maybe you were raised by your grandma. Two women who are connected. Now I am connecting to the older one. The one who would have helped to raise you, your grandmother. Became a mother figure for you. They are very much connected together. Annie is your dad's mom. She was feeling old. She was in her sixties but she felt like she was in her eighties. She is sending you love.

Your mom seems to be with your dad's family. Pauline has organized your family. Annie became your surrogate mother. That's who you went to when your mom passed. There is a motherly feel with Annie and that's how she wants you to think of her. You would have that softness with her.

There is a George, still living. He has not passed. He is somebody you are both connected to. He has his own business. He works on his own. He is the owner. Your mom goes with you there, to the place near George. There's a farm connection. They're showing me a pitchfork. It's current. Someone lives in the country. There's lots of space. A farm feel. Current and now. There's a barn near it.

Your mom goes with you. You were just there. That's where she spends time with you, in the country. In a big open space. That's where your mom comes to see you so know that she is there with you. You have a separate structure on your property separate from your house. At the back. Free standing.

Our log home in the woods was surrounded by farms. Behind the house was a large wooden shed that we used for storage of our picnic tables and kindling for the fire pit. Barry and our neighbour George had just brought the picnic tables into the shed. George lived next door to our log home and looked after our home and property as if it were his own.

There's a lot less emotion with your family than with Lynda's. There's a free-standing structure at the back of your house. You didn't build it. You're not very handy because your mother is laughing at you. But you try. But you're not what we call a tool man.

George was extremely handy and when we bought the house, Barry went to Home Depot and bought an array of tools to have at our cottage. They were all beautifully organized and displayed on a tool rack in our garage. We all laughed, because he wanted to be handy and he liked doing odd jobs with our neighbour George, but he was really not very good with tools.

She's talking about pulling the tree out. She knows you did that on your property. You aren't the handy guy—you had somebody do it for you. Some trees pulled out. Not so long ago.

George told us that we had to remove a tree that was leaning towards our house. It was way too big and too dangerous for Barry and George to cut down with George's chainsaw, so we had a local toothless farmer come over with his rickety pick-up truck and remove it. It had just been done a few weeks earlier.

I'm connecting to the eleven year old again. Carla. She's very talkative. She's describing a falling sensation, of going from up high to low. She says I'm falling, I'm falling, I'm falling. This is in an airplane. She says it was an airplane crashing from the sky. An airplane crash. Movement. Impact. It hit the ground. It hit something else on the way down. An impact before it hit the ground. There was an impact.

The plane had landed on the runway for a few seconds and then the Pilot decided to take off again and attempt a second landing.

The plane crashed on the land. They were going someplace. They were on their way. They weren't returning from somewhere. They are all fine now. I see them all standing together.

Talk to them. And your dad says to pay attention to your black dog. He says there's an M connection, a strong M sound in both dogs.

Simba and Amber.

Your sister is telling you to remember that there are two birthdays in September.

Carla's birthday was September 16th and my mother's birthday was on September 23rd.

There is a name that starts with SH. Not Shirley. No. But it sounds like that. It's your fathers name, but it's an SH sound. I can't seem to get the name. Please tell me what his name was.

I told her it was "Shloime".

Yes. That's it. That's the SH sound. The SH name. I never would have gotten that right.

Your mother is acknowledging a painter. Not a house painter. An artist. There's an artist connection in your family. Your daughter. She is not just a little girl drawing. We're talking about somebody going to an arts school. Very interested in art.

Kimmy was in an arts school. She was highly talented in art, singing and drama. Almost all of the art hanging at our cottage was done by Kimmy.

She really draws a lot. Your mom is around her. She does know your kids. There's an Angela in your family too. Very connected to you. Important to you.

I had sponsored Angela to come to Canada as our live-in nanny. We were in regular contact with her and were anxiously awaiting her arrival.

Seven. The number seven is important.

Oh my God. The number seven. As if I had ever forgotten about the number seven.

They're pulling back now.

BARRY AND I could not move off of our chairs. We were completely spent. Emotionally and physically depleted. This experience had been the most incredible, emotional, moving and surreal experience we had ever been through.

Sandy said that the reading was different than any of the others she had done, probably because there were so many young people we were connecting with. She had never done a reading where the people on the other side were so emotional.

As we sat there, in awe, she asked us to come back and said she would not charge us. She felt it was important that we do another one in a few months. We booked the next meeting and walked out of her house. We were both drained and excited. But mostly, we were in shock. Happy shock. Elated.

Barry needed to stop at the first restaurant we could find so he could have a glass of wine. For someone who was always even-tempered and proud of having no vices, I thought it was funny that he wanted a drink.

I can't imagine that any drug would have given us the high we felt after that encounter with our family. We talked for a while about some of the messages we could remember, and then we called home to tell the kids. They put us on speaker and we told them about the visit, passing the cell phone back and forth.

After school the next day, Kimberly and I sat at the computer and transcribed the tape. I typed while she pushed the play and pause buttons accordingly. Hearing the messages again, and having it all on paper made it all the more real. I never tired of reading it over and over.

For weeks, our contact with the other side dominated my thoughts during the days, and then showed up in my dreams. By constantly talking and thinking about my family who I missed terribly, I had found a place for them in my current life where I could finally feel connected to them. I now had proof that they never were completely out of my life.

No matter how many years had gone by, I still ached for them. I tried to imagine what life would have been like if they were alive. I envisioned their lives through the years, as if they hadn't died. My favourite image was visiting my parents' house with my husband and children, being greeted at the door by my parents, smelling the familiar aroma of my mother's cooking, seeing the inside of our home and all of the furniture and pictures on the walls.

I couldn't help but daydream about all of us sitting around the dining room table, laughing, talking, celebrating. My parents with my kids, interested in everything my kids had to say. I wondered what my sisters would have looked like as adults, married with children, all of us together in that noisy house that was filled with love and happiness. My dad teaching all of his grandchildren how to whistle. The kids banging away on the piano, serenading us. Everyone talking at the same time, excited to be in that dining room, so proud of each other. And then all in the kitchen cleaning up, putting things away, washing, drying, scrubbing the sink with Ajax.

Sometimes I just needed to get totally lost, swallowed up, in that imaginary life with all of them alive.

WHILE WAITING TO go back to the medium, I had to remind myself that I was alive. I had a family, a job, a life, and I couldn't spend so much time thinking about my family members on the other side. I had to keep myself balanced, and stop from endlessly searching for signs, messages, opportunities to talk to them, and confirmation that they were around.

No matter what, I did feel their presence. I thought about Wendy and her favourite song, *Sugar Sugar*, would play on the radio. I'd be in a quiet room and hear my dad whistling. There were many instances where I swore I heard my dad giggle when I was at the park with my dogs and Amber, the black one, did something funny. I hadn't heard that giggle for so many years, and there it was. The first time it happened, I actually had to look around to see if someone was there imitating my dad's giggle. No, it was just me and the dogs. And my dad.

I could hardly wait to go back. To connect with everyone was comforting and electrifying. Barry and I both agreed that as sceptical as we were, it seemed impossible to discredit Sandy. She had said things that she never could have known—even if she had done some research, which we didn't think she did. No amount of digging could have come up with me being Number One. That had been deeply buried for over thirty-five years.

CHAPTER 2

O NCE AGAIN, ON the day that we were due to visit Sandy, I had a quiet conversation in front of the bathroom mirror, with both of our mothers. I told them how excited I was to be going back to the medium, and I asked Barry's mother to please tell him how proud she is of him. He is a wonderful husband, a great father, a good brother to Mitchell, an amazing person, and a successful professional. Barry never got the recognition he deserved, and I asked her to please give him some acknowledgment of his many accomplishments.

This time, driving to Sandy's house felt different. I knew what to expect, but I feared the experience would not be as successful as the first one, and all of our belief would come undone. Maybe we should not try it again. What if they don't talk? What if we don't get any messages from them?

Neither of us were talkative, lost in our thoughts. I told Barry that I had asked our mothers to say a few specific things today to prove to me that they really were around. I told him that I had asked them to talk about what he has done with his life and to let him know how proud they were.

WE SAT IN the same chairs as the last time. Sandy turned on the tape recorder.

Today is February 22, 2005.

She looked at Barry.

There is a mother vibration coming through. She is saying I'm sorry, I'm sorry. First thing she is doing is acknowledging two boys. You didn't say goodbye to her. She says it's okay. Her passing was a surprise. It was very quick.

She is saying something about offices, doors, a business where you are the boss. She is giving you the thumbs up. You boss people, but in a good way. She visits you at work and when you travel. You travel with your business. On planes. She goes with you. She is very much protecting you. Very much with you. You go and you talk about your business. You do presentations. She sees you going up the stairs to do presentations. Speaking in front of groups. Your mom is very proud of you.

There is a two boys connection. She wants to acknowledge him too. He acts younger. She is surrounding both of you with love. She knows and really wants to talk about what you've done with your life. She sees it. You're going up higher. You're not quite done. She feels like there's a promotion that you may already

*know about, that somebody has talked to you about. And your mother feels like
you are getting it. Your mother wants to be sure you know that she knows. There
is an S place that you go to. A place with a strong S sound—that you go to with
your business. Israel. She's protecting you over there too.*

The head office for Barry's company is in Israel. He travels there a couple
of times each year, often doing presentations to groups of executives.

*I feel another mother around but it's your mother who is the strongest one
right now. She's got your dad there too. He passed after her. He remained alone.
He never remarried. He was a man on his own, alone, for a long time. She was
there to get him. They are very much together now.*

*There's a Ruby. She's acknowledging Ruby. Ruby is a friend, but he hasn't
passed. He's still here. He is somebody connected to the older generation.
Somebody your parents knew. She goes to see him. Both of your parents go to see
him, but not here in Ontario.*

Ruby, who was Hyman's best friend, is still alive, close to ninety years
old, and living in Montreal.

*She is giving you a hug today. She keeps saying that she is very proud. They
are both proud of you. She wants you to know that she knows what you are doing.
And this is big about your business. She keeps saying it's big, big. A big business—
it's pretty important. She's not only saying it as your mother. It's a big, booming
business. There are different businesses. She doesn't seem to want to stop talking.
She's right around you. You're teaching others to do what you want them to do.
Your mother has not left you. She's always been right there. She keeps saying that
she is sorry that she passed. She keeps saying I'm sorry, I'm sorry. She wants you
to talk to her, feel her, sense her. She hasn't left you. She says that Jon is just like
you. Jon has the business head like you.*

Our son Jon was so much like Barry it was incredible. Sincere, kind,
and very bright. He was in a business program at University.

*Now she's going to bring through Lynda's mother. She's saying thank you to
you, Lynda. She is your mother-in-law and you really called her in today. She's
done what you've asked her to do.*

The tears were pouring down my face. All I could do was nod. She was
absolutely right, but I couldn't speak.

*Your mother says that you've been going to the hospital—back and forth to
the hospital—and back and forth to doctor's visits. Your mother is going with
you. She knows, and she is with you. Right there with you. It's not just one visit.*

There is something going on that you are getting tested or checked out. Well your mother is right there giving you a hug.

And your mother-in-law too. Your mother-in-law is really sending love. She says you brought her in today. She didn't want to come today. She wanted your mother to be here, but you asked her, so she's here.

Your mother is saying that this medical thing is recent. It happened since the last visit here. This is new stuff. Your mother is very much with you. She has not left you. Both of them keep saying they have not left you. And she knows that you are struggling with this medical thing. I don't get any blackness around this. I don't feel like there's a heaviness or a worry. Your mother doesn't think so either. There's one more visit that you're going to be making–she says you're not finished—but she's going with you.

I had badly dislocated my shoulder in January, a bit more than a month ago, falling on the ice in front of our cottage. I was rushed to the hospital and they had to completely anaesthetize me in order to put the shoulder back in. Because of the damage to the shoulder, I was now seeing an Orthopaedic doctor.

Your mother is talking about Miriam. She is like family to you. Older than you. A mother vibration to you. That's who your mother is thanking. She was somebody you trusted as a mother. Miriam had cancer. She is also connected to your father. You stayed connected to her. Your mother and Miriam are together on the other side.

My relationship with Miriam had grown even closer as I got older and especially once I had children. I trusted and loved her deeply, and was able to talk to her about anything. In many ways, she was like a mother to me.

The last time Kimmy and I were with her in Florida, she was quite sick, but well enough to hit the malls with us. Someone referred to me as her daughter. She looked at the woman and told her that I was not her daughter, but she loved me as if I were. She died a couple of months later.

Your mother wants to acknowledge the April birthday. She's really welcoming you Barry the same way that your mother welcomed Lynda. She's going to be there for the birthday in April.

Barry's birthday was April 9th.

There's an R around both of you. An R name connected to both of your mothers. Rebecca. Your oldest. A smart girl.

Rebecca was named in memory of both of our mothers, Rita and Ruth. *Your mother says there is some drinking around her. Yes. Alcohol and a party. There's a black truck connection here. Both of them are watching over her. They know that she has a black truck. The truck isn't at home right now. Like she's away or something. It's here with you. Both your mothers came with you in the black truck.*

Rebecca was in Cuba for her university reading week, with a big group of friends. They were at an all-inclusive, with unlimited alcohol. We drove her black Honda SUV to Sandy's house.

Both mothers wanted to be here together. They are acknowledging Jon or Jonny. Your middle one.

Even though his real name is Jonathan, most people call him Jon. I'm the only one who calls him Jonny.

Your mom is fine. She is calm today. Barry's mother is keeping her calm. She was very emotional in life. She cried very easily.

Oh, she cried easily. We used to tease her about crying even when she was watching a comedy show.

Your mom is bringing her dad in. Jack. Your mother is with her family and her friend Miriam.

The mothers say that you call your daughter Becky or Becca. They are very much around her. She must be gone somewhere because your mother keeps saying I go away to see her.

She was away at school in London, Ontario, about a two hour drive from our house.

Both your moms met on the other side. They didn't know each other in life. They heard you when you talked to them this morning. That's the subject they want to talk about. They are listening to you. You asked for them to do it so that's what they are doing. They are saying that sometimes you go with Barry on his business trips. Your mothers went too, to the States. Both of them. Work related, not holiday trips.

So even they knew that I had finally started joining Barry on some business trips.

Your mother says you just came back from Arizona. The Arizona desert. You flew there. They were on the plane with you. They are always protecting you.

Barry had just been to Arizona on business.

There's a connection to Mexico. They know you both love Mexico.

Mexico is our favourite place to go on vacation.

There is an England connection. Big Ben. Away from work. They say you are going to England.

Yes, we had a trip to England planned. Nothing was booked yet, but we knew when we were planning to go.

There's a C or K name. A daughter. The teenager, or almost thirteen. She just had her birthday in the month of December. She's a big girl. She seems older. She sort of feels like a teenager. Pretty mature.

Kimberly. Her birthday is December 31st.

All three of your children have been acknowledged.

Your sister Carla is here. She is standing behind your mother, pushing your mother forward. She watches over your daughter.

I have an N name here. I can't get the name. It's an unusual name. Starts with an N and has an M sound. She is connected to your mother. She is her sister. She's here too.

Naomi.

They are saying that they all passed at the same time in a plane crash, but your little sister—they found her first. They identified her first and your father knew that. The little one. The baby. They were watching and they know what you guys went through.

I vividly remembered standing on the bathtub, looking out of the window onto the backyard where my father was given the news. They had "found" Wendy. "Identified" her.

There is an S name, not yet on the other side. She was with your dad. A lady friend, an S person.

Sonia.

Your mom is saying she is sorry. You didn't get along with her. It was a heart-ache for you. Your mom says that she is sorry that you never clicked with her. It pulled you and your father away from each other. She knows that. This lady is living but you don't see her. She is showing me a break from her. You didn't get a replacement mother.

Oh my God. Oh my God.

But your mom says there were others who were mother figures for you. You had Toby.

My grandmother, Toby.

Both mothers are standing together. And both dads. But the women are talking today. Your little sister is quiet on the other side. These two mothers are very much front and centre. They have both been to your house. They say you have two houses. They are showing me two houses. You use both homes. Your family goes to both. One is up north near the water. They say it's not a cottage. It's a house. They are making a big deal about it. They say it's a beautiful house. Not a little cottage. It's next door to an empty lot?

We call it our cottage, but compared to the cottage we had when I was a child, this is more like a house. It is a very big log home. And yes, there is an empty lot right next door.

Barry, your mother says you looked after your father. Your mother is saying thank you. You did enough. Your brother doesn't live in Ontario. He is away. They go there too. He is on his own. You feel older even though you're younger. You grew up more. And she knows.

They both are here. Both mothers. They want to talk more about the two houses. They are a united front, your mothers. Very much together. Like friends.

She looked at Barry.

Your father lived in Montreal. He says you looked after him in some way. He passed very quickly. He didn't get to say goodbye. He wants to acknowledge the other watch. Not the one you are wearing. His watch. He knows that you have the other watch.

Barry keeps his fathers watch in a small box in our bedroom. He has never worn it.

He sends you a lot of love. He says you helped him.

The mothers say there's some building coming soon. Construction. Something new and exciting.

At the time, we had no idea how accurate they were about the construction they were referring to. Little did we know that we would soon find out.

Everyone has pulled away.

The session had ended.

CHAPTER 3

I HAD ALWAYS felt as if I had the most amazing job in the world. I loved it. Even though I was not the owner, I gave it everything I had, as I did with every undertaking, small or large. Being a camp director was not just what I did, it was who I was.

I was totally committed to the campers, the parents, the young leaders, and the organization. I was driven by a sense of purpose and worked hard to cultivate a culture of compassion. My favourite expression when coaching my staff was that "actions speak louder than words." Young, easily influenced staff members had the opportunity to fully participate in good deeds and events that inspired them, and motivated them.

I never hesitated to reach out to anyone in our camp community who needed some help. When any of my campers or staff members were going through a rough time, I was there for them, providing support, giving them tools and strategies. When it came to teens in crisis, I could certainly relate to them. I could make a difference in their life because I held a position that enabled me to intervene and direct them towards making good choices.

Despite what people thought, I didn't have many "difficult" people as customers. My attitude was to talk with people about challenges, connect with them and work through the problems together. I easily took an empathetic and sincere approach, rather than being defensive, and it inevitably paid off.

Within only a few years, I built this day camp into a thriving business where people had to register their children for camp many months in advance of the actual start date.

IN THE MID 1990s, I was sitting at my desk in a large open office packed with staff members rushing to finish the last minute planning for the camp's first day, when a man walked in. He spoke quietly to the first person he saw, and was immediately ushered to my desk. After shaking his trembling hand, we found a quiet corner to talk. He told me that his wife had just been diagnosed with terminal brain cancer and he needed camp for his two boys. The camp was full and we had been turning people away for months. Without skipping a beat, I assured him that his boys could come to our camp and that we would do everything we could to help his family.

Regardless of how busy it got, I was in regular contact with this dad, and made sure that the counsellors in each of the boys' groups had ongoing coaching to help the boys have the best summer they possibly could, considering everything that was going on in their lives.

At the end of the camp season, we invited families to a Family Night which included a performance and ended with everyone singing along to well-known songs.

I was moved beyond words when this family arrived, walking slowly alongside the dying mom. It was heart-stopping to see her there, so ill, so delicate, yet obviously determined to be there for her children. That evening, we played "That's What Friends Are For" as the last song of the summer.

Despite the large audience, as that song played and everyone started to cry, I found her from my spot on stage and our eyes locked for what felt like sixteen seconds. If there really is such a thing as a telepathic message, then she certainly got my message.

From that summer on, "That's What Friends Are For" became our traditional last song for the summer.

In 2006, a number of changes were made in the structure and organization of the camp and, as a result, it became obvious to me that I could no longer stay at the job where I had been for almost seventeen years. Deep down the whole situation had that distinct feeling of being the beginning of the end.

The changes set off a chain of events for me and those around me. As a result, a few months prior to the summer of 2006, I cut my ties with the organization.

It was not simply leaving a job. It had not been just a job—it was an emotional commitment, my identity, my sense of worth and accomplishment. It was who I was.

Having to deal with loss again, albeit with different players, brought back memories and feelings that I thought were buried deep down, never to resurface. But they did. With a vengeance. Grief, anger, sadness. They feel the same. Pain is pain and, while you can't compare the pain of losing a job to that of losing a family, the passing of such a defining chapter of my life brought back those all too familiar emotions. Having suffered so much loss as a child, it was always a huge challenge for me as an adult to cope.

THE SUMMER OF 2006 was a summer I would never forget. My biggest issue with leaving my job was handling the emptiness left by the absence of the personal and professional relationships I had with the people with whom I had spent so many summers. Campers, families and staff members.

Thank God my key full-time staff members, also my very dear friends, quit their jobs as a show of solidarity and our shared vision. Almost immediately we began to receive an endless number of emails and calls. I was moved to tears by the emotional kindness that poured in, flooding us with support and compassion.

Together, we all worked on healing our wounds. We spent hours at my cottage, connecting with nature, eating, drinking wine, talking, laughing, crying.

We spent many evenings around the campfire, and many days digging for rocks and uprooting dead trees to chop up as firewood. Our time together was healing and restorative. There's something therapeutic about going into the woods with two dogs, shovels, a wheelbarrow, heavy work gloves, and steel toe boots, and digging up rocks. All shapes and sizes. Some were too big to budge, but our deal with each other was that if we could get the shovel underneath it and move it, we could find a way to get it into the wheelbarrow.

Sometimes in life, you feel like you're pushing a huge boulder up a hill. That's how we felt while moving those rocks. We were armed with shovels, a wheelbarrow and a huge amount of determination. We listened to the birds singing, watching us from the trees, swooping down, and darting in and out of the bird houses. My dogs romped though the forest, chasing the squirrels and coming back to us every few minutes to dole out some kisses and then take off again.

Sure, we spent a lot of time overthinking and overanalyzing what we were doing and decided that the rocks and trees were meaningful symbols. Rocks were solid, permanent and strong, so digging for them felt analogous to digging for answers. And pulling dead trees out of the ground was a symbol of how we all felt: uprooted.

HAVING LEFT A job after almost seventeen years of incredible dedication and commitment, I was sick of hearing the same thing over and over again. One door closes and another door opens. Something better will come along. Everything happens for a reason.

What door could possibly open that would be better than a job that I had loved for so long? My kids were raised in that camp, right by my side. It was my identity. My reason for getting up every day. A big part of my social life. I had given my entire adult life to that place, to that job, to the campers, their families, the staff members. I tenaciously grew that camp from a small village of two hundred, to a city, a huge community of twelve hundred.

I watched little toddlers grow to be teenagers. I helped families who were struggling. They confided in me. They trusted me. And I did everything in my power so as not to let them down.

I handpicked teens who were struggling with crumbling self-esteem, awkward social skills, the need to belong somewhere, to feel wanted and valued. I took them under my wing and gave them responsibilities and roles, and the opportunity to rise to the occasion. To step up and to feel great about themselves. I believed in them. I knew they could succeed. They just needed to believe in themselves.

With all my talk about ploughing forward, picking up the pieces, dreaming, focusing on the good stuff and staying positive, when I left my job I was a complete mess. Grief and all its nasty accompaniments had come back to rear its ugly head, as it did at every dark opportunity. I felt betrayed, hurt and rejected. I spent so much time staring at that closed door, still feeling the draft long after it was slammed behind me, that I couldn't see what was right in front of my face. How could I see ahead when my head was twisted back, still totally focused on what was? On anger. On resentment. On sadness.

Finally, my stubborn will to fight for happiness, to come alive again, to feel the pain of loss and move beyond it, began to fight back.

Everything people were saying about opportunities, looking behind door number one, was true, but only partially true. What was missing from all of the free advice was that the only way to see new opportunities, to see the reason for something having happened, the opportunities now available, was to look ahead. To stop looking back, staring at that closed door.

To believe that the best was yet to come. To feel grateful. To feel the power to be whoever you wanted to be. To trust that things happened for a reason and that there was a purpose and a plan for all things.

Someone had sent me a story, the author apparently unknown, that helped me tremendously. Resonated with me. A story that reminded me to turn towards the front, focus on the good things, and stop fuelling the lousy feelings.

A TRUTH

One evening an old Cherokee told his grandson about a battle that goes on inside people. He said, "My son, the battle is between two "wolves" inside us all. One is Evil. It is anger, envy, jealousy, sorrow, regret, greed, arrogance, self-pity, guilt, resentment, inferiority, lies, false pride, superiority, and ego. The other is Good. It is joy, peace, love, hope, serenity, humility, kindness, forgiveness, benevolence, empathy, generosity, truth, compassion and faith."

The grandson thought about it for a minute and then asked his grandfather: Which wolf wins?"

The old Cherokee simply replied, "The one you feed."

WITHIN A SHORT time of leaving my job, I had found a location just perfect for starting my own camp. I had to keep it quiet for the whole summer of 2006 as my lawyer pursued my lawsuit, but the moment the lawsuit was settled, I started Adventure Valley Day Camp.

CHAPTER 4

D ETERMINATION CAN BE incredibly powerful. With my children by my side, and Barry doing as much as he could, we started a brand new business. It was a huge risk which took a lot of courage, but we were determined to follow through on this dream of finally owning our own summer day camp.

By September 2006 we signed a long term lease and began major renovations to the building and property. There was a whirlwind of fast-acting support and compassion from friends and relatives who opened their hearts, generously offering, and then actually demonstrating, their genuine willingness to help us.

Since we were starting completely from scratch with not a single customer, we put forth a massive effort into building the business and getting as much exposure as possible. Forging ahead, we all rolled up our sleeves and got to work, exhausting ourselves in order to succeed. Here it was again, that gut level determination to move forward, that tenacity to beat the odds, to make a difference and create something our family would be proud of.

We learned something new every day, stretching ourselves, filled with a sense of possibility, constantly uncovering a new set of challenges. We worked, we slept, we went back to work.

We didn't have time for fun. We worked every single weekend, while everyone else was out enjoying themselves. We were completely and totally consumed. Our diets consisted of anything that was fast and easy because every minute was spent at Adventure Valley.

There were moments when the fear and anxiety seemed to overload my body, and I was tempted to give up, but through all of the effort and events, our family felt connected. It was a soul-stirring family time, filled with moments worth savouring. And that made it all worthwhile.

The property was like an oasis in the city, with acres and acres of lush green fields and nature trails. In addition to a summer day camp, Adventure Valley was a perfect venue for weekend events, both large and small. We were almost instantly busy with birthday parties, outdoor education programs, charity events, and corporate events.

On an excessively hot day in July, every inch of our grass fields was covered with booths, tables, barbecues, kiosks, and portable shelters. The comfortable capacity for the facility was about a thousand, so we were quite shocked when people continued to arrive by the hundreds and hundreds for a Chinese festival. It was like a giant flee market with what we later learned had been four thousand people in attendance.

We had staffed the day for what we thought was a usual corporate event, so we were grossly understaffed. The bathroom lineups were endless, and garbage bins overflowing. Not knowing if we should laugh or cry, we did everything we had to do just to keep up with the basics. With clean garbage bags draped around our necks, each of us did our best to keep up with the garbage, removing the overfilled bags and dragging them to our garbage area. We were dirty, sweating profusely and nauseous from the smell.

Looking uncharacteristically scruffy in filthy jeans and a t-shirt, Barry was struggling to pull an overflowing plastic garbage bag out of the bin when someone approached him. "Excuse me, but aren't you the President of Novopharm?"

Barry seemed puzzled when he responded with "Yes, sorry, but have we previously met?"

"I work for you. I work in the shipping area. Do you need some help?"

When Barry told us this story, we laughed so hard, we were almost on the floor.

Adventure Valley was a new beginning. Another chance to repair my rainbow. To make a difference to others through help, guidance and kindness.

We integrated both children and staff with special needs, hosted charity events, and invited children who, without our help, would otherwise never experience summer camp.

I know that every camper and staff member was moved by the opportunity to get to know Robert, a nine year old boy who was a camper during our first summer. He was fully deaf, and only able to communicate with sign language, so we modified some of our programming to include the teaching of sign language. We had a sign language word of the day and watched as people referred to the guides and books throughout camp with some common words and phrases. Robert was definitely one of the most popular kids at camp.

Giving back to our community, reaching out to families in crisis and doing as much feel good stuff as we possibly could, nurtured our souls and provided our family with a huge sense of pride.

Eventually, I learned that leaving my last job and starting Adventure Valley was truly a gift. I cherished the lessons learned through this time in my life where so much had changed. And best of all, here was another chance for my family to leave big footprints.

CHAPTER 5

IT WAS NOT over, even after so many years. It was never over. I missed them all the time. I still cried and had to hold back tears when I talked about them. Having discovered a remarkable way to communicate with them, I was obviously drawn to the medium.

Amidst the renovations, the construction, and just a few months before our first camp season, our whole family met with Sandy.

TODAY IS FEBRUARY 5th 2007

This time she looked at me first.

Mother vibration coming through. She says you've been worried about some-thing. Says she is worried about you. You've been struggling with something, but it's okay, it's okay. She's been around you—wrapping her arms around you. Not something personal, but related to your family. Something of concern. Don't worry so much. It's all okay. You're doing the right thing, so let it go. Close the book on the other thing. Don't worry so much about it.

Exactly what everyone had been telling me. Forget about it. Stop think-ing about the job I had left. Let it go.

She knows about the birds. Listen to the birds. Watch them. They're important.

The birds.

Then she looked at Barry.

Your mom is here. She is telling you to lighten up. She says you worry too much. Everything is good. She's talking about money again, finances.

Something about the bank. She knows that you're spending a lot of money now, but it's a good thing. Your mother is wrapping her arms around you right now.

Now she is saying hello to the kids. She says that Rebecca is a lot like her dad. She has made a stop in school, thrown her school books away, decided not to go back. That is a good thing for now.

Rebecca had graduated from university and had decided to hold off on graduate school and, instead, help us get the business off the ground. And yes, she was a lot like Barry.

She says there were lots of secrets in your family when you were a child. Things that were kept quiet. Nobody talked about your mom to you. She passed when you were young. There's lots you didn't know about her. She says that you get phone calls from your brother in Montreal about money. He wants you to send him money, and you ask him questions. Something is going on that is connected to your brother, involving boxes.

There is somebody else that he is looking after. Some kind of care-giving going on there, that is out of your hands. This is your older brother. You're the baby. But it's your brother she is worried about, even though you worry too much. For some reason, he is older but you look after him in some way.

He has a lady there with him. A relationship lady. But it's on again and off again. Very troubling. You can't control it, or him, but he drives you crazy, frustrates you. The lady isn't really bright, but it's okay. She doesn't treat him nicely. You can't control the relationship and you can't control her. He lives in an apartment, not a house. Your mom goes to his apartment to see him. He spends time moving in and out.

Your mother wants you to know that she sees all of that and, for some reason, it's all put on your shoulders. Don't let it. He will get mad at you. But the money keeps flowing. She likes to spend, his lady friend. Your mom says she's not really worried about you because you're comfortable, but you don't want to throw the money into the air and let it go. For a purpose it is okay. It drives you crazy and you and Lynda talk about it sometimes, the money with your brother and this female. The money helps him. His balance is off. He is not an alcoholic, but his mobility and speech are affected in some way. Something is wrong with him. He has a mental incapacity, he acts young, he doesn't act his age. A lot has been put on you for a long time.

MITCHELL AND TINA. Now there's a long story.

During the spring of 2002, Mitchell told us that he had met a woman named Tina. He described Tina as wonderful and caring, and he said they were madly in love with each other and were going to get married. He sounded so excited.

For Mother's Day weekend, we sent Mitchell and Tina train tickets for a trip to Toronto. We had a minivan that could seat seven, so the five of us went to pick them up at the train station. They walked off that train absolutely beaming, arm in arm, and kissing each other. Mitchell was dressed in his usual clothing, a torn black t-shirt that looked like it had never been washed and worn-out army pants. His shoes were tattered and missing the laces.

Tina was no more than five feet tall, quite chubby, wearing a smock-style dress, white knee socks and old filthy sneakers. Her hair was dishevelled and greasy.

Mitchell was so proud to introduce all of us to "Auntie Tina", and after about three rounds of hugs, since he was uncontrollably elated, we all piled into the van. The two lovebirds did not stop kissing and fondling each other the entire thirty minute drive home. And the kids could not stop giggling.

Since neither of them had ever really been on a vacation, we had arranged for them to sleep at a hotel quite close to our house. We wanted them to have a special weekend, so we also made reservations for Sunday Mother's Day Brunch at a lovely restaurant.

We sat with them in the kitchen of our house hearing all about how they had met. They told the story together, each one adding to the information to make sure no detail was left out. They discovered each other through a dating service that was specifically geared for people connected to the program that provided vocational services for the mentally challenged. After speaking to each other on the phone, they agreed to meet at a coffee shop. Tina said that she was waiting at the coffee shop but Mitchell never showed up. She went home and blocked his calls.

Mitchell admitted that he had shown up, but when he saw Tina, he changed his mind. And then, typical of Mitchell, he regretted that decision and tried to call her to apologize. He called her several times every single day, but could not get through because she had blocked the calls. When she finally, months later, removed the block, he got through to her and apologized as only Mitchell can do. Over and over and over again. So they met, fell in love immediately, and were planning to get married.

Throughout this story, Barry and I had to remind them that there were children in the room and they had to stop fondling each other so intimately. We told them that we could see how in love they were with each other, but their behaviour was inappropriate.

Rebecca and Kimmy offered to take Tina to the mall. I slipped Rebecca my credit card since I knew that she would be buying Auntie Tina some badly needed new clothes, and off they went.

I could not have been more proud of my kids. Jonathan stayed in the kitchen talking, well mostly listening to his Uncle Mitchell. The girls came back with bags of clothes that Tina had chosen, and a fresh new hair cut. They scurried upstairs with her and brought her down about half an hour later sporting one of her new outfits and a face full of make-up. When Mitchell saw her, he wanted to jump her right there in the kitchen. We knew that because he told us so.

The weekend continued as it had started. They were constantly making out, and we had to keep reminding them to control themselves in public. They talked incessantly about their plans for marriage, and we agreed to help in any way possible to plan and organize, and of course pay for their wedding.

We brought them back to Toronto in July for their engagement party. The entire Fishman and Alpert family arranged to come to the party which would be held in our backyard on a Saturday evening. Jonathan had set up speakers for music, he put up plenty of outdoor lighting, and we had prepared a variety of salads to go with the chicken, steak and fish on the barbecue.

We had bought an engagement ring for Mitchell which he wanted to give to Tina at the party, in front of all of his aunts, uncles, cousins and some of our friends who we had invited. He got down on one knee and formally proposed. We were so touched by his gesture, which he said he had seen on television and always wanted to do. So sweet.

Tina had one cousin living in Toronto, who came to the party with her husband. Unusual people, to be polite. They didn't really speak to anyone at the party, and at the end of the evening, I saw the aunt filling her purse with all of the candy and assorted nuts that were in the living room.

While the party was successful, their relationship quickly began to deteriorate, and they continuously broke up and got back together. On and off. On and off. The wedding was cancelled primarily because Mitchell found out that Tina would lose her welfare cheques if she married Mitchell.

We further discovered that Tina was taking a variety of anti-psychotic drugs, and that one of her biggest issues was her paranoia.

In Mitchell's usual, unique way, he had been obsessing about Tina since the day they met. When things were "on" she was the greatest person in the world. When they were "off" he told us about all of the things he couldn't tolerate about her, including the details about their sex life, which was way more information than we wanted.

He was constantly asking us for money, which we knew he was using for Tina, but we couldn't say no to him.

He tried so hard to improve his life, and sadly, his life had been so unlucky, so pitiful. The one great thing, maybe the only thing about his life that had been positive, was that he kept his job at the same place for twenty years. That was a major achievement for anyone. For Mitchell it was incredible.

He still lived in a one-room apartment with no carpets, a basic table and chairs, a bed and a reclining chair that no longer reclined. Every bit of furniture that we bought him through the years had been damaged and replaced, over and over. Mitchell worked so hard to live his own life, in his own way, with strong determination to be out of the shadow of Barry's life. When we bought him nice clothes, he refused to wear them. When we gave him advice, he got angry.

He undoubtedly appreciated the love and attention from our kids, the fuss we always made about him at our family events, and the money we constantly sent.

He told us that he visited Tina at least three times a week, and that her recent deterioration was due to the progression of her Multiple Sclerosis.

So we sent him money and tickets for trips to Toronto and, each time we saw him, we had the exact same experience. The visit started off with a positive tone and quickly descended to strained and uncomfortable. He became agitated and restless as those familiar emotions of jealousy and resentment rose up and choked him.

SANDY CONTINUED, TALKING about Barry's family.

There's a grandmother here, standing beside your mom. On your dad's side. She wants you to know she is watching over you. You jumped around as a child a lot. Annie is sending you a lot of love. She just couldn't look after you any more. She didn't mean to leave you too. Both of these women left you but they didn't mean to. Well they want you to know that they haven't left you. They've stayed with you, and with your brother too. You'll be going to France soon, and she will be going along with you too.

That was true.

Your dad's with her too, but he's got a bit of a wall around him. He is saying he did his best. He did his best. You were young when your dad passed, a teenager.

She looked at Jonathan.

They call you Jonny. Your grandpa is saying hello. He walks with you. He wants to acknowledge a brown dog connection. The brown dog goes into your room. You have two dogs, and one is lighter brown. He's been making the dog do weird things. Just know that.

Simba, the older brown dog had recently started going into Jon's room when Jon was home for a weekend, lying down or nudging Jon. This was highly unusual behaviour for him.

You go to school out west. He follows you to school. You are out of residence, into a house or something where there's a group of four of you in the house—four boys. A fifth one may be staying there temporarily, a girl, who needs a place to stay. And you have a friend, more like a brother, named Matt. Your grandpa says he knows Matt. He likes Matt. Matt makes him laugh. Matt is very special to your family.

All of this was absolutely true.

Then she looked at Kimmy.

You are the Christmas baby. You are fourteen. Your grandma is saying hello. She is fine. She passed very quickly. Crumbled down quickly. Bleeding inside. Nobody's fault. Nobody could have fixed it. In case you wondered. There were two incidents that happened to her. Brain and heart. She fell and hit her head. She had some signs but didn't tell anyone. She ignored them. She apologizes. She was busy with the baby.

I looked around at my children who sat stock still and teary eyed.

There's something about the black dog. A problem with its leg.

Amber had recently been attacked at the park by another dog, where she suffered a gash in her leg. She had required surgery and had to wear a bandage on her leg for a while.

Sandy addressed Barry again.

Your dad didn't bring in another woman to help raise you. No step-mother. You missed the mother thing. She is sorry about that. Do what you can with your brother and let the rest wash off your back. He is very stubborn. And you're not going to change him. He's not very good with money. He works in a factory. She is sorry she wasn't there to help you look after him. You got the physical work, she got the spiritual work. She keeps telling you to lighten up. Laugh. Enjoy your life.

Before your mother leaves, she wants to remind you that she is bringing your dad along when you go out west.

Barry was going out west on business.

Your dad is here. He talks about you getting up on stage. Some kind of speaking engagement. Where you're going to be teaching people something. Not like a teacher in the traditional sense in a classroom, but a speaker up on stage, front and centre. He hears you. He is proud of you. He wants to put a red ribbon on your chest. You're the boss in a lot of ways. He is mentioning pills. Not bad pills. Legal pills. Good pills. You have something to do with medications. Your dad knows what you are doing.

I glanced at Barry, my logical, practical Barry, so moved by what was said.

Sandy cleared her throat and turned to Kim.

Kim, your grandmother is acknowledging your singing and that you have a nice voice. There's a lot of music around you. Not typical teenage music. Like you are up on stage. A little actress. Not on stage like your dad. Your grandma knows that. She says you have a very nice voice.

Kimberly had just been in a school play where she sang a solo.

There's a boy here. A friend. A younger male who passed. He's not a child. He's here for one of you. He says you never got to say good-bye to him. Something was wrong with him. He was sick. It was a sudden change for the worse. A cancer connection. He wants to say hello. He's young—20ish. Not a boyfriend—just friends—friends for a while. He was still in school. He hadn't thrown the books away. He liked school. He is talking about a girl. A girlfriend who you're connected to. He is saying hello to the S name. You still see her. Sarah.

Rebecca's friend Alex had recently died after a long battle with cancer. His girlfriend's name was Sarah.

He went over very easily and he is fine. He was in the hospital, getting better and people thought he was going to be ok, and then he went quickly. He's okay now.

Carla is here. She's got the younger sister with her. She sees you, Kimberly, dancing at school. A dance that will be up on stage. She knows that you never met her, but she knows you.

She is teasing Rebecca that she still lives at home.

This was an ongoing discussion in our house, since Rebecca had moved back home after being away at university. She was eager to move into her own place.

She sees the black room at work.

Rebecca had just painted one of the walls at work black.

Jon, she is saying she knows that you go to a school in Kitchener or Waterloo. You may not know me, but I want you to know that I have been with you. I know each of you. She is a very bright girl. She says she always did well in school, read a lot of books and wanted to be a doctor.

That was Carla.

The little sister is here too. She acts young.

There's a Mary connection saying hello to everyone. Not a blood link, but a friend of the family. Same age as your mom. She was sick before she passed. Tired. Visited your house. Knows your house. Like a mother or aunt to you. Big energy. Her real name is Miriam, but she is calling herself Mary. She is laughing about the name "Mary."

Kimberly and I looked at each other. "Mary" was an inside joke between me, Kimmy and Miriam.

The three musketeers are stepping forward. All friends. All of the same generation. Three of them, standing together. We are all here. There's an Omie too. She is there too.

Oh my God! Naomi. We all called her Auntie Omie. In fact, she referred to herself as Auntie Omie. Her grave, which is in the back of our cottage, says her full name, as well as "Auntie Omie" right below it.

Yes, her grave. She had been cremated and had asked for her ashes to be sprinkled over my mother's, sisters' and grandparents' graves. Since that is not allowed, my uncles didn't know what to do with her ashes. She never had kids, and she had tried so hard to mother me, albeit in her own outlandish way. I asked my uncles to send me the ashes and we would make sure they were properly buried. We engraved a slab of limestone, dug a hole in back of our cottage in a beautiful spot near the pond, had a little family ceremony, and buried the metal box.

Three women of the same generation. They were really good friends. They both became mother figures for you. You talked to them a lot after your mother died.

My mother, Miriam and Naomi. Everyone always called them "the three musketeers."

There's another purchase of a house or a business. You've been talking about it. Another significant place in your life. More money going out. There's been discussion about it.

Yes, Adventure Valley. We had just started the business and had already spent a huge amount of money getting it up and running. We poured our heart and soul into that business, working seven days a week.

The big fish. A pet fish. A fish just passed. Your mom's got the fish. You just lost a fish and there was talk in your house about the fish going really quickly. Your mother knows about it. She had a funeral for the fish. Recently happened. It was an S fish. You named the fish. The one that passed. They are laughing about it too. Sam. She's got Sam. Not orange. Not a goldfish. It was dark, more of a black colour. She's got it in a little box.

We were all laughing and crying at the same time. This was unbelievable. It had literally been a few days since one of our fish, who we actually named Sam, had died. He was an ugly, dark fish, a bottom feeder who was supposed to help keep the tank clean. We only had him for two days when he died. His short time with us had been the source of a lot of jokes, and when he died, we laughed about having a proper funeral for him.

Someone just hurt their finger. She knows about that too.

Rebecca had broken a finger a few weeks earlier.

They know that Jon will be heading right to school after this.

Jon had driven his own car and was driving to school directly from Sandy's house.

There's an Elisabeth or Lisa. Someone current. She says she talks a lot.

For almost ten years, I had worked with and become very good friends with Lisa. And yes indeed, Lisa talks a lot.

You switched offices. You changed offices in the last little while. Your mom is here. She's been here the whole time. She says she knows about the book. There's been some talk about writing the book. She wants you to write it. She says you should start it already. They are sending their love to all of you and are pulling back now.

CHAPTER 6

Mᴀʏ 10, 2007. The morning of my fiftieth birthday. It was a tough one. If I hadn't committed to driving Kimberly's carpool that morning, I probably would have stayed in bed. I just couldn't believe that it was my fiftieth birthday and, even after all the years, I still longed for my parents and sisters at such a significant milestone.

No matter how much time passed, there was always that painful awareness that they were not with me to share in both the happy and difficult times. Reminder after reminder that they were not here and not coming back. Sadness and celebrations, each so different yet both triggered such sorrow: reawakening that slumbering ache for my family.

People always say that time heals. It doesn't. To heal suggests to cure or restore something back to health. Yes, through time, you make progress and improve, but you never fully recover from losing a mother. When you lose a mother, particularly when you are a child, you spend the rest of your life grieving and longing for her. The effects appear and reappear. It is unpredictable. It never goes away. Because no one in the world cares about anything as much as a mother cares.

I never got over losing my mother and sisters. The effects of those profound losses at such a young age continued to resurface throughout my life. I moved on, and did eventually create a wonderful life, but the underlying emptiness was always there, just not always heard. Even though it's not every minute of every day, there has always been an emptiness inside that never has, and never will be filled by anyone else. Losing them affected everything significant I ever have done. It's erratic. Sometimes their absence causes such intense pain, it's almost unbearable. Other times, I manage to be strong and positive, and ride the wave of resolve rather than get pulled under the water, and struggle to not drown in my own despair.

I ꜰɪɴᴀʟʟʏ ᴡᴇɴᴛ down to the kitchen and started making coffee and feeding the dogs. I opened the sliding door, leaving the screen ajar to let in some fresh air. The dogs had barrelled through the screen so many times that we didn't even bother replacing it. The actual mesh was still partially attached and blowing in the light breeze. It was already a gorgeous day.

I stood by the door watching the dogs as they played together in the yard, and admiring the purple lilacs that were starting to flower. While I wasn't able to plant purple lilac bushes at the cemetery, I did plant them at every house we ever owned.

I started to cry softly as I thought about my mother and sisters. I wondered what we would have done together to celebrate a milestone birthday, when suddenly a bird flew right past me and into the house.

Rebecca and Kimberly saw it fly into the living room and immediately announced in unison that there was a bird in our house. I said that I knew, yet I could not move. I was totally stunned.

Angela walked into the living room, easily picked up the bird and walked into the kitchen. It was cupped gently in her two hands with its' little head peeking though.

She walked right over to me and said, *"Look. It has a white head just like a little angel."*

I just stared at this bird, which didn't even try to get away from her or show any signs of distress. Angela walked over to the screen door, opened her hands and the bird flew into the tree. Then it just sat there looking at us as we stood in the doorway staring back at this little angelic bird.

Weakened from heartache and disbelief, I slumped into a chair in a state of shock. I couldn't move. Rebecca had to drive the carpool for me.

SOME THINGS ARE just unexplainable. Not necessarily irrational events, but not rational either. I realized that the bird was quite a special fiftieth birthday present, unmistakably from my mother. Instead of being upset, I chose to see it as an unusual, interesting, and comforting gift. A sign with important messages. It made me think about the lessons my mother and I had learned from the movie "The Birds", the uncanny connections between my life and the movie: birds fly, planes fly, and I had to fly alone. I even overanalyzed it to come up with the analogy that the plane crash "clipped my father's wings" prohibiting him from continuing to fly.

But the most meaningful message of all, was that the love between a mother and daughter is truly forever. The strongest possible bond.

Deep down, I always knew that she had never really left me.

CHAPTER 7

I HAD BEEN waiting impatiently for this fourth visit to Sandy, and wanted to go alone. Sandy had made it clear to me that she would not see me again. I had used up my limit and was banned from further visits after this one.

I wanted to connect to my family on the other side and not have to share it with anyone else. But Kimberly insisted on coming. She badgered me with all the right reasons, until I finally agreed.

During the drive to Sandy's, Kimberly said that she wanted to see if Wendy would talk to her, since everyone always told her that she looks and acts exactly like Wendy.

Today is April 16th, 2008

Sandy looked right at Kimberly.

There is a young girl here who is around you a lot and this little girl is following you. This is the youngest sister that is coming through, the baby one. She is very much with you, she walks with you. She guides you. You feel her and sense her and, if you wonder who you are sensing, you are really sensing that little girl. She was with you when you were a child, so I don't know if you felt her with you.

This is Wendy. She's the one that walks with you. You're not crazy when you feel somebody. Strong energy. She became your guide. She says that you just changed schools. Different than going off to university. We are not talking about that, we are talking about a switch in schools for you.

She is with you when you go up the steps and onto the stage. She says you are always talking, that you never stop talking. You are doing some kind of speech on stage, different than getting an award. Different than just singing, and she is very proud of you for doing that. She says she sees you acting in a play. In a little theatre school, an acting school. Now she is just giving you a hug.

Yes, Kimberly had changed schools for that school year.

Have you seen a picture of Wendy? She wants you to look at her picture. She walks with you a lot. She is skipping. She loves to skip. She's happy. She is teasing that she doesn't have to get old and you do.

My heart just stopped. Wendy was a champion skipper.

There's an Ann connection to you. Angela. Your best friend. Hangs out with you a lot. All the time. Wendy is dancing around you and Angela. Angela is at your house a lot. She's more than just a school friend. She's older than you. She moved into your house. But she is your best friend. You really like her. You get along really well together. She's older than you but she feels young. They know that she's in your house.

As soon as Angela's name came up, I started to cry. Angie had not only been our Nanny for three years, but she was totally involved in our new business, helping us in so many ways. It felt as if she had been with us forever. I had never met anyone quite like Angie and I was overflowing with gratitude for everything she did for everyone in our family.

A few weeks after the bird had flown into our house on my fiftieth birthday, Angela called me at work to tell me the most bizarre story. She was out walking the dogs and a bird flew onto her shoulder and remained there for the entire walk. She said that the bird was now in our house, just sitting on the washing machine in the laundry room. I raced home and sure enough, there it was. We took pictures of the bird and then she brought it to the door and it flew away. Unbelievable.

To show my appreciation for Angela, I began buying angels for her, since I truly believe that she is an Angel on this earth. I started an extensive angel collection for her. Angels made of glass, crystal, pottery, fine china, carved in wood. Kimberly and Angie have a special relationship. A friendship. An indescribable bond.

Wendy says you have to keep your marks up at school. She is talking about your Sweet Sixteen in December.

Yes, Kimberly was turning sixteen that upcoming December. And yes, we were planning to have a Sweet Sixteen party to celebrate the occasion.

Then Sandy looked at me.

This is your little sister. She says that she is really very much around you as well.

An older man is coming through. It's your father. Your dad wants you to know that he is very proud of you. Very proud of what you've done with your life.

He's proud of the two businesses. He needs to tell you because in life he didn't tell you. He was closed off. He is very proud that you own a business. That you've done it. He says your husband is at your office a lot. Your dad likes to listen to you when you're talking to people. In life he didn't hug you. He wants to now.

Your dad is acknowledging the 28 connection. The 28th of the month. He says he is talking about the other dad, Barry's dad.

Barry's father had died on April 28th.

Your dad had a very difficult time in his life, and he wants you to know that it is easier there for him now. He is with your mom and is glad to be with her. He is whistling. He is happy. Don't worry about him. If you hear any whistling, it's your dad.

The tears were pouring down my face.

He gives you the thumbs up for what you have done. It's a family business and there are many bosses in the business. He is laughing about that.

The joke in our family has been that there were so many bosses in the business. Me, Rebecca, Jon and, of course Barry, even though he still has his own job.

He says you have to have patience. Your dad is really proud of you. Your dad's got your mom with him. They are all together. He missed her. He is glad you keep your family close. It's good.

She looked at Kimberly.

He is acknowledging the tattoo. There's been talk about a tattoo. He knows. He says that no, you don't have to get a tattoo. Your mom still has control, your grandfather says, and he heard the conversation about it. He's laughing about it.

Kimberly had recently and persistently asked for a tattoo, and we consistently said no.

Sandy turned to me.

Your mom wants you to know she's been with you. She goes to the place by the water. The rock. She sits by the rock. She is with you by the rock. She wants you to go there and have some peace there. She says you work too hard and it's a place where you can go to relax. She follows you there. There's water and some sand, but there are rocks. At the cottage. She says you've been really tired lately. You're exhausted. Working too hard. Talk to your mom when you are near the water. She will listen.

We have a pond at the cottage and the entire pond is surrounded by rocks. I love rocks. Rocks of every shape, size and colour. There are some huge rocks that I love to sit on, and many smaller ones that I dug up myself and lugged over in the wheelbarrow.

Something about the curtains. Down. At the cottage. Something was wrong with the curtains. That was a sign from your mom.

The last time we went up north, the shower curtain in one of the bath-rooms was on the floor. I just assumed that the pressure rod had somehow slipped and the whole thing had fallen.

Continue to pay attention to the birds. Your mom says she sends you messages through the birds.

The birds. The movie. The bird that insisted on nesting on Rebecca's window sill. The bird that flew into my house on my fiftieth birthday. The bird that landed on Angela's shoulder. And Oliver...

It was September 23rd. My mother's birthday. I picked Kimberly up on that sunny day and she said she wanted to go to the big plaza near her school. We walked into Petsmart and fell in love with a green and turquoise Parrotlet, a miniature parrot. Before I could catch my breath, Kimberly was begging me to buy the bird she had already named "Oliver."

We left the store with a fully loaded cage, bird food, toys and, of course Oliver. The sales staff did not know anything about the bird. The date of birth, the sex, the name of the breeder. They suggested we call the next day to get the pertinent information.

Happy birthday, Mom. I told her that she didn't have to send wild birds into my house anymore, because now we had a bird in our house. Oliver. Bought on September 23rd, my mom's birthday. And the next day I discovered that Oliver was born on May 10th. My birthday.

There really are so many signs when you are open to seeing them.

Watch the little bird. The hummingbird. It will be a sign from your mother too.

A few weeks after this medium visit, I was sitting on a bench in front of my house with both dogs, waiting for Barry to come out so we could go for a walk. A hummingbird flew right up to me and fluttered in front of me for at least ten seconds. The dogs and I just looked at it. They didn't even bark. And then it flew away. Unusual. Unexplainable. Comforting.

That's your mom. She is taking credit for those signs, just to let you know that she is with you, near you. You know this already, she says. You have to keep trust-ing, believing, being open to it, feeling it.

There's a sadness about the 5th. A passing. The 5th of the month. They are with you on that day. They are all with you.

The plane crash was on July 5th.

There's also a birthday connected to five. The fifth month. Not a sad time. It's a happy time—a birthday. Your mom is always there for your birthday.

They are all there.

My birthday is in May.

You have to stop feeling guilty. It's not your fault that you are still here. She's really happy that you are, and she's been around you all the time. There's a Robyn connection. Your mom knows her. She says you should listen to Robyn. She has helped you and your mom is happy about that.

I had been searching for some spiritual explanations for all of the recent changes in my life, and had been seeing a life coach named Robyn for the past year. She had done so much for me but the key lessons I learned from her were related to the Law of Attraction. Basically, we attract into our life whatever we think about. So if we think positive thoughts, we attract them; if we focus on negative thoughts, we will attract those too. In many ways, I had always intuitively known and understood the Law of Attraction. Robyn reinforced that knowledge, and added deeper levels of understanding. She always said that we have all of the answers we seek, and that we get to choose the direction we take. It is all within our power.

They want you to do this by yourself. They want you to get it. When you get the signs, believe them. They are there. Know that they are with you. Go home and feel them. Pay attention to your dreams. Your mom comes to you in your dreams. But know that they are not going to come to you all the time. You have to live your life here.

You can't be more connected to them than you should be. They will come when you need them. They want you to enjoy your life. It's a good thing. Your mom wants to see you smile.

They will all be waiting for you when you get there, but in the meantime, they will connect when you need them to.

They know that you miss them. Talk to them when you need them. They will go home with you.

You have to know that.

It's Never The End

Believe

We slipped away, to another place
So close, and yet so far
Whatever we were to each other
That we still are

Please call us by our names
In the way you always did
Don't forget us because we can't be seen

Let our names be household words
Speak to us
Share your thoughts

Life still means all that it meant

Don't hold onto sorrow or pain
Search for joy and happiness
Purpose and meaning

Embrace life

Laugh as we always laughed
Listen for our giggles
Smile when you think of us
We are smiling at you

EPILOGUE

SEVERAL YEARS AGO, I was tracked down by an author, living in California. At his request, we met to discuss his keen interest in writing a book about my story. He was eager to write about it, because it was almost his story as well. Well, his father's anyways. He, his mother and sibling were booked on the same fatal airline flight as my family. At the last minute, they changed their flight to a day earlier. They were already in California when they heard about the Air Canada DC-8 flight 621 plane crash. Their relatives and friends didn't know about their change in plans and, until they heard otherwise, thought they were on that doomed flight. Incredible luck. Fluke. Fate.

As tempting as it was to have a proven author write the book, with his vast writing experience and already established reputation and connections, I couldn't let him do it. It was my story to tell. The facts, the emotions, the choices, the way it all unfolded, all of that was in my head and in my heart. And there was way more to my story than the plane crash in 1970. But I wasn't ready yet.

IN NOVEMBER OF 2008, I started to write. Five months later, in April, 2009, my Auntie Nicky called me from Montreal to tell me about an article she just read in the Montreal Gazette about the family members of victims in the 1963 plane crash that occurred just outside of Montreal. I got in touch with the reporter who then put me in touch with Bob Page. Bob is about ten years older than me and, at age sixteen, lost his father in that 1963 plane crash. Seven years before ours.

Bob and I had that instant connection and comfort with each other that comes from having found someone with whom you have an understanding. No need to explain. I had finally spoken to someone else who had lost a family member in a plane crash. Not cancer. Not a heart attack. A plane crash. It gave me goose bumps.

We talked about losing family in a plane crash, and the effects we have endured and continue to deal with. We obviously had so much to share.

Bob and I both agreed that writing about our experiences was tough. No matter how many years passed, the tragedy has continued to affect us and our families.

We both felt that these two airline disasters were important and rare parts of Canadian history. If Air Canada's objective, years ago, was to "bury" these incidents as quickly and quietly as possible, they succeeded. But for the families left behind, the impact and ensuing fall-out never went away. We both believed that Air Canada dropped the ball, letting down countless many families. Back in those early days, months, and even years, they should have made sure we had appropriate grief counselling, financial and emotional support, and some compassion—whatever the form.

The most amazing part about connecting with Bob was discovering that he too began writing his book in November 2008. So many years later for both of us, and yet we chose the exact same month and year to start writing. There has to be a message in that incredible coincidence. Confirmation for both of us that it is time we told our stories.

FRANKLY, IT WAS hard for me to start the process. Aside from being a very personal story, and questioning whether to take it public, the biggest challenge was my ability and strength to relive the deep pain and hurt. Open the wounds that had been so carefully nursed all these years. And my keen awareness about how difficult it would be to pull myself away from this "good place" in life, full of joy, gratitude and love, to that horrible time when my whole world had fallen apart.

But the more I thought about it, the more committed I was to sharing my story and all of the lessons I learned through the years, in the hope that I could help those faced with the same choice I had to make over and over: the choice to live.

Since November of 2008, I was instantly and completely immersed in writing. That's me. Whatever I take on, I do with my whole heart and soul. I devote myself completely. There were times during my writing, where I had put myself so completely into the past that I forgot about the present. I was actually disoriented, back in time, hurting so badly I could not control the tears.

But the journey was both difficult and cathartic.

Along with the struggles and sadness came important lessons. As I reflected, it became obvious to me that the life lessons have been endless. My hope for the book is that readers will learn the value of growth in the face of tragedy. If my experiences can help light the way for others, then the intensity of the writing was all worthwhile.

Repairing Rainbows reveals my positive and determined view of life. There's a crucial difference between truly living and the existence that is often mistaken for being alive.

At every juncture, I had to decide whether to succumb to or overcome the sorrow. You always have choices. You can give up or you can go on. I chose to go on. I chose life.

The most meaningful lesson for me has been the importance of focusing on the good, finding the rainbow in every storm. And in that rainbow, there is gratitude and appreciation. "Thank you" as a predominant idea and feeling was critical for me.

Even when life completely collapsed around me, and hope seemed so far away, I took baby steps. I refused to give up. I replaced fear and panic with hope and dreams. I believed that somehow things would get better. Instead of dwelling on all of the 'bad' things that I had to endure, I chose to acknowledge the good things, even when it felt like I was grasping at straws. I did my best to search for and find some form of peace and love in my life.

Most importantly, I never let go of my hope and faith in the future. Somehow I intuitively believed that despite the pain, I could make some good choices, write my own story, create my own life.

There's no template to follow that will determine the course of any tragedy and its effects. But the toughest decision people have to make is whether or not they respond to a crisis with hope. It is a choice. It's a choice about whether you want to live or die. I chose life.

Lynda   *Carla*   *Wendy*

Wendy, Lynda and Carla

Dad with Lynda on his back and Wendy and Carla in his arms.

Acknowledgments

THIS BOOK HAPPENED because of the endless love and support from my devoted husband Barry, our precious children, Rebecca, Jonathan and Kimberly, and because of the editing skills and dedication from my amazing editor, Nancy Davis. From the moment Nancy and I started working together, she showed me her true commitment to my story, to our book.

I can't even begin to imagine what my life would have been like without Barry. He has been by my side as my dearest friend, my pillar of strength, my lover, my confidant, my therapist...my everything. We each experienced terrible childhood tragedies and prevailed. Together, we reassembled our shattered lives into something new and wonderful.

We are incredibly proud of our children, Rebecca, Jonathan and Kimberly. They support each other, and are truly honest, kind, capable and caring people.

Barry and I often talk about the many teachers we've had along the way: our parents, my grandparents, Mitchell, Julie, Uncle Len, Angela and so many other wonderful people who have been role models, angels disguised as people. They've been there to carry us when we didn't think we could take one more step forward. They provided courage, inspiration and guidance.

My grandparents taught me about generosity, kindness, accepting individuals for who they are rather than judging them.

I may have only had my mother with me for thirteen years but her impact on my life has been strong throughout my life. She showed me how to give, how to care, and how to trust. She taught me to find the strength and daring to soar like a bird above life's seemingly insurmountable obstacles. She was a woman who left huge footprints for me to follow, a mentor and a guide. Her mother had shown her the path to living life with beautiful values and integrity. I only hope that these important lessons continue to be learned and appreciated for generations to follow.

Mitchell passed away in December of 2009. Mitchell taught us so many life lessons. He had a heart of gold and, despite all of his limitations and difficulties, if he could, he would have done anything for anyone. I think he faced more challenges in his life than anyone else I've ever known, yet he carried on, doing the best that he could to make his life, and Tina's, more meaningful.

I AM SO grateful for having had the privilege of spending time with a medium. This wonderful woman, who I have learned to trust and treasure, has the unbelievable ability to connect to spirits on the other side. She has confirmed over and over again, that throughout the years, our family members, *on the other side*, have stayed very close to us, helping and protecting us, guiding us, comforting us. When she told me that my mother was encouraging me to write my book, that gave me the final push I needed to find the time to sit down and start to write.

The Fishman family

About The Author

IN 1970, WHEN she was thirteen years old, Lynda's life came to a disastrous halt when her mother and two younger sisters were killed in an Air Canada plane crash.

As a young teen, Lynda made a conscious decision to become happy and to lead a fulfilled life. Lynda chose to live. She was committed to learning, growing and making a difference. Determined to find meaning and purpose in her life, she managed to muster up the courage and strength to dream big, to be idealistic, to strive for more, and to live a meaningful life where she could make a difference in the lives of others.

Lynda Fishman is a trained clinical social worker who has spent over twenty years as a camp director. In the early 90s, Lynda was one of the first camp directors in the Toronto area to incorporate children with special needs into mainstream camp life. Lynda has devoted a lifetime to organized camping and is passionate about the positive role of camping in a person's life. She is the owner and director of Adventure Valley Day Camp.

Lynda is a motivational and inspirational speaker and facilitator. She has published articles and training manuals on leadership, teamwork, bullying, trust, childhood health and wellness, communication and customer service.

Lynda's husband, Barry Fishman, has his own amazing story to share, having been orphaned at age 17 and left alone to care for his brother with special needs. Lynda and Barry met as teenagers and have been together since then. They have three grown children, and the whole family is heavily involved in supporting children dealing with tragedy, cancer or other life-threatening diseases, fund-raising and charity events.

Barry has spent his entire career working in the health care and pharmaceutical industry. He is the President and CEO of the Canadian operations for the world's largest generic pharmaceutical company, Teva Pharmaceuticals. Barry serves on the Board of Directors of the Childhood Cancer Foundation.

Lynda is a woman of action. She has incredible enthusiasm for life. She is persistent, focused and faithful to her dreams and goals. She is willing to work for everything with patience, optimism and determination. She finds ways to be grateful and positive. Lynda goes out there and does what she has to do with a CAN DO attitude of gratitude, positivity, compassion, and honesty.

Mom and Wendy

Mom and Dad

Carla with Tiger, Lynda and Wendy   *Dad and Wendy*

Carla

Wendy's birthday

from the recipe file of **Rita Weinberg**

Florentines:

½ cup whip cream
3 table. butter. ½ cup sugar
1¼ cup finely chop. almonds
⅓ cup sifted flour ¾ cup chop. candied peel
melted semi sweet choc. any coloured candies

Combine Cream, butter, & sugar in
saucepan & bring to boil. Remove from
heat & stir in almonds, flour & peel.

Drop by tablespoons onto greased & floured
cookie sheet, keep 3 in. apard. Bake 350°F
for about 15 min. Remove with spatula
Cool - & cover bottom with melted choc.

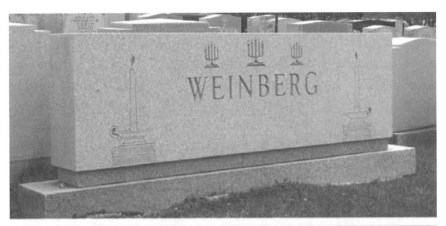